St Luke's gospel

St Luke's Gospel

An Introductory Study

E. V. & K. G. Barrell

John Murray

© E. V. and K. G. Barrell 1982

First published 1982
by John Murray (Publishers) Ltd
50 Albemarle Street
London W1X 4BD

Reprinted 1983, 1985

Typeset in Great Britain by Inforum Ltd, Portsmouth
Printed in Hong Kong by Wing King Tong Co. Ltd

British Library Cataloguing in Publication Data
Barrell, E. V.
    St. Luke's Gospel: An Introductory Study
    1. Bible. N. T. Luke – Commentaries
    I. Title   II. Barrell, K. G.
    226'.4'07   BS259.3
ISBN 0-7195-3903-X

Contents

v

Jesus' last visit to Jerusalem (19^{28} to 24^{53})   141

viii *Contents*

Illustrations

Maps

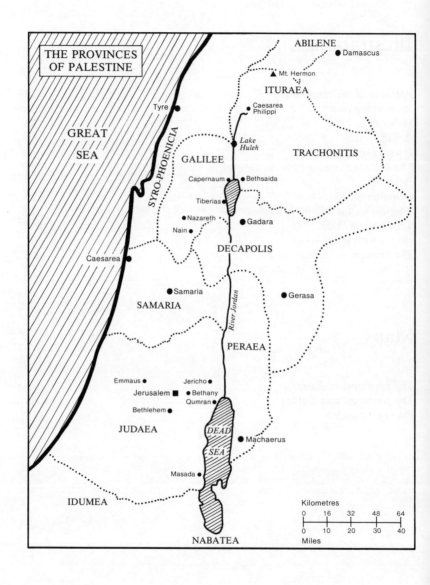

THE PROVINCES
OF PALESTINE

ABILENE

● Damascus

▲ Mt. Hermon

ITURAEA

Tyre ●

Caesarea
Philippi ●

GREAT

SEA

SYRO-PHOENICIA

Lake
Huleh

TRACHONITIS

GALILEE

Capernaum ● ● Bethsaida

Tiberias ●

Nazareth ●

Nain ●

● Gadara

DECAPOLIS

Caesarea ●

● Samaria

SAMARIA

River Jordan

● Gerasa

PERAEA

Emmaus ●

Jericho ●

Jerusalem ■ ● Bethany

Qumran ●

Bethlehem ●

JUDAEA

DEAD

SEA

● Machaerus

Masada ●

IDUMEA

NABATEA

Kilometres

0   16   32   48   64

0   10   20   30   40

Miles

X

The Life and Teaching of Jesus in the Gospels: Mark and Matthew

After the Crucifixion and Resurrection of Jesus, his followers expected that he would return soon to rule over the Kingdom of God in a new age. They set out to gain more followers by teaching and preaching. There were many who had known Jesus personally and could tell others about him, so for a long time no one saw any need of writing a gospel. People of that time did not rely on reading as we do today, they were used to remembering and repeating things accurately. Also it was much better to hear about Jesus and the things he had said and done from people who had seen and heard for themselves. These spoken testimonies brought others to a belief in Jesus and the Church developed and spread.

At last, when persecution and old age brought about the deaths of many of these eye-witnesses and leaders, it seemed wise to preserve their testimonies safely by writing them down. Added to this from A.D.66 many of the Jews in Palestine were revolting against Rome. The Christians did not feel involved in this and many left Palestine to live elsewhere. This made many people aware, for the first time, of the fact that Christians were not really just another group of Jews. As the gospel spread to the Gentiles more and more Christians had no personal knowledge of Palestine, where Jesus had grown up and worked.

Luke 1^{1-4} tells us that there were many attempts at writing accounts of all that had happened. Fragments of some early copies of these writings are still in existence, others were lost or never gained the popularity necessary to continue, so we rely on the gospels in our New Testament as sources of information about Jesus. They were not intended as biographies, for they leave out details which a modern biographer would consider important, such as the date of Jesus' birth and a description of what he looked like. They did not attempt to tell us everything that Jesus said and did. John (20^{30-31}) says that the gospel's purpose was 'that you may come to believe that Jesus is the Christ, the Son of God, and that believing this you may have life'. This purpose makes the gospels different from any other kind of literature.

According to the speeches of Christian leaders in the Acts of the Apostles their gospel proclaimed that Jesus was the fulfilment of Jewish history and that his coming brought in a new age for all people. For listeners who had not known Jesus it was necessary to say something about his coming, his life and teaching, his death and Resurrection. The first preachers must have used stories about Jesus to illustrate their sermons, and memorized his sayings to answer the challenges and criticism they had to meet, particularly from religious Jews like those whose criticism Jesus often answered. The written gospels perhaps echo the ways in which those early preachers used their material. Certain stories seem to serve mainly as a way of leading up to an important pronouncement of Jesus, e.g. Mark 12^{13-17}, Luke 12^{13-15}, 17^{20-21}. Some were about events in Jesus' life or about people with whom he was concerned, e.g. Luke 2^{41-51}, Mark 1^{9-11}, Luke 10^{38-42}, 19^{1-10}. Others showed how he used his power to heal, e.g. Mark 1^{40-45}, Luke 7^{11-17}.

A closer look at the gospels shows that each writer selected his material carefully and presented it in the way best suited to his particular purpose and the particular people for whom he was writing. Sometimes the writers linked a saying of Jesus to a different background story, cf. Matthew 8^{11-12} and Luke 13^{28-30}; Matthew 13^{31-33} and Luke 13^{18-21}.

The different treatment each writer applies to the same event or saying helps us to spot the purpose and meaning of that particular gospel. Each gospel-writer gave a large amount of space to describing the last few days of Jesus' life in Jerusalem and events after his death, events witnessed by many people and obviously considered by all to be a very important part of the story. We cannot be sure who wrote the gospels or when they were written, for information is scarce and often open to more than one interpretation. For instance, a church historian named Eusebius, writing early in the fourth century, claimed that Papias, who was a bishop in Asia Minor about A.D. 130, had said that the apostle Matthew made a collection of Jesus' sayings in the Hebrew (or Aramaic) language, and that everyone interpreted these as well as they were able. It doesn't seem that he was speaking of what we now know as Matthew's gospel. Papias also mentioned Mark, saying that 'Mark became the interpreter of Peter and he wrote down accurately, but not in order, as much as he remembered of the sayings and doings of Christ'.

It is thought that Mark's short gospel was written for the Gentile Christians of Rome and that it was circulating about A.D.65. For this reason Mark did not quote much from the Scriptures of the Jews, and he explained any Jewish words or customs mentioned. Mark's gospel showed Jesus as a man of action and mighty works, a teacher, the Messiah expected by the Jewish nation, God's Servant who was destined to suffer in order to complete his mission. Mark's mother's house in Jerusalem became a meeting-place for the early Christians (Acts 12^{12}), and there possibly Jesus and his disciples ate their last supper together. In Mark 14^{51-52} is the only mention of a youth who just managed to escape from the soldiers who arrested Jesus in Gethsemane, and it has been suggested that Mark himself was the unnamed youth in the olive-orchard, for he could have overheard the plans for the evening made in his mother's house. Later Mark was allowed to accompany his uncle, Barnabas, and Paul on their missionary journey to Cyprus. He deserted the group when they decided to cross to Asia Minor, and the angry Paul would not take him again, but Mark was with Paul in Rome to comfort the great missionary as he approached the last days of his life (Acts 13^5, 13^{13}, 15^{37-39}, Colossians 4^{10}). In A.D. 64 the emperor Nero blamed the Christians for the terrible fire that engulfed Rome, and it is thought that both Paul and Peter were put to death in the persecution that followed. The loss of leaders like these made it the more necessary to write a gospel, and Mark's was probably completed before A.D. 70, since he shows no knowledge of the Roman destruction of Jerusalem which came in that year.

Mark's gospel has several references to Peter (1^{16}, 5^{37}, 8^{29}, 9^5, 14^{66-72}, 16^7), and sounds like the personal memories of someone like Peter who saw it all happen from the time of Jesus' baptism, which is where Mark's gospel begins and about the time when Jesus and Peter met. The first part of Mark's gospel seems to set out to answer the question, 'Who was Jesus of Nazareth?' From the beginning Mark assures his readers that Jesus was the Christ, and at 8^{29} he tells how Peter openly recognized Jesus as the Christ. The second part of the gospel concerns itself with the question, 'What does it mean to be the Christ?' and answers that it meant suffering, death and resurrection for Jesus. Jesus' own words and the events of Easter Day made this clear. Finally Jesus answered in the affirmative the High Priest's question, 'Are you the Christ?' Many scholars have seen Mark's gospel as a gradual unfolding of the fact that Jesus was the Messiah, with the climax coming when Jesus answered the High Priest, 'I am'. They refer to this unfolding as the 'Messianic Secret' of Mark's gospel.

John's gospel is easily seen as quite different from the others, but the first three have a great deal in common and are known as the Synoptic Gospels since they have the same viewpoint. In fact, 95 per cent of

Mark's gospel is repeated in Matthew's gospel, and about 65 per cent of Mark's gospel is repeated in Luke's. Mark's order of events is followed by Matthew and Luke. If Matthew and Luke differ, one of them always agrees with Mark. There are little differences, but often it is because they were trying to improve on what Mark had written. For instance when Mark's sentences are clumsy or might be misunderstood they improve them, and when Mark suggests that Jesus was angry or when Mark's words seem critical of either Jesus or the disciples they tone them down (Matthew 8^{23-27}, cf. Mark 4^{35-41}, Luke 8^{22-25}). Luke, however, is more independent than Matthew in his use of Mark. His gospel from 6^{12} to 8^4 and 9^{51} to 18^{14} has no Markan material in it. He makes no use of Mark $6^{53}-8^{10}$, perhaps because he feels he has already included similar stories in his own material.

Both Matthew and Luke include a lot of material not found in Mark's gospel, and of this extra material there are about 200 verses which are amazingly similar, so similar that it is believed their authors must both have used some written source that Mark did not know. Compare Luke 3^{7-9} with Matthew 3^{7-10}, and Luke 10^{13-15} with Matthew 11^{20-24}. Matthew and Luke have made such different use of the material that it doesn't seem likely that one copied from the other. The written source has never been found. German scholars called it 'Quelle' (German for 'source'), and we usually know it as 'Q'. If we take Mark's material and Q away from the gospels of Matthew and Luke we are left with material which is found only in Matthew's gospel ('M'), and material found only in Luke's gospel ('L'), so the two gospels are made up as follows:

Matthew's gospel   = Mark + Q + M
Luke's gospel   = Mark + Q + L

As the gospels are compared it becomes obvious that each writer wanted to present Jesus in his own particular way, with a particular purpose, for particular people and circumstances. Probably Luke's gospel was written before Matthew's, but since Luke's gospel is the main concern of our study, we shall look at this separately in the next chapter.

If Matthew's gospel had been written by Matthew the tax-man disciple, who knew Jesus well, surely he wouldn't have needed to use so much of Mark's gospel. Perhaps the disciple Matthew collected some of Jesus' sayings, as Papias said, and these were developed by an unknown author to become our present gospel. Perhaps the material developed in a church which had close links with Matthew himself. However, in those times writers were not beyond using the name of someone well-known to give importance to the work and to persuade people to read it. A disciple's work would be more likely to get read than that of an unknown Christian. For the sake of convenience we continue to refer to the gospel-writer as 'Matthew'.

Matthew was very disappointed when so many of Jesus' own countrymen, the Jews, failed to recognize and accept him (Jesus) as the Messiah for whom they had waited so long. He felt that their history and their prophets should have made them prepared for Jesus' arrival. Matthew took every opportunity of showing how Jesus fulfilled Old Testament prophecies and belonged to the descendants of King David, from whom the Messiah was expected to come (e.g. 1^{23}, 2^5, 11^{4-15}, 12^{17-21}, 15^{22}, 21^9). By the time this gospel was being written there was great hostility between the Jews who accepted Christianity and those who rejected it. Perhaps this is why Matthew bitterly condemns the Pharisees, scribes and Jewish leaders (3^{7-8}, 21^{43}, 23), many of them good and well-intentioned, but hampered by their devotion to the many rules which had grown up around the Mosaic laws. He saw that Jesus' life of love for other people was a simpler and better way, and in this way Jesus drew out more depth of meaning from the Command-ments than all the rules could do (3^7, 21^{23-30}, 21^{43}, 23). On the other extreme there were people within the Church itself who felt that all they had to do was preach and perform miracles in the name of Jesus. They thought they could dispense altogether with the teachings of Moses and the prophets (5^{17-19}, 7^{15-23}). Matthew reminded them that Jesus himself stressed the importance of the Law which must never be neglected, but he also showed that a real concern for the welfare of other people ensured the best possible way of keeping the Command-ments. In order to emphasize this, Matthew includes more of the teaching of Jesus, and also reminds Christians that belonging to the Church does not excuse them from God's judgement (13^{41}, 13^{47-50}, 22^{14}). Matthew seemed to be writing a considerable time after the destruction of Jerusalem, when the Church had had time to become well-established and had accepted the fact that Jesus might not return for some time (22^{6-7}, 28^{15}, 24^{24}). It has been suggested that the gospel was written somewhere between Palestine and Syria about A.D. 85 or even later. The writer seemed to be a Jewish Christian who believed that Judaism should develop naturally into Christianity and that Christians were God's new Chosen People.

What Do we Know about Luke and his Gospel?

The third gospel and the Acts of the Apostles are two volumes which together form a continuous story. The gospel tells the story of Jesus, the Saviour who was determined at all costs to love mankind back into God's Kingdom, even those who were considered by other people to be lost beyond all hope. His chosen way of life, led by God's Spirit, caused him to be crucified, but also brought resurrection and ascension; so his apparent disgrace and failure really led to success and triumph. The Acts of the Apostles traces the spread of the good news about Jesus from the Jewish capital of Jerusalem to Rome, the capital of the world known at that time. It seems to be saying, 'Jesus has completed the work he was sent to do. Now the Church must complete its work of taking his gospel to all other nations'.

Both volumes were written in excellent Greek, and both were dedicated to someone named Theophilus. The writings may have been intended for a cultured Gentile official who was already interested in Christianity, or the name may have been a cover-name for someone who wished to remain anonymous. The name 'Theo-philus' meant 'one who is loved by God'. Perhaps the writer meant it to signify that he was writing to everyone in the world, for God loved not only the Jews but all nations. The gospel has many examples of the writer's concern to show that Jesus welcomed Gentiles. Stories like the Centurion's Servant, the Good Samaritan, the Great Feast showed Jesus' concern for non-Jews (7^{1-10}, 10^{25-37}, 14^{15-24}). The gospel-writer avoided using Jewish words like rabbi and scribe, using instead the Gentile equivalents, teacher and lawyer. He dated events by reigns of Roman emperors and officials as well as Jewish leaders (2^{1-2}, 3^1), and was keen to show that Jesus was not a political rebel challenging Rome. Indeed, Pilate only condemned Jesus under pressure from the Jewish authorities, and even made attempts to free him ($23^{4,14,20-22}$), and the Jews, not the Romans, were blamed for his death (23^{25}, 24^{20}). Whereas Matthew 1^{1-16} traced the ancestry of Jesus back to Abraham, forefather of the Jews, Luke (3^{23-38}) traced Jesus' ancestry back to Adam, supposed forefather of the human race. Although neither of the two records is reliable, Luke's intention is clearly to say that the gospel must be universal, a point made also at 3^6 and 13^{29}.

Tradition says that the writer of both volumes was Luke. Some second-century writings said that Luke was from Antioch in Syria, an unmarried doctor and a companion of Paul, and that he died in Greece at eighty-four years of age. Some people have wondered, however, if he came from around Troas or Philippi, an area he seemed to know well. The Acts of the Apostles tells its story using the third person 'they' as far as 16^8, but at verse 9 it suddenly changes to 'we' as if the writer had just joined Paul's travelling missionary group there at Troas. From there on the writer alternates between using 'they' and 'we', seeming to indicate his own presence on the journeys by using 'we'. It is noticeable that 'they' is used whenever Paul's group visits the area around Troas and Philippi (e.g. Acts 20^6). Perhaps at these times Luke was given leave to visit his home, but wrote about what had happened in his absence (using 'they'), then continued the story as an eye-witness again (using 'we'). Some scholars have questioned whether Luke was the real author. Sometimes a famous person was claimed to be the author so that people would want to read the work, but since Luke was not a famous or outstanding person there was no point in saying that he was the author unless this was true. We have little reason to doubt that he wrote both volumes, and was the only Gentile amongst the gospel-writers.

The missionary journeys would provide Luke with opportunities of meeting many Christian leaders who had known Jesus personally. Paul preached at Ephesus where, tradition says, the disciple John cared for Jesus' mother, Mary. Perhaps Mary herself told Luke the stories of Jesus' birth and childhood. When Paul was kept in custody for two years at Caesarea his visitors probably included many who had known Jesus and were able to speak of events not mentioned in Mark's gospel. Luke was with Paul at this time (Acts 27^1).

During one of his times in prison, probably at Rome or Ephesus, Paul wrote to a friend named Philemon, whose slave had run away from his home at Colossae, hoping to find refuge with Paul. The letter mentioned those who were working with Paul and the list includes the name of Luke (Philemon v.24). Paul's letter to the Christians at Colossae (Col. 4^{14}), included greetings from his 'dear friend Luke, the doctor'. When winter was near Paul wrote from prison asking his young friend Timothy to bring a warm cloak and some notebooks. He mentioned that his only companion then was Luke (II Tim. 4^{11}).

The excellent Greek of both volumes is what one would expect of an educated man like a doctor. A doctor was usually a slave, educated to serve his master's family and friends. Perhaps Luke was given his freedom as a reward for good service, and was called in to help when Paul was ill. Acts $16^{6\text{-}12}$ suggests that seeing a man of Macedonia made Paul decide to go and preach there, and one wonders if the man were Luke himself. In verse 12 Luke speaks with pride of Philippi, perhaps again because it was his home district. Some people have suggested that Luke's medical knowledge is obvious in his writing; at Luke 18^{25} he uses the Greek word for surgeon's needle. He spoke of Simon's mother-in-law being in the grip of a high fever (4^{38}) and of a man with an advanced case of leprosy (5^{12}), but many ordinary people speak that way too. Luke had a natural interest in Jesus' healing miracles and shows concern for anyone who was unhappy. He describes Jesus' concern for poor and needy people ($1^{46\text{-}55}$, 2^8, $6^{20\text{-}25}$, 6^{30}, $9^{46\text{-}48}$, $12^{13\text{-}34}$, $14^{7\text{-}24}$, 16^{13}, $16^{19\text{-}25}$, $18^{9\text{-}30}$, $21^{1\text{-}4}$), and for outcasts of society ($5^{12\text{-}14}$, $5^{27\text{-}39}$, $7^{36\text{-}50}$, $8^{43\text{-}48}$, $9^{52\text{-}56}$, 15, $17^{11\text{-}19}$, $19^{1\text{-}10}$, $23^{29\text{-}43}$).

The Roman world showed little respect or concern for women. Amongst the Jews they received more care, but had less rights than the men, who often prayed, 'Thank you God for not making me a Gentile, a slave or a woman'. Luke uses every opportunity to show Jesus' concern for women, and the gospel mentions Anna the prophetess, Simon's mother-in-law, the widow at Nain, a woman at a Pharisee's house, women amongst Jesus' followers, a woman with a haemorrhage, Mary and Martha, a crippled woman, women on the Crucifixion route, women at the tomb. The Annunciation story is told from Mary's point of view ($2^{36\text{-}38}$, 4^{38}, $7^{11\text{-}17}$, $7^{36\text{-}50}$, $8^{2\text{-}3}$, $8^{43\text{-}48}$, $10^{38\text{-}42}$, $13^{10\text{-}17}$, $23^{27\text{-}31}$, 24^{10}). In his commentary *Epistles of St Paul: Paul's epistle to Philippians* (Macmillan, 1879), pp. 55–6, Bishop Lightfoot wrote that in certain parts of the Roman Empire, especially in Macedonia, a woman's 'social position was higher than in most parts of the civilized world. . . . The extant Macedonian inscriptions seem to assign to the sex a higher social influence than is common among the civilized nations of antiquity'. Sir William Ramsay makes a similar comment in *St Paul, the traveller and the Roman citizen* (Hodder & Stoughton, 1925) and remarks on the prominence given to women in the Macedonian cities visited by Paul. In *The First Three Gospels* (SCM Press, 1966), William Barclay suggests that if Luke were a Macedonian it would account for his gospel mentioning women more than the other gospels do, but Barclay thought it more likely another indication of the wideness of Jesus' love and graciousness.

Luke's concern for Gentiles did not mean that he was unconcerned about the Jews. He wanted them to recognize Jesus as their Messiah, or Deliverer, sent by God. Jesus was their new Temple, their meeting-place with God. The gospel was to spread from their city of Jerusalem to the whole world. Luke chose and presented material to show how Jewish history and the prophecies of the Old Testament led to Jesus. No prophet had visited the Jews for many years, but prophecy came again with John the Baptist. God's Spirit had brought about Creation and now it was bringing about a new Creation. Luke gives great importance to the Holy Spirit whose guidance Jesus constantly obeyed and which his followers must also obey ($1^{15,35,67}$, 2^{25-26}, $4^{1,14-18}$, 10^{21}, 11^{13}). Judaism's natural progress should be towards Christianity. Luke's style is influenced by the Greek version of the Old Testament (the Septuagint) and often he uses words which spoke there of God's ways of helping His people. Used in his story of Jesus they mean that Jesus is God's way of intervening in history to help His people now, e.g. 'deliverance' (Ex. 14^{13}, Ps.37^{39}, Is.26^1, Luke $1^{69\ 71}$), 'peace' (Is.55^{12}, 66^{12}, Luke 2^{14}, 19^{38}, 8^{48}), God's visit (Ex. 4^{31}, Ps.106^4, Jer.10^{15}, Luke 19^{44}, 7^{16}). The stories of Jesus' birth and childhood would remind them of other times when, in strange circumstances, children were born who brought God's help to the nation, e.g. Isaac, Samson, Samuel (Gen. 17^{15-19}, Jud. 13, I Sam. 1^{1-20}). The songs of Mary and Zechariah emphasized that Jesus brought God's deliverance; their language and literary style are those of the Old Testament, e.g. the song of Samuel's mother, Hannah (I Sam. 2^{1-10}). Luke was keen to show that Jesus was a descendant of King David, from whose family the Jews expected the Messiah to come.

Until recently Luke was thought of mainly as the historian amongst the gospel-writers. Other people had written accounts, but Luke wanted to concentrate on writing accurately, carefully checking all details and setting the story in its historical background (1^{1-4}, 3^1). This makes it difficult to explain why his versions of Paul's speeches in Acts do not seem consistent with ideas expressed in Paul's own letters. Acts 15 and Galatians 2 are an example of this, and some people think that Acts 17^{22-31} sounds most unlike Paul. Luke also presents a picture of peace and goodwill in the early Church, omitting to mention disagreements like those between Peter and Paul. Obviously he felt that the Church must present a united front if it were to continue the work that Jesus had begun, and in Paul's speeches it seems that Luke was expressing his own rather than Paul's ideas. This means that as well as being a historian he was a theologian with definite ideas of his own.

Luke saw the life of Jesus as one long journey towards crucifixion at Jerusalem as God's Suffering Servant. Jesus was the new Israel who would not fail God as the old nation of Israel had done. Though rejected, he made that journey with majesty and serenity, the perfect example for mankind and one his followers could remember when they were being persecuted. The tragedy and sadness of the Crucifixion is not mitigated but muted in the light of the joyous Resurrection and the triumph of the Ascension. Luke's gospel is full of praise and joy, and he alone attributes four great songs of praise to Mary, Zechariah, the angels and Simeon (1^{46-55}, 1^{68-79}, 2^{14}, 2^{29-32}). Praise is the essence of 7^{16}, 13^{13}, 17^{15} and 24^{52}.

The first Christians had expected Jesus to return almost at once to collect his people into God's Kingdom. Disappointment could have left them disillusioned, but Luke gave meaning to the delay of the parousia, (Greek for 'arrival'). The delay was to allow time for the Church to do its work for the spread of the gospel. God's Kingdom was not to be thought of as a visible, geographical place, but as anywhere and everywhere where people followed the example and teaching of Jesus. It was not something in the dim and distant future, for it began with Jesus and is present whenever his influence is seen (17^{20}, 9^{27}, 21^{8-36}, 12^{38-46}). The destruction of Jerusalem was in the near future (21^{32}), and would be seen by many who were listening to Jesus, but no one could know when the Son of Man would return. The only way to be ready for him was to use every moment so that one would never be worried about being taken by surprise (18^{1-8}, 17^{20-30}, 12^{32-48}, 21^{34-36}). To be in this constant state of readiness one must know God's will and be guided by the Holy Spirit, hence the need of prayer. Luke's gospel emphasizes the importance of prayer, showing how Jesus prayed at every important event in his life (3^{21}, 5^{16}, 6^{12}, 9^{18-19}, 9^{28-29}, 11^{1}, $22^{32,41-46}$, $23^{34,46}$). Only in this gospel do we find the parables of the Friend at Midnight, the Unjust Judge and the Pharisee and the Publican (11^{5-13}, 18^{1-8}, 18^{9-14}). By going frequently to God in prayer Jesus opened himself to the guidance of God's Spirit (4^{16-19}) and his followers would find the same (Acts 2^{1-4}).

As we read Luke's gospel we find that he has used about 65 per cent of Mark's gospel. Like Matthew, Luke tidied up some of Mark's phrases as he went along, e.g. Mark 4^{38-40}. The disciples said to Jesus, 'Master, we are sinking. Don't you care?' and Jesus replied, 'Why are you such cowards?' Luke (8^{24-25}) makes the whole thing more reverent and respectful – the disciples cried, 'Master, Master, we are sinking', and Jesus asked, 'Where is your faith?'

Luke seems to have arranged sections of Mark's gospel alternately with sections of his own material (L) and Q. Most scholars think he was using Mark's gospel as his foundation, inserting extra material as he worked. In 1921, however, the scholar G.H. Streeter argued that Luke's first gospel was made up of Q and his own collected material, i.e. Q + L. This could be referred to as 'Proto-Luke'. Then, Streeter suggests, Luke wrote a second version adding sections from Mark, i.e. Q + L + M. Streeter's Proto-Luke theory is not generally accepted. Many manuscripts of Luke's gospel in the original Greek still exist and sometimes they vary at certain points. Some Bibles include footnotes drawing one's attention to the different translations possible. Usually these do not make much difference to the sense, but occasionally there is a difficulty, e.g. 22^{19} – is Luke referring to one or two cups at the Last Supper? (While some versions of the Bible include verse 20, others leave it out.) The present availability of so many versions of the Bible means that they may present us with somewhat different interpretations, e.g. Revised Standard Version, Jerusalem Bible, New English Bible, Today's English Version, etc.

Since Mark's gospel is considered to have been written about A.D. 65, Luke's writing must be later than this. Luke (21^{20}) suggests that he knew about the siege of Jerusalem which took place in A.D. 69–70. Either he did not know of Paul's letters or chose to ignore the ideas Paul expressed. He doesn't tell us what happened finally to Paul, but perhaps he did not wish to take the story beyond the time when it reached Rome. On the other hand, Luke may have intended to continue writing about the spread of Christianity in a third volume. Considering the facts as we know them it is thought that he must have been writing about A.D. 75 to 80.

The Coming of Christ (1¹ to 4¹³)

First read each section from your Bible.

Introduction (1¹⁻⁴)

This gospel and Luke's other volume, the Acts of the Apostles, were dedicated to someone he called 'Most excellent Theophilus'. (See comment on p. 6.)

These four verses were written in excellent Greek. William Barclay described them as 'the best bit of Greek in the New Testament'. Obviously Luke wanted his writings to be accepted by someone who was cultured and educated. The style was one used in the important documents of the time and showed the writer's concern for accuracy. Luke knew that many other writers had already written about Jesus from stories told by people who had seen the events happen. He carefully checked all the details and wanted to write his own orderly account to provide Theophilus with reliable information.

General note concerning 1⁵–2⁵²

This section, written in the style and vocabulary of the Septuagint (the Greek translation of the Old Testament), was a way of showing the Jews that God sent John the Baptist. For about 500 years there had been no prophet, but 1¹⁵,⁶⁷, 2²⁶,³⁶ show that prophecy was beginning again. Read Isaiah 21¹, 35¹⁰, Psalms 50¹⁵, 116¹⁶, and see how Luke's words are reminiscent of them. Read the second introductory chapter (pp. 8–9) from 'Luke's concern for Gentiles did not mean . . . John the Baptizer'. It particularly concerns 1⁵ to 2⁵².

Although John arrived six months before Jesus, Luke puts their birth stories together and makes it clear that Jesus was first in importance. John was filled with God's Spirit from the time he was born, but the very conception of Jesus was the work of God's Spirit (1¹⁵⁻³⁵). At that time people described a religious experience as the visit of an angel, a being thought of as God's messenger. The Jews' ideas about angels often seem to have been influenced by the religions of neighbouring countries like Babylon and Persia. Later, when Jesus had an experience of God's closeness at his baptism, Luke describes it in tangible form as God's Spirit appearing 'in bodily form like a dove'. The essence of this section is Semitic, written to appeal to the Jewish people.

Zechariah the priest has a vision in the Temple (1^{5-25})

The Romans were established in Syria and their general, Pompey, sent an army to sort out a civil war in Palestine where two brothers, Hyrcanus and Aristobulus, were fighting each other. Eventually Pompey established Hyrcanus as High Priest in Jerusalem and put King Antipater of Idumaea in charge of Palestine to keep the peace. From 40 B.C. Antipater's son, Herod, took his father's place. Herod comes down through the pages of history as a monster of brutality. He was married ten times. Later he became obsessed with suspicion that people were plotting to take his throne and had three of his sons and his favourite wife, Mariamne, put to death. According to Matthew's gospel the babies of Bethlehem were massacred for the same reason. He must be credited, however, with keeping the country at peace for thirty-five years and for organizing great building schemes. He agreed to observe the Jewish Law and built a magnificent Temple for the Jews. He rebuilt an old port, naming it Caesarea in honour of the Roman emperor. He ruled over Judaea, Samaria, Peraea, Galilee and some territory to the north-east.

The Jews were allowed to continue their own religious system. Their priests were chosen exclusively from families who claimed descent from Moses' brother, Aaron. By now, there were so many priests that each was allowed to serve in the Temple for only two weeks of the year. They were organized into twenty-four groups. In the eighth group, known as Abijah's group (I Chron. 24^{10}), was the elderly Zechariah.

Some of the duties in the Temple were more popular than others, so the priests drew lots to decide which duty each would do. On this occasion Zechariah was honoured to carry out the duty given to a priest only once in his lifetime, that of burning the incense at the altar in front of the Holy of Holies. He would do this before morning and evening worship and it was said that the incense smoke carried the prayers sweetly to God. The same priest would say the prayer of blessing at the end of the day's worship.

Zechariah was alarmed to see an angel standing to the right of the altar (see General Note above). The angel reassured Zechariah saying that God had heard his prayers and his wife, Elizabeth, would have a baby son whom they must name John (meaning 'God has been gracious'). John would bring joy and gladness to many people and he would do great work for God. He would not drink anything alcoholic. This meant he would be following the example of people like the Nazirites and Rechabites who regarded wine as the product of foreigners, pagans like the Canaanites who lived in Palestine before Joshua brought the Israelites there. To abstain from wine was a sign that the man's life was dedicated strictly to God's work. From babyhood John would be guided by God's Holy Spirit, God's way of using someone for His purposes. John would also be filled with the spirit of the great prophet, Elijah, and he would guide the people back to God and prepare them for His coming.

The Jews believed that they had been specially chosen by God and that He had controlled their history. They expected Elijah to return to warn them when God was coming to keep the promises He had made to them as a nation (Malachi 4⁵). Then He would send somebody like their great king, David, to save them, a Deliverer or Messiah (Greek – 'Christos'), who would defeat all their enemies and make them a ruling nation under God's control. They would bring the other nations of the world to God.

Now, it seemed, John was to do the work expected of Elijah.

Zechariah and his wife, Elizabeth, who was the daughter of a priest, were devoted to God's work. No one could understand why this saintly old couple had not been blessed with children, for barrenness was regarded as a punishment for sin. Yet they continued to serve God faithfully even though He seemed to have withheld His blessings from them. Now they were much too old to have a baby, so it was natural that Zechariah found it difficult to believe the angel's words. The angel told him, 'I am Gabriel, God's attendant, and He has sent me to tell you this good news.' Gabriel means 'hero of God'.

Isaac, Samson and Samuel had been born to parents who had long since given up hope of having children (Gen. 17¹⁷, Jud. 13³, I Sam. 1⁵). Luke wanted the Jews to realize that God was again intervening in their history by sending John, and later Jesus, to His people.

The angel went on, 'Because you disbelieve, you will be unable to speak until these things have happened. When the time comes, my words will be proved true.' Zechariah's dumbness was both sign and punishment to him. The people outside, who had waited a long time for the evening blessing, could see that something had happened to Zechariah. Unable to speak, he made signs hoping that they would understand. People today might have come to the conclusion that he had suffered a stroke.

With his duties finished, Zechariah went home. Soon Elizabeth realized she was pregnant. For five months she did not go out in public, but she was pleased to be expecting a baby. No longer would the people be able to say that God was displeased with her.

Thus Luke began his story at the Jerusalem Temple, and there, finally, he will end it with the friends of the risen Jesus praising God. The Jews believed that when God came He would appear first at the Temple (Malachi 3^1 and 4^{5-6}).

The Annunciation (1^{26-38})

Six months after Zechariah's vision Gabriel was sent to Nazareth, a town near the lake of Galilee, to a girl named Mary who was betrothed to the local carpenter, Joseph. Luke says that Joseph was a descendant of King David, yet he says that Jesus was conceived through the agency of the Holy Spirit, not through Joseph. Jewish Law, however, made the children of a marriage descendants of the husband's family, thus making Jesus a descendant of King David, from whose family the Messiah must come, but also the direct creation of God.

The angel said to Mary, 'Greetings, most favoured one. The Lord is with you'. Then he told the bewildered and frightened girl, 'Do not be afraid, Mary, for God is pleased with you. You are to have a son whom you will name Jesus. He will be great and people will know him as the Son of the Most High. The Lord God will give him David's throne and he will rule for ever. His kingdom will never end.' (The name Jesus is the Greek form of the Hebrew name, Joshua, and means 'God saves' or 'the deliverer'.)

Mary asked, 'How can this happen? I am still a virgin.' The angel told her, 'God's Holy Spirit will come to you, and the child will be holy – God's child. Despite her age, your relative Elizabeth is also expecting a baby. You see, nothing is impossible to God.' Mary replied, 'I am God's servant. I will accept whatever He says.' Then the angel left her. Mary's answer echoed Old Testament phrases like Psalm 116^{16}, 'O Lord, I am thy servant!'

Betrothal, which lasted for exactly a year, made Mary the legal wife of Joseph. Betrothal could be cancelled only by divorce. If the man died during the year, the girl was referred to as a widow. The betrothal year was spent in preparing what would be needed for the home.

The possibility of the virgin birth is often questioned. The births of children like Isaac, Samson and Samuel were seen as miraculous interventions of God to help His people. Luke presents the birth of Jesus in the same way, but as much more important for Jesus' birth was the great climax of them all. He was the long-awaited Messiah himself, sent even more directly from God. In Matthew 1^{18-25} is the only other reference to a virgin birth.

Mary visits her relative Elizabeth (1^{39-45})

Mary travelled south to the hills of Judea to her relative, Elizabeth. When Elizabeth heard Mary's story her own baby jumped inside her, as if with joy. This is, again, one of Luke's ways of emphasizing that Jesus was greater than John, for the story suggests that even in the womb John recognized and acknowledged that Jesus was the Messiah. It confirmed that these events were God's doing.

Elizabeth cried out, 'God has blessed you more than all other women! What an honour that the mother of my Lord should come to visit me! You must be very happy, knowing that God will keep this promise to you!'

The Magnificat, Mary's song of praise (1^{46-56})

Luke's gospel is full of joy and praise and thanksgiving. Only in his gospel do we find the songs of praise of Mary, Zechariah, the angels and Simeon. Of these the Magnificat is perhaps best known, for it is said between the Bible readings at Evensong in Anglican churches. The songs express Luke's own ideas so they tell us something about him. They are composed in similar ways mainly from phrases from the Old Testament. Mary's song, which magnifies or praises God, seems to have been modelled on the song of Samuel's mother, Hannah (I Sam. 2^{1-10}). Hannah had belonged to old Israel, Mary was the mother of the new Israel.

The song tells how the prophecies of the past are being fulfilled, e.g. Isaiah 5^{6-12}. As always, God was keeping His word in caring for the Israelite people. He had caused the collapse of many mighty empires that threatened them. God was the champion of the poor and oppressed. The gospel of Luke reflects over and over his concern for the poor, the hungry and the oppressed.

The birth of John who would become the Baptist (1⁵⁷⁻⁸⁰)

Mary stayed with Elizabeth for three months and then went home. When Elizabeth's son was born the neighbours and relatives were delighted at the birth, and it was arranged that he would be circumcized and named on the eighth day after his birth, according to custom. When Elizabeth said that he would be named John, they were horrified. Surely he should be named after his father or someone in the family? They asked what Zechariah felt about it and, still dumb, he wrote on a writing-block, 'His name is John!'

Immediately the old priest found himself able to speak again. The amazed neighbours had soon told everyone in the hillside villages. It was all very strange, and must mean that the baby was destined to be a great person!

Zechariah's doubts were over. The song of praise ascribed to him is often used in church services and is known as the Benedictus. Like Mary's song it uses many Old Testament phrases, thanking God that at last He is going to send a descendant of David to save His people. God is keeping the covenant, or agreement, made with Abraham when the nation began (Gen. 17⁵). God would protect His people from enemies so that, free from fear, they could concentrate on serving Him, keeping themselves holy and upright.

Zechariah said of his son's future, 'You, my child, shall be known as the prophet of God. You will go ahead of the Lord, to prepare His way and lead His people to salvation through knowing Him and having their sins forgiven. God's tender compassion makes the sun shine on us; the heavenly sun will help those who seem doomed to darkness [evil] and death, and will guide our steps to the way of peace.'

Circumcision was the sign of a boy's entry into the bond between God and the nation. The Jews had given a religious meaning to the old eastern custom. It was a sign of their agreement to belong to God, much as baptism is to a Christian.

The Benedictus used phrases from Psalms 41, 105, 106, 107, 111, 132; and from Isaiah 40 came the words, 'Prepare a road for the Lord through the wilderness; clear a highway across the desert for our God.' When the Jews were in exile in Babylon nearly six centuries before this, an unknown prophet, whose sayings have been added to those of the prophet Isaiah in chapters 40–55 of our work, comforted the people. This prophet is often known as 'the Second Isaiah'. He wrote promising that God would save them and would bring them back to Jerusalem by an easy and safe roadway made across the desert from Babylon to Jerusalem. Now Zechariah's son, John, was to prepare the way for the arrival of their Messiah. John was the forerunner, or herald. God was about to visit His people, to decide which of them deserved punishment and which should be saved.

Malachi (4^{5-6}) prophesied that Elijah would come back to warn the people of the arrival of 'the day of the Lord'. Now it would seem that John was meant to do the work expected of Elijah, for he was to warn the people that the Lord was coming, and they should clear their lives in readiness.

As John grew up he was filled with the Holy Spirit and spent his time in the deserts until he was ready to begin preaching his message. The deserts were near to the Dead Sea and one wonders if perhaps he had joined the Essene monks who lived at the monastery of Qumran. The Essenes were not happy with the way the Jewish religious authorities organized worship at the Temple, so they formed a self-dependent community in a valley near the Dead Sea, a bleak and desolate area. They hand-copied the Jewish scriptures and wrote about their own beliefs, which included frequent baptisms for those who wished to confess sins. This may have led John to recommend baptism in the Jordan river as a sign of repentance for all people and the beginning of a new way of living in preparation for the Lord's arrival. Perhaps by now John's elderly parents had died. John's life in the desert reminds one again of the way in which Elijah had lived, though Luke tells us no details of his food and dress.

Mary and Joseph travel to Bethlehem (2^{1-7})

The gospels of Matthew and Luke say that Jesus was born at Bethlehem, which was seventy miles from Nazareth. Micah (5^2) had prophesied that, although Bethlehem was not large nor important, it would produce a governor for Israel.

Quirinius became the area-governor in A.D. 6 and organized a census then. The Romans seemed to expect a census every fourteen years, so perhaps there had been one in 8 B.C. The dating of our years was not decided until the sixth century A.D., and by that time it was difficult to fix the year of Jesus' birth with accuracy. Romans did not usually expect people to register at their ancestral homes. The Jews themselves may have insisted on this and such arrangements could delay a census considerably.

Joseph made his way to Bethlehem, the old home of his ancestors, the family of King David. By now, Mary must have been Joseph's wife, and we wonder why she chose to accompany Joseph for she was in an advanced stage of pregnancy.

Registration usually served to tell the Romans how much they could expect from local taxpayers and how many local men could be conscripted for the legions, but Jews were not conscripted because of their religious rules which forbade them to work or carry weapons on the sabbath.

The guest rooms of Bethlehem were already full when Joseph and Mary arrived. This would necessitate using the lower room, usually used for travellers' animals, for the travellers themselves, and it may have been in such a shelter Mary's baby was born. The eating-trough served as a makeshift cot. From his birth Jesus was to share human difficulties. Mary wrapped him closely in the 'swaddling' bands she had brought, a custom which was thought to help a baby's limbs to grow firm.

The shepherds and the angels (2⁸⁻²⁰)

Palestinian shepherds were often hired to look after the sheep which belonged to a town or village. It has been suggested that the flocks reared on the hillsides near Bethlehem were intended to become the unblemished lambs for Temple sacrifices. A shepherd's work was demanding and dangerous, for he had to protect the flock day and night from robbers and wild animals. He must provide proof of the fate of any sheep missing from the flock. These men, like most of the working-class people, were unable to keep the Torah, the many regulations of Judaism, and they were regarded with contempt by the religious leaders. Such people were called 'the people of the land'. Yet Luke shows how the news of Jesus' birth came first to these lowly men as they were doing their ordinary everyday work. The birth of a boy was usually celebrated by a party at his home, but Mary and Joseph were away from family and friends and those who came to rejoice at his birth were ordinary working shepherds.

Again Luke expresses the wonder of the coming of Jesus by saying that angels were present (see General Note above). The appearance of a bright light and an angel naturally frightened the shepherds until the messenger said, 'Don't be afraid. Listen, I have joyful news for you and for all people, for your Saviour has been born in David's town. He is Christ (Messiah), the Lord. You will know him for he is wrapped in swaddling clothes and lies in a manger.' The title 'Christ' meant he would be acknowledged by the Jews; the title 'Lord' meant he would be acknowledged by Gentiles too.

A crowd of angels appeared, singing, 'Glory to God in Highest Heaven; and on earth His peace among men with whom He is pleased.' The angels' song, another of Luke's songs of joy and praise, is often known by its first words in Latin, 'Gloria in Excelsis Deo'.

When the angels had gone, the shepherds hurried to the town to see what had happened. As promised, they found the baby in the manger and Mary and Joseph nearby, and they told the amazed people what had caused them to come. Mary, however, pondered about these strange events, probably wondering what the future was going to bring. Luke travelled with Paul the missionary who established a church at Ephesus (Acts 18^{19}), where tradition says the disciple John cared for Mary after the death of Jesus.

Luke does not tell of the Wise Men's visit nor the massacre of the children under two years old in Bethlehem, nor of Joseph taking the family to safety in Egypt (Matt. 2). Herod the Great, who ordered the killing of the children in the hope that Jesus would be amongst them, died in 4 B.C. If Jesus was at the toddler stage by then, he must have been born about 6 B.C., about the time when a delayed census beginning in 8 B.C., could have taken place. The accuracy of dating is unimportant when one considers the more important things Luke's gospel has to say. God's work was not to be frustrated by the difficulties of the time. Luke prefers to tell of ordinary workmen who recognized God's signs and readily obeyed. He knew that all the world over men and nations longed for an inward peace and an answer to their search for life's meaning. Jesus was more than the Messiah for whom the Jews waited, he could be the Gentiles' Saviour too. Many believe that in the birth of this baby, God was coming to live with His people. This is what is meant by the word 'Incarnation'.

The child Jesus (2$^{21-40}$)

Again it is only Luke who records the stories found in this section, which he may have learned from Mary herself.

Luke, who was a Gentile, makes a point of telling us how Jesus was brought up in a good Jewish home, where his parents obeyed the Jewish religious laws. In later years, Paul, the great missionary to other nations, also remained faithful to Jewish ways.

Primitive people had all kinds of strange taboos about childbirth and menstruation (see Leviticus 12$^{1-8}$). A new mother must attend a ceremony of purification and the Jews circumcized baby boys on their eighth day, even if that day fell on a sabbath. The name Jesus, or Joshua, meant 'the deliverer' or 'the Lord is salvation'. The first male baby of human and animal belonged to God, and in ancient times would have been given as a sacrifice, but the Jews redeemed or 'bought back' a baby by giving five shekels instead. The mother was expected to give an offering of a lamb and a pigeon or turtledove. If she could not afford a lamb she gave two birds, and this is what Mary gave.

Having done what the law demanded, Mary and Joseph took their baby to the Temple at Jerusalem 'to present him to God'. As they arrived they were met by an old man called Simeon, who, guided by the Holy Spirit, took Jesus in his arms and praised God. He had always believed that he would see the Messiah before he died, and he said, 'Now, Lord, let your servant depart in peace, for my eyes have seen the means by which the people will be saved. He will be a light to heathen people and glory to your people, the Israelites.' Simeon longed to see the Jewish people serving God as they should. He told Mary, 'This child is a sign whom many will ignore, and you yourself will be heartbroken by what will happen to him. Because of him many will be saved or will fall, and the secrets of many hearts will be known.' When Jesus became a man he set high standards, putting spiritual matters before material things. He called people to purify and discipline their lives. Some loved him and changed their ways. Others hated him because they could not meet his challenge.

Also in the Temple was an eighty-four year old woman, Anna, who was said to be a prophetess. She was a widow whose husband had died seven years after their marriage, and Anna spent most of her time around the Temple, worshipping, fasting, and praying. When she saw the child she thanked God and began to talk about him to everyone who longed to see Palestine a land wholly devoted to the service of God.

Having obeyed all these religious laws, the family went home to Nazareth in the Galilee district. Jesus grew big and strong and wise, living in a way which pleased God and the people living around him.

The boy Jesus in the Temple (2^{41-52})

The twelfth birthday marks the beginning of preparation for adult life for any Jewish boy, even today, and in whatever country he grows up. For a year a rabbi gives the boy special lessons in the history and religion of his people and he practises reading in Hebrew. The climax

A Bar-mitzvah ceremony in the old part of the city of Jerusalem.

of the year comes at a special synagogue ceremony when he wears a cap and talith (prayer-shawl), and reads the Scripture. He has then become a member of the synagogue, or Son of the Law (Bar-mitzvah) and can take his place with the other men of the synagogue.

Every year Joseph and Mary went to Jerusalem for the most important of the Jewish religious festivals, the Passover. Every Jewish man living within fifteen miles of the city was expected to attend the festival, which commemorated the time when the angel of Death 'passed over' the houses of the Israelite slaves in Egypt during the time of Moses. The Jews still celebrate the festival wherever they live.

The people of Nazareth would travel together, the children playing together along the way. At the end of the festival week people from various towns and villages would meet to travel home again. Perhaps the men walked together discussing religion and national affairs. Perhaps Mary thought that her growing son would be with the men, while Joseph thought he must be with the other children, near to their mothers.

Probably they didn't miss him until the families got together for the evening meal towards the end of the first day's journey, and when they did they hurried back to the city, but didn't find him until the third day. He was still in the Temple, deep in conversation with the learned leaders and rabbis, who were amazed at his questions and his ability to understand difficult matters of religion. At twelve, he would be allowed inside the Temple and had the right to discuss the interpretation of scripture with adults. It was clear that Jesus, as a special servant of God, was already adult and mature and able to dispute with the greatest of the Jewish scholars.

Like any mother, Mary expressed her relief in anger, and she said to Jesus, 'My son, why have you treated us like this? Your father and I have been searching for you and we were worried!' Jesus replied, 'Why did you search? Surely you realized that I was bound to be in my Father's house.'

Mary referred to Joseph as 'your father', but Jesus deliberately referred to God as his Father. Some people feel that, even at this early age, Jesus was aware of his unique relationship with God. Others would say that Jesus had a serious attitude towards religion which was perfectly natural at his age and that all Jews referred to God as 'Father'.

Mary and Joseph seemed unable to understand their son's attitude, but Jesus went home with his parents and accepted their authority. As with previous strange events, Mary stored these memories in her mind. Meanwhile Jesus grew up and developed in wisdom and 'in favour with

God and man'. Jesus believed that his first and foremost duty was to God, but he also realized that Mary and Joseph had a responsibility as parents, and he obeyed them.

The historical place of the story; The message of John; John is arrested (3¹⁻²⁰)

Luke obviously regarded the beginning of John's preaching as an important point in history. From then on nothing would ever be the same again, so he marks the point in the story's historical background by telling his readers of six rulers in power at the time. From these facts both Jews and Gentiles would be able to pinpoint the time when John offered his news to anyone who would listen. The six mentioned by Luke are the emperor Tiberius, Herod Antipas, Philip, Pontius Pilate, Lysanias and the Jewish High Priest Caiaphas.

Tiberius took over from the Roman emperor, Augustus, in A.D. 14. He was now in the fifteenth year of his reign, which would make it A.D. 28 or 29. This dating would be especially helpful for non-Jewish readers.

In 4 B.C. Herod the Great died and his territory was divided up between his sons. Abilene was not in Herod's territory but was under the rule of Lysanias. Herod Antipas received Galilee and Peraea which he held until A.D. 39. Jesus lived and preached most of his time in Galilee. Until A.D. 33 Philip ruled over Ituraea and Trachonitis. He built Caesarea Philippi. For a while Archelaus ruled in Judaea, Samaria and Idumaea, but the Jews asked to have him removed, and he was replaced in A.D. 6 by a Roman governor. Pontius Pilate was the fifth of these Roman governors and was in power when John the Baptist was preaching. Pilate continued as governor until A.D. 37. The most powerful religious leader was the Jewish High Priest. The position had been hereditary, but by this time there was competition and intrigue to obtain it. Caiaphas was now officially High Priest, but his father-in-law, Annas, the previous High Priest, was very influential still and the two were often named together.

Having dated the event in detail, Luke wrote, 'The word of God came to John in the desert.' Similar words had been used to describe God's call to the Old Testament prophets. For many years the Jewish nation had been without such a prophet.

John preached in the Jordan valley to anyone who would stop and listen. He called them to repent so that God could forgive their sins, and asked them to make a public witness of starting a new life by being baptized in the waters of the Jordan river. Perhaps the idea was that it is more difficult to go back on a promise when we have made it in front of other people. Mark and Matthew were keen to point out how John was a second Elijah, even in the way he dressed, but Luke does not tell us what John looked like. He is more concerned to show John as the last prophet before the Messiah, but emphasizes that John was not as important as Jesus. Luke shows how Jesus held John in high regard and said that anyone who ignored John's message and baptism was ignoring God's purposes (7^{30}), and that whereas the people of the past had the Law and the Prophets for guidance, people now had John (16^{16}).

All four gospels used parts of Isaiah (40^{4f}) to describe John the Baptist, but Luke quoted most fully. John's was the voice crying aloud in the wilderness, 'Prepare a way for the Lord, clear a straight path for him. Every ravine shall be filled in and every mountain and hill levelled; the corners shall be straightened and the rough parts made smooth, and all mankind shall see God's deliverance.' God had brought back the Jewish exiles safely from Babylon, as Isaiah had promised. The quotation would tell the Jews that God was coming again now to deliver them. The people must tidy up their lives for the Messiah as they would tidy up the local roads for the arrival of a king. Luke always emphasized the universal character of Christianity, and here he uses the words 'all mankind'.

Attracted by this strange desert preacher, crowds came to see John and many felt moved to be baptized. John was no flatterer and had no sweet words for them. The Jews tended to take for granted their privileges as God's Chosen People, so John shouted at them, 'Who warned you about the trouble to come, you snakes, you viper's brood! Prove that you are sorry by living better lives. Don't imagine that you are safe and privileged just because you are Jews, descendants of Abraham. God can make children for himself out of the stones around us. Already He has put the axe at the bottom of the tree. Unless you produce good results he will cut you down!' John's message emphasized punishment for sins, Jesus offered forgiveness of sins.

To those who asked what they could do John said, 'If you have two shirts give one to somebody who has none. Share your food, too.' To publicans, who were tax-collectors for the Romans and often cheated their countrymen to line their own pockets, John said, 'Do not ask more than the rightful amount.' To soldiers he said, 'Don't bully or blackmail people into doing what you want. Manage on the pay you get for being a soldier.' Roman soldiers often carried heavy packs and were allowed to order a foreigner to carry the pack, but only for one mile.

Winnowing corn. In many parts of the Middle East the age-old method is still used

John's message had his listeners keyed up with a feeling that something important was about to happen. They wondered if John himself were the Messiah and they asked him, but he replied, 'I can only baptize you with water, but when he comes he will baptize you with the Holy Spirit and with fire.' Fire may have meant God's punishment for those who did not live by His ways, or perhaps the giving of the Holy Spirit, or a purifying experience. John continued, 'He is mightier than I. I am not fit to unfasten his shoes.' The lowest of the household slaves usually removed the sandals of tired guests and washed their feet. Palestinian farmers used a large winnowing-fork to beat the gathered corn, then they would use the fork to throw the wheat in the air in an exposed windy place so that the wind would blow the light husks or chaff, leaving the heavier wheat kernels to be gathered to make flour. The chaff was then destroyed in a fire. John imagined the Messiah coming to judge the people, separating them, like good wheat from useless chaff, and burning the wicked people in Hell, which the Jews thought of as an ever-burning fire.

John demanded social justice, fair play for all people. The idea is characteristic of Luke's gospel. A while later John was arrested because he openly criticized Herod Antipas, who divorced a Nabataean princess in order to marry Herodias, the wife of his brother. The whole affair is found in greater detail in Mark 6^{14-28}, and Matthew 14^{1-12}, where the brother is named as Philip. This man was not the Philip who ruled over Ituraea and Trachonitis. The entangled relationships of the Herod family make the matter a confusing one. The behaviour of Herod Antipas infuriated the Jewish people and caused war between Palestine and the Nabataeans. When Herod Antipas and Herodias were staying at the Machaerus castle, near John's place of preaching, John was arrested and kept in the castle dungeons until Herodias found an opportunity of getting him beheaded.

Jesus is baptized (3^{21-22})

Amongst the crowds who came for baptism was Jesus himself. As he stood in the Jordan river, he was praying. Whenever Luke wants us to realize that an event was particularly important in Jesus' life, he tells us that Jesus was praying, for even Jesus would not make any important step or decision without God.

Luke does not actually say that John baptized Jesus. Perhaps he was afraid it would sound presumptuous of a person like John to baptize someone as unique and sinless as Jesus; and Luke wanted there to be no doubt whatsoever that Jesus was the more important of the two. The story says that the Heaven opened and the Holy Spirit 'in bodily form like a dove' came down on Jesus and a voice from Heaven said, 'You are my beloved son. I am well pleased with you.' Perhaps there really was a dove flying around at the baptism, or perhaps it means that God's Presence was experienced in a very real and definite way. In the Noah story the dove symbolized safety; the rabbis sometimes spoke of God's Spirit at Creation like a dove brooding over its young, protectively. Some would say that it simply means that Jesus had a feeling of inward peace, knowing that he was starting out to do what God wanted him to do. He marked his decision by being baptized, identifying with others who were starting out to obey God's will, as if saying, 'I am one of you. I will set the example. I respect John and by being baptized I am showing that I think his idea is a good one.' In his mind Jesus was sure that he was taking up a unique job as God's Servant, and it seemed to him that God was voicing His approval of the step Jesus was taking. The words of the voice are similar to various parts of the Old Testament (Is. 5[1], 42[1], 62[4], II Sam. 22[20], the coronation Psalm 2[7]). The book of Isaiah contains four poems known as the Servant Songs (Is. 42[1-4], 49[1-6], 50[4-9] and 52[13] to 53[12]). The first poem begins, 'Here is my servant, whom I uphold, my chosen one in whom I delight.' The report of the words Jesus heard at his baptism can only have come from Jesus himself, showing that he thought of himself as the Suffering Servant described in the poems rather than the militant Messiah expected by the Jews. The poems seem to describe perfectly the way Jesus took, even to his death.

Luke 9[28-36] tells the story of the Transfiguration and students should be careful not to confuse the words heard at the two events. At the baptism it would seem that the words were spoken to Jesus as he humbled himself to be baptized. The Transfiguration showed the glory of Jesus and the words were addressed to Peter, James and John.

Jewish priests began their training at eighteen years and were considered ready to be priests at thirty years of age. Jesus was about thirty at this time when his baptism marked the beginning of his full-time work for God. We know nothing about him between the time he was twelve and the time he was thirty. He was often addressed as 'Rabbi' or 'Teacher' (10[25], 12[13], 20[21,28,39]), but there is no suggestion that he was trained as a teacher, and his authority was queried (20[2]).

Now Jesus needed to go away by himself to consider just how he would tackle the great work ahead of him. The words heard at his baptism suggest that he was now fully aware of his unique relationship with God. Ahead of him lay a task never before given to any person. It was for him alone.

The genealogy (family-tree) of Jesus (3^{23-38})

Matthew (1^{1-17}) traces Jesus' ancestry through his legal father Joseph back to Abraham, forefather of the Jews. Matthew wrote particularly for Jewish Christians. Luke traced the family through Joseph to Adam, father of the human race. Luke wrote for world-wide Christians. With Jesus came a new Creation; he was the new and sinless Adam. Both show how Jesus was a descendant of King David, but further comparison shows that the two accounts have various differences. Neither genealogy is accurate. One would expect inaccuracy in the absence of ancient records.

The temptations of Jesus (4^{1-13})

When one is full of enthusiasm to begin a task it is easy to make serious blunders by rushing into the work without sufficient thought. The work that Jesus had to do was too important to risk making blunders, so he went alone into the wilderness to consider how he could best accomplish God's task. To the Jews 'three days' often signified a short time and 'forty days' a long time, but it may also serve to remind us that the Israelites called out of Egypt wandered for forty years in the desert before settling in Canaan as God's People.

Since Jesus went alone this story can only have come from him and it is valuable in helping us to understand what he believed about himself and his work.

The wilderness between the inhabited parts of Judaea and the Dead Sea was known as 'Devastation'. It is still a hot forbidding area of dust, limestone and jagged rocks. There in the silence, absorbed by his thoughts, Jesus didn't think about food until he became aware that he was very hungry. Then 'the Devil came and tempted him'.

Modern readers may argue that the Devil is not a physical being, and the phrase may well mean that a battle was going on in Jesus' mind. We realize, however, that temptation is very real and comes to us in subtle ways, just as temptation came now to Jesus. Originally, the Jews had thought of the Devil as an angel who tested people's loyalty to God (cf. Job). Later, they thought of him as a power of evil setting himself against God in every possible way.

If Jesus really were God's son, surely he must have the power necessary to produce bread from the stones lying at his feet. Their round flat shapes were similar to small Palestinian loaves. The word 'if' may mean that Jesus was beginning to have doubts about himself, but he decided that the Devil was putting such ideas into his mind, and he answered from Deuteronomy 8[3]: 'Man shall not live by bread alone.' On the Exodus journey the people's faith had been sorely tested when they suffered hunger. They learned what dependence on God meant and He provided their 'manna'. Would God now provide food for Jesus? Eastern people lived in poverty and Jesus could soon attract a following if he offered them food, but Jesus rejected the idea. Bribery was no way to attract people. Jesus trusted God and had no need of such proofs of God's power. Man has no dignity when only concerned with satisfying his appetite.

It may have been some time before the next idea came into Jesus' mind. The Jews expected a militant Messiah who would drive out the Romans. Great empires had existed under the power of Assyrians, Babylonians, Persians, Greeks and Romans. Jesus imagined all the kingdoms of the world before him. If ordinary men could gain such empires, how much more could Jesus do if God's power were really in him? He could conquer the world and bring its people to God. This, however, would necessitate lowering his standards, using means that were not always good or honest. He would be using the Devil's method, not God's. On the Exodus journey the Israelites had lowered their standards, paying homage to a calf idol. Jesus could make no such compromise with the Devil, and he answered from Deuteronomy 6[13] and 10[20]: 'You should worship the Lord God and Him only shall you serve.'

Then in imagination Jesus seemed to be high up on the pinnacle above the Jerusalem Temple, 450 feet above the sheer drop into the Kedron valley. Many Jews expected that the Messiah would make his first appearance there, accompanied by angels. If Jesus jumped from there and landed unhurt they would accept that he had come from God. If he really were God's Son, then angels would hold him safely, making sure that he didn't hurt himself on the stones. Such protection had been promised in Psalm 91[11-12]. However, this might suggest that Jesus was asking for proof of God's presence. Such a feat would be a temporary sensation and quickly forgotten. The people of the Exodus journey had required sensational signs, like water coming from rocks, to reassure them of God's presence, but Jesus found an answer from Deuteronomy 6[16]: 'You shall not test the Lord your God.'

Jesus rejected such methods of gaining a following and decided to live according to the poems of Deutero-Isaiah, which described a Suffering Servant of God. Through love and service, even to death, he would bring people to God.

Then we are told that the Devil left Jesus 'until an opportune time'. In his lifetime there were other occasions when he had to resist temptation. The crowds of Capernaum tempted him to stay with them; there he could have been a popular wonder-worker. The crowd to whom he gave bread and fish tempted him to become their king. Peter tempted him to resist arrest. The crowd that greeted his entry into Jerusalem asked him to lead them to military victory. At Gethsemane he was tempted to run away from his destiny. Even during the Crucifixion he was tempted to use his power to 'come down from the cross'.

Jesus' Ministry in Galilee (4^{14} to 9^{50})

Galilee (4$^{14-15}$)

Jesus' baptism had marked his great decision to give all his time to God's work. In the wilderness he had worked out how he would tackle the job. Now he must decide where to begin.

He decided to begin in the area called Galilee. The Jewish historian, Josephus, who lived from A.D. 37 until at least A.D. 100, tells us about Galilee. 'Galil' meant 'a circle' and so area or district. Around it lived many foreigners whose ideas and customs influenced the Galileans. Galilee's two hundred towns and villages were densely populated, with about three million inhabitants who liked the wonderful climate and benefited from the fertile soil and plentiful water. Trees of all kinds grew in abundance and the lake itself provided good fish.

The Galileans were not as set in their ways as the Judaeans who lived close to the ritual and tradition of the Temple and its priests. Ten was the minimum number of men who could constitute a synagogue and there the local men discussed and argued about the Scriptures. 'Synagogue' means a meeting, or assembly. Discussion was often led by scribes and Pharisees, whom Jesus accused of grabbing the chief seats in the synagogues. The 'chazzan', or attendant, was a minor official who seemed to organize just about everything in the synagogue, from cleaning the building to teaching in the school. He organized the service of worship, asking various people to read from the Hebrew scrolls. As the reading progressed it was translated into the more familiar Aramaic or Greek, a few verses at a time. An interesting visitor might be invited to give his interpretation of the reading. In Judaea the priests with their set legalistic ways would be suspicious and resentful of Jesus; Galilee was where he would most likely get a hearing. When he was asked to read and explain the Scriptures, his interpretation came like a breath of fresh air. Josephus said that the Galileans had the reputation of being quick-tempered and trouble-some but they were also known as honourable and courageous, more impressed by a man's bravery than by his wealth.

Eventually the synagogues made Jesus unwelcome, and many Galileans, like those in the next section at Nazareth, turned against him, but he also gained crowds who supported him, at least for a while. Animal sacrifices could only be offered in the Jerusalem Temple. Local synagogues concentrated on teaching and discussion. Most of Jesus' ministry took place in the towns and villages and country spaces of Galilee.

Jesus in his home town, Nazareth (4^{16-30})

The quiet town of Nazareth lay hidden between the slopes of the Galilean hills. From the top of nearby Mount Tabor one could see over the old battlefields of the Jezreel valley (Greek – 'Esdraelon') to Mount Carmel which overlooked the Great Sea (the Mediterranean). Busy thoroughfares ran in all directions, one road south to Jerusalem, another the trade-route between Syria and Egypt. Along the road to the east came Roman legions and camel-caravans from Arabia.

Jesus had been healing and preaching in various Galilean towns when he came back at last to Nazareth. The gospels of Mark and Matthew put this much later in the ministry, (Mark 6, Matt. 13), but Luke may have included it here so that his readers would realize why Jesus spent his time at Capernaum and not at Nazareth, where everyone recognized him immediately as the son of Joseph who had been the local carpenter.

When Jesus turned up at the Nazareth synagogue on the sabbath, the 'chazzan' or attendant handed him the scroll of Isaiah, asking him to read. In the synagogue service the first scripture-reading came from the first five books of the Scriptures, the Law or Pentateuch. The second reading was taken from the books of the Prophets. Whether Jesus was given this second section to read, or whether he chose it himself, we cannot know, but he read from the scroll of the prophet Isaiah, 'The Spirit of the Lord is upon me because he has chosen me to bring good news to the poor. He has sent me to release captives, to give sight to the blind, to free those who are oppressed, to proclaim that the awaited time has arrived.'

In our present Bibles these words are found at Isaiah 58^6 and 61^{1-2}. Our book of Isaiah contains the words of at least three writers, probably more, and these chapters come from an unknown writer whom we call the Third (Trito) Isaiah. Many of the Jews who came back from exile in Babylon struggled against hardship and disillusionment in Palestine. Their faith and early enthusiasm began to fade as the years brought no fulfilment of the promises of earlier prophets. This situation seems to have been the background of an unknown writer (or writers) whom we know as the Third (Trito) Isaiah who offers comfort and hope to the depressed people. The phrase translated in RV and RSV as 'the opening of the prison' (Isaiah 61¹) is given at Luke 4¹⁸ as 'the opening of the eyes' as in the Septuagint. By the time of Jesus the Jews regarded the words as referring to the new age to which they looked forward.

Having read, Jesus handed back the scroll to the attendant and, like all eastern teachers, he then sat down to teach. When everyone was looking his way he said, 'This prophecy has come true for you today.' At first his friends, neighbours and relatives were pleased and impressed, then they began to doubt and question. Surely he was only the son of Joseph the local carpenter? Jesus, knowing that they would have heard about the healings he had performed in other towns, said to them, 'Of course you are going to remind me of the old saying "Physician, heal thyself". You will want me to back up my claim by performing some wonder before you. Well, there were many widows around here during the famine in Elijah's time, but the only one he helped by a miracle was a foreigner, a widow living at Zarephath in Sidon. There were many lepers around here in Elisha's time, but the only leper Elisha healed was a foreigner, Naaman the Syrian.' (These two incidents are told in I Kings 17 and II Kings 5). Jesus added, 'No prophet is ever appreciated in his own country.' The prophets certainly had been treated cruelly by their own countrymen and Jesus knew he could expect no better. It was obvious that they wouldn't see many of his healing miracles at Nazareth!

His listeners were furious. If, as he claimed, he was sent by God, then surely he should do something for the town where he had grown up! Jesus, however, had sensed the disbelief as they had remarked, 'Is not this Joseph's son?' This same lack of faith Jesus was to find throughout his own nation. Jesus' references to Elijah's and Elisha's dealings with foreigners implied that non-Jews might be in a more favourable position than the people of Nazareth. They became so angry and violent that they pushed Jesus through the town and hustled him to the top of a hill, intending to throw him down headlong then stone him, but somehow Jesus walked through the crowd and went on his way. This violence is mentioned only in Luke's gospel.

Mark (6¹⁻⁶) says bluntly that Jesus, astonished by the people's lack of faith, was able to do only very few miracles at Nazareth. Matthew (13⁵³⁻⁵⁸) says that Jesus did not choose to do his miracles there because the people lacked faith. Luke suggests that Jesus had no intention of performing miracles there. Matthew and Luke often smooth away Mark's bluntness which readers might take to be a criticism of Jesus. The incident at Nazareth seems to prepare one for Jesus' final rejection and death at Jerusalem, but his time to die was not yet, and would be decided by God, not by these people. It has been suggested that the crowd, realizing that their unruly behaviour might be punished by the Romans, allowed Jesus to walk away. Others suggest that the angry and disorganized crowd somehow lost Jesus.

Jesus at Capernaum (4^{31-44})

Examination candidates are sometimes asked to tell the story of the sabbath day Jesus spent at Capernaum, the day described in this section. Sometimes they are asked to compare Jesus' stormy reception at Nazareth (the story above), with the welcome he received at Capernaum.

Capernaum was a busy fish-market town on the northern shore of Lake Galilee. Here the fishermen-disciples Simon-Peter, Andrew, James and John lived. Such people, like the shepherds of Bethlehem, belonged to those known as the 'people of the land', people whose everyday occupations made it impossible for them to keep the Law. These people were treated with contempt by many of the Jewish religious leaders, to whom religion was obedience to the rules.

Jesus offered a radical view of religion which broke through the strict conventional demands of orthodox Judaism and met the needs of all people everywhere, whatever their circumstances.

People living in Capernaum met many foreigners from the countries around the northern border of Palestine, so they were familiar with ways and opinions avoided by orthodox Jews and were more open-minded and ready for the teaching of Jesus. Many of them soon supported him with enthusiasm and their faith in him grew. His way of speaking was direct and refreshing, for instead of quoting from great rabbis or scholarly writings he usually began by saying, 'I tell you . . .'. He seemed to have first-hand knowledge of God and His Kingdom and to understand the everyday problems of ordinary people.

One sabbath day Jesus was invited to speak in the Capernaum synagogue. (This synagogue was rebuilt about 200 A.D. and the remains can still be seen.) As Jesus was speaking, a man who was insane (or perhaps epileptic), shrieked at him, 'What do you want of us, Jesus of Nazareth? Have you come to destroy us? I know who you are . . . you are the Holy One from God!' It was believed that this man was possessed by demons.

At that time people believed that a man's whole personality could be taken over by demons who had managed to get into him, perhaps with his food and drink. Jesus answered the demons, which seems to suggest that Jesus himself believed these things. Anyway, the sick man believed it and, if Jesus were going to get the man's confidence, it wouldn't help if he wasted time arguing about demon-possession. Luke (11[19]) shows that there were many people, apart from Jesus, who exorcised demons. (For some interesting information on the subject read p. 51 of William Barclay's *Gospel of Luke* in the Daily Study Bible series, published by St Andrew Press, 1975.)

Jesus commanded the demons, 'Be silent (or 'Be muzzled'), and come out of him!' The man may have been epileptic, for he fell writhing on the ground, as if the demons were struggling to hold on to him, then he became still and cured. Genesis 1 described how God spoke and the world was created. When the Old Testament prophets spoke their words made a thing happen. Here the word of Jesus cured the man without the strange magic rites of the popular exorcists. Demons were thought to be the agents of Satan, the Devil. The fact that Jesus was driving out the demons meant that God was taking over the world from Satan's clutches. God's Kingdom was beginning. The year of the Lord had arrived! Jesus' exorcism of demons was seen as one of many things he did in fulfilment of prophecies about the Messiah, e.g. Isaiah 35[5ff].

Again Luke describes the reaction of the onlookers. They were deeply impressed and asked one another, 'What kind of words are these? With authority and power he gives orders to unclean spirits, and they obey!' Jesus' fame spread all around the countryside.

At the end of the synagogue service Jesus went home with Simon Peter, much as we might go to a friend's house for lunch after being together at church. They got home to find that Simon's mother-in-law had been taken seriously ill, for Luke describes her as being 'in the grip of a high fever'. The people in the house asked Jesus to help her. He stood over her and 'rebuked' the fever, as if rebuking the demon believed to have caused it. Then, seeming to need no time to recuperate, she got up and began to serve them. Here, in a family, Jesus was just as ready to help as he had been in a crowd.

The eastern day ended at sunset, when the new day officially began. Jews were forbidden to do any work on the sabbath. They were taught that after six days of creating the world, God had rested on the seventh, and they should do the same. Probably the people of Capernaum didn't want to put Jesus in an awkward position by asking him to heal anyone else on the sabbath, but at sunset they brought their sick folk to him. By now, all Capernaum had heard about Jesus curing the demoniac and Simon's mother-in-law, and crowds came to Simon's house for cures. The 'demons' in people who were mentally ill shouted at Jesus, 'You are the Son of God!' but Jesus discouraged this, perhaps afraid that the Jews, longing to overthrow the Romans, would see in him the charismatic leader they were seeking to lead a revolution. During their history the Jews had suffered at the hands of many powerful nations, such as Egypt, Assyria, Babylon and now Rome. Even during the reigns of their kings they had regarded God as their true King, and they looked forward to the time when He would vindicate them. They awaited the Day of the Lord, brought in by a Messiah sent from God. He would defeat and punish their enemies and establish a Kingdom ruled over by God. The nation would be restored to the greatness and prosperity it had known under King David, and would be the leading power in the world. There would be a great Day of Judgement in the future, after which the Kingdom would be complete and perfect, made up of those who deserved such a reward. It would be celebrated with a Messianic banquet in Heaven.

To be such a military Messiah was as far from the mind of Jesus as was a suffering and dying Messiah from the minds of the Jews. It was necessary to change their conception of the Messiah before they would acknowledge him as Messiah. Obviously Jesus identified himself more as the Suffering Servant of Isaiah 53. Until his death even the disciples imagined him ruling over a kingdom on earth (Luke 18$^{31-34}$, 22^{24}, Mark 10^{37}). The Kingdom of God was the theme of Jesus' teaching. He taught that time and place had nothing to do with it for the Kingdom was already in existence in people's hearts, where God already ruled (17$^{20-21}$). His healings and exorcisms were signs that, through him, God was already reclaiming the world from the powers of evil. The Kingdom was not a visible place but was inward and spiritual. It was not simply for the Jews, but was universal. It was not something that people could earn through any merit of their own, but a gift which God longed to give to them and one to be received gratefully with the trust and humility characteristic of a little child (12^{32}, 18$^{15-17}$). It was already developing rapidly without people being conscious of its growth. Some would see it come with power during their natural lifetime, (9^{27}), and this was perhaps so on the Day of Pentecost described in Acts 2.

The difference between this concept of the Kingdom and the Jewish one explains Jesus' reluctance to be openly acknowledged as the Jewish Messiah.

Early next morning the people began to arrive again, but Jesus couldn't be found. At last they found him alone in an isolated place, probably because he needed to be alone with God his Father. The people begged him to stay at Capernaum, but he decided to leave, and told them, 'I must take the good news of the Kingdom of God to other towns. That is what I was sent to do', and he went away to preach in the other synagogues of the land.

At the end of the Temptations story we were told that the Devil left Jesus until another opportunity should present itself. Here at Capernaum Jesus must have felt tempted to stay where he could become a beloved and famous wonder-worker, but he resisted the temptation, determined that his miracles should be signs that God had come to His people, not means by which he himself could become famous. His main work must be to teach.

Luke's story follows Mark 1^{21-39}. and it is Luke's first obvious use of Mark's gospel.

A great catch of fish; Called to catch men (5^{1-11})

Jesus was preaching to great crowds on the fertile plains of Gennesaret, south of Capernaum. (Gennesaret and the Sea of Tiberias were other names for Lake Galilee.) Jesus saw two empty boats by the lake. The fishermen were washing their nets nearby. The local fishing industry was a prosperous one; some of the fish was salted and exported as far afield as Rome.

Jesus got into the boat which belonged to Simon Peter and asked Simon to push it out a bit from the land. It became a convenient floating pulpit from which it was easier to speak to the people.

When Jesus had finished speaking he told Simon to take the boat out into deep water and let down the nets. Simon told him, 'Master, we have been out fishing all night and we caught nothing.' Nevertheless, he agreed to try what Jesus had suggested. The result was that they caught so many fish that the nets began to tear. Simon and his brother Andrew were in partnership with the brothers, James and John, sons of the fisherman, Zebedee. James and John rushed along with their boat to help bring in the great catch. Even then the fish were so many that both boats were in danger of sinking. Perhaps Jesus had been able to see the movement of a large shoal of fish from where he was standing. When the boats came in, Simon fell at Jesus' feet and said, 'Go and leave me, Lord, for I am a sinful man.' Simon's words suggest that he found something disturbing in Jesus, the power and presence of God.

These modern fishermen are using equipment very similar to that of New Testament times

This made him shrink away. Simon felt embarrassed, unworthy of receiving help from such a good man; but instead of turning away, Jesus invited Simon to join him, saying, 'Don't let this scare you. From now on you will not be catching fish, but men!'

When they reached the shore, the four men left their fishing business and went with Jesus. These first disciples, Simon and Andrew, James and John, were to bring in great numbers of people of all nations for God's Kingdom. They left homes, families, comfort and security for a life which would be rough and lonely. They launched out with Jesus, becoming his closest friends. Like all friends they kept him company in sad and happy times, they admired, helped, misunderstood, chided and even failed him at various times. Despite their human failings, they were the friends upon whom he relied.

Luke's account should be compared with Mark 1[16-20], Matthew 4[18-22] and John 21[1-13]. As a non-Jew, Luke saw the story as meaning that the great net of God's Kingdom was large enough to hold people of all nations, a point which John's gospel makes even more clearly.

Luke makes no mention of Andrew here. Peter, James and John seemed particularly close to Jesus, and accompanied him on some occasions when the other disciples were not present, e.g. the healing of Jairus' daughter, and the Transfiguration. We are told that Jesus himself gave to Simon the nickname 'Peter'. Peter (in Greek 'Petros', in Aramaic 'Cephas') means 'stone' or 'rock' (see Luke 6[14], Mark 3[16], John 1[42]). Peter had become the great Christian leader by the time Luke was writing this gospel.

Leprosy and law-breaking (5[12-16])

In another town a man came and fell down before Jesus begging for help. The doctor, Luke, describes the man as being 'covered in leprosy'. Biblical descriptions mentioning 'leprosy' often meant all kinds of skin diseases like impetigo, ringworm, eczema and leucodermia. These could be serious and difficult to cure, but were not as terrible as the paralysing and rotting effects of true leprosy as we think of it today. The physical suffering was dreaded, but perhaps more dreaded was the ritual 'uncleanness'. A leper was a social outcast banned from coming anywhere near a normal Jew. The priests had the responsibility of deciding the identity of the illness and whether it necessitated isolating the sufferer. Leviticus 13 and 14 gave instructions for dealing with these cases, and there were detailed instructions given for the ritual necessary before any cured sufferers could resume their place in society.

Yet this man dared to approach Jesus and say, 'Sir, if only you will you can heal me.' Jesus dared to do what no ordinary person would risk, for he actually touched the man and said, 'Indeed I will. Be clean again.' Contact with this man meant that Jesus himself would be considered ritually unclean, an outcast of society. Mark's version of the story says that Jesus could no longer show himself in any town (Mark 1⁴⁵), and the reason may have been that he had touched the leper. The man's leprosy disappeared immediately. Jesus ordered him to keep silent about what had happened. Such stories could encourage the crowds to recognize Jesus as Messiah, but they expected a militant Messiah. Rebellion could only result in mass-crucifixions and would hasten his own death before his work was half done.

Jesus told the cured leper to go and do what the Jewish law demanded of one claiming to be cured. He must ask to be inspected by a priest. If the priest considered him cured there would be a special ritual at the Court of the Lepers. He would be sprinkled seven times with running water into which had been dipped cedarwood, crimson and hyssop and the blood of a sacrificed bird. A second bird was allowed to fly away, presumably carrying away the evil. The man must bath and cleanse his clothes, repeating this a week later. The priest then touched the man's right ear, right thumb and big toe of the right foot, first with the blood of a sacrificed ram then with oil which also was put on the head. The cured man could now resume his normal place in society. Only a priest could touch such a man without himself being considered ritually unclean.

Despite Jesus' wish to keep the matter quiet, great crowds soon arrived to see the healer who could cure lepers like Moses and Elisha had done (Num, 12⁹⁻¹⁶, II Kings 5). Luke's gospel suggests that the presence of such crowds were Jesus' reason for staying out of the towns. Jesus withdrew to the wilderness where in this, another crisis, he could seek God's guidance in prayer.

Later, at his trial, Jesus was accused of encouraging people to rebel against Moses' laws. This story shows that he encouraged people to keep those laws.

(Information about leprosy today can be obtained from the Mission to Lepers, 50 Portland Place, London, WIN 3DG.)

General note about the Pharisees

The Pharisees were pious people who avoided anything or anyone who might prove a bad influence. They aimed at keeping a very high standard of moral conduct, so in many ways were the best amongst the Jews. They stayed usually amongst their own kind and obeyed every detail of the Law with meticulous care. The Ten Commandments had been elaborated so as to give guidance on how one should behave in any situation which might arise in daily life. The hundreds of rules were passed on from one generation to the next and these were known as the 'oral tradition'. The Pharisees tried to do better than each rule demanded, just to be on the safe side. Luke (18^{9-14}) describes a Pharisee who was pleased to think that he fasted twice a week instead of once a year. The Pharisees were descendants of brave and sincere Jews who, in the second century B.C., gave their lives rather than give up their religion.

Alexander the Great, who died in 323 B.C., had been anxious to spread Greek civilization, language and culture throughout the countries he conquered. This process was known as 'Hellenization'. After Alexander died his empire was divided between his generals. Seleucis took the eastern part, making Syrian Antioch his capital. His rival Ptolemy seized Egypt. Each of them struggled to get Palestine. By 175 B.C. Syria had come under the power of a ruler known as Antiochus Epiphanes, who marched into Palestine determined to subject the Jews to his will. He tried to force them to accept Hellenization. Some Jews accepted, others refused. At the village of Modin the priest Mattathias refused to set up an altar for Greek gods. He and his five sons fled to the mountains where soon they were joined by other patriotic Jews including a religious group known as the Hasidim ('the Pious Ones'). From the mountains the Jews made raids on the enemy and, when Mattathias and two of his sons died, the third son, Judas, led the fight and earned for himself the nickname Maccabeus ('the Hammerer'). When, eventually, the Jews were able to cleanse their Temple of heathen altars and use it again to worship God the Hasidim felt that the fighting should cease, but it continued and Judas was killed. The rest of the family, now known as the Maccabees, went on with the struggle which now entailed much foreign intrigue, another source of complaint from the Hasidim. Eventually Judas' brother, Simon, achieved peace without fighting and became High Priest at Jerusalem. The Pharisees had developed out of that group of the Hasidim who refused to associate with the Maccabees, believing that the aims of the Maccabees were political rather than spiritual. Undoubtedly it was the Pharisees who were responsible for the preservation of Judaism against the influx of Greek thought. They believed there would be a future Day of Judgment.

From what we can gather many Pharisees were poor, but no doubt there were some who used religion as a cloak to hide their preoccupation with worldly gain, thus deserving the name of hypocrites which Jesus is said to have given to them. They praised almsgiving and set themselves up as superior examples of piety, but could not live without wealth and security as Jesus himself did. Their concern for holiness resulted in a 'holier-than-thou' attitude towards 'the people of the land', those whose work and conditions made it impossible to obey all the rules of the 'oral tradition'. They avoided any dealing with foreigners. Jesus appreciated their genuine keenness and anxiety to please God, and realized that in many ways they were good and admirable, but unfortunately self-righteous and misguided about what was most important in life. Their legalistic ways made them forget that, after all, the Law was made to benefit humanity. By the end of the first century the Pharisees were in control of justice and education. The criticism of them found in the gospels probably reflects the division which by then had developed between them and the Christians. The Law had been given to improve people's lives, but the Pharisees made it an extra burden. The rabbis calculated that a tradition of 613 rules had developed around Moses' Law. The oral law is contained in the Mishnah, which dates from about A.D. 200. Later this was expanded with comment and the work is known as the Talmud, which dates from about the fifth century A.D. (see also p. 48 for specific rules). Rules can make us do the right thing; it is much better when we want to do the right thing.

General note about the scribes

A scribe is a writer. Jewish scribes were trained in the copying and interpretation of the religious Law, so Luke refers to them as lawyers. They served as lawyers and judges in courts such as the Sanhedrin and gave their professional advice to anyone who required it.

Many of them kept the laws very strictly so belonged to the groups of Pharisees. They had little sympathy for those ordinary people whose work made it very difficult for them to live according to the details of the oral tradition. Jesus told the lawyers that they were making religion a burden for the people (11[46]). As the experts who decided how the Law should be kept, they sometimes regarded themselves as more distinguished than the Pharisees who obeyed their instructions.

Later Jesus said that the lawyers enjoyed parading in long robes, receiving the respect of the people and sitting in places of honour wherever they went. They were supposed to give their advice freely and earn a living from ordinary jobs but often they themselves broke the law and also exploited the poor and helpless by accepting money for legal advice given, yet they tried to impress people with their goodness by reciting lengthy prayers (20^{45-47}).

Jesus heals a paralysed man (5^{17-26})

Jesus was teaching and healing in a house which was packed to capacity with people who had come from all over Palestine. Among them were Pharisees and scribes.

Some men, carrying a paralysed friend on his stretcher-bed, tried to get him in to Jesus, but failed to get through the crowd. Determined to seek help for their friend they carried him up the outside stairs to the roof in which they made a hole big enough to let down the mattress on which he lay. Palestinian houses had flat roofs made of poles laid across, the spaces between them crammed with reeds and twigs held together with a kind of mortar. It was very easy to clear a space between the poles.

Looking up, Jesus realized that they had no doubts about his ability to help their friend. He was also aware that the Pharisees and scribes were looking for any opportunity to criticize him.

It was generally accepted that God gave illness as a punishment for sin. Like many people today, some had physical illnesses caused by fear, guilt or worry. These are called psychosomatic illnesses. This man's illness may have been caused by his mental state. As long as he felt guilty, he would be paralysed, so Jesus must first remove his fear. Jesus told him, 'Your sins are forgiven you.'

Immediately Jesus sensed the disapproval of the Pharisees and scribes who were thinking, 'Whom does he think he is? Only God can forgive sins!' Jesus asked them, 'Why are you thinking that way? Is it any easier for me to say, "Your sins are forgiven" than to say, "Stand up, take your bed and go home"? To prove to you that the Son of Man has authority to forgive sins –[then he turned to the man] – Stand up, take your bed and go home!' The man immediately did what he was told and, carrying the mattress, went off home, praising God (see General Note on 'Son of Man', pp. 77–8).

The critics had seen the punishment for sin removed by Jesus. This must mean that he could forgive the sin which had caused the paralysis! Whatever they felt, the Pharisees were in no position to comment. Jesus had not answered their question, 'Whom does he think he is?' in words, but his action forced them to decide for themselves about his identity.

Luke tells again of the reaction of the people who saw the paralysed man cured. They were amazed and said, 'No one would believe the things we've seen here today!' and they praised God. Luke has taken this story from Mark's gospel, but Luke speaks of a roof of tiles, the kind which may have been more familiar to Gentile readers.

The tax-collector, Matthew Levi; Criticism from the Pharisees (5^{27-39})

Jesus was now gathering around him a group of disciples, men who would learn from him, help him and go on with his work when his life here was over. When they managed to get away alone, Jesus taught these chosen men privately and intensively, for eventually they themselves would be sent out as teachers, or apostles.

One day, Jesus invited a tax-collector, or publican, called Levi to join the group. Matthew (9^9) calls him Matthew; perhaps his full name was Matthew Levi. Like us, the people of those times disliked paying tax. It was sometimes difficult to find money to pay the Temple tax, but they deeply resented paying tax to the Romans, who were unwelcome there anyway. The Romans' tax system was called tax-farming and we assume they used this system in Palestine. A man could buy the right to collect the taxes in a certain area, and the job usually went to the highest bidder. As long as he handed over to the Romans the amount they demanded he kept whatever extra he managed to get from the people, so all tax-farmers were regarded as corrupt, dishonest and not respectable people at all. Local people had to pay a tax to live in the area, they were taxed on the grain, wine and oil they produced, on the amount of fish they caught in the lake, they paid to use roads, markets and harbours. The tax-farmers were regarded as traitors, collaborators working for the army of occupation. Religious Jews saw them as outcasts and sinners working for pagan Gentiles. They classed them with thieves and murderers and didn't allow them to attend the synagogues.

One can imagine the people's amazement when Jesus approached the collecting-table where Levi was working and said, 'Follow me!' They were further amazed when Levi left everything and went with Jesus. Levi himself couldn't have enjoyed being so unpopular and he must have been deeply moved by Jesus' offer of friendship and trust. He gave a party so that his colleagues could meet Jesus. He had found something good and he wanted to share it with his friends.

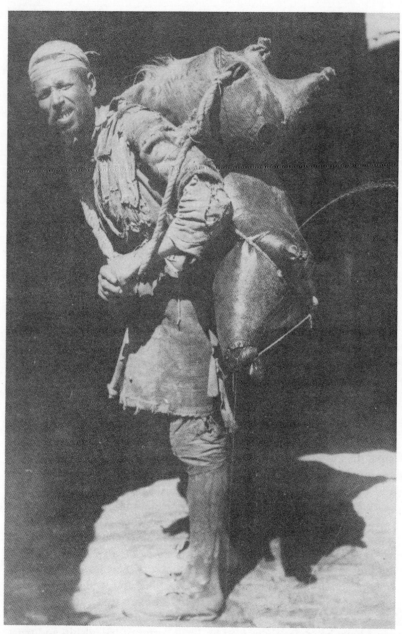

In New Testament times wine was contained in 'bottles' made from skins of animals. These were efficient only when new and supple enough to stretch when the wine fermented. When they became dry, cracks appeared and the wine leaked through as it is doing in this picture of a modern wine-seller

The Pharisees and scribes were disgusted and asked the disciples, 'How can you eat and drink with tax-collectors and sinners?' but it was Jesus himself who provided the answer. 'Healthy people don't need a doctor; sick people do. I don't need to teach people who are already good. I have come to persuade sinful people to repent.' Jesus was saying that the Pharisees considered themselves so good that they had no need of forgiveness. As long as this attitude prevailed he could do nothing for them.

Jesus did not condone sin, but his loving and forgiving ways gave wrongdoers the opportunity to 'turn over a new leaf', whereas the attitude of the Pharisees tended to cause resentment and rebellion, driving the wrongdoer away to do more wrong.

Some of the Jewish people were loyal followers of John the Baptist who was then in prison. The Pharisees said to Jesus, 'The followers of John and those who follow the ways of the Pharisees fast and pray a lot, but your disciples seem to eat and drink normally. There were annual days, particularly the Day of Atonement, when Jews were required to fast, but many religious Jews privately chose to fast on the market-days of Mondays and Thursdays (cf. Luke 18^{12}), and sometimes whitened their faces so that the people would comment on their suffering and piety. They thought that to be religious one had to look solemn and miserable. Jesus found joy in prayer and in serving God. To him it wasn't just a matter of obeying rules.

In an eastern wedding the bridegroom's friends entertained the company and added to the merriment of the occasion. They would be considered rude and churlish if they looked miserable or refused to eat and drink at the celebration, for fasting was a sign of sorrow or shame. Jesus reminded the Pharisees of this and he told them there would be time enough for sorrow when the bridegroom was no longer with his friends. The Jews thought of God's Kingdom as a celebration party, so why should they fast in sorrow when Jesus (the bridegroom) had arrived to announce and begin that celebration?

Jesus, however, was beginning to realize that the orthodox Jews would not adapt to his new ideas. He said it was like trying to patch an old worn garment with a piece of strong, new cloth. The new piece would look out of place and soon it would tear away a bigger hole in the garment. In the same way it was as useless as putting new wine into old leather wineskins. The skins, already fully-stretched, would burst as the new wine fermented, and then the skins and the wine would be lost. The strict Jews preferred the old ways to which they were accustomed; they were afraid of changes. They were rejecting Jesus' teaching.

The Pharisees criticize Jesus for sabbath-breaking (6$^{1-11}$)

This section describes two incidents when Jesus offended the Pharisees by breaking the laws about the sabbath day. Moses commanded, 'Keep the sabbath day holy', but people have different ideas about the meaning of this. The sabbath had been intended originally as a regular rest-day to benefit the people. It commemorated the seventh day when God had rested after the work of Creation and the Jews were expected to remember, every sabbath, how God had brought them out of slavery in Egypt. The Jewish authorities had issued many rules about what could be done and what couldn't be done on a sabbath. No one could light a fire or do any cooking. Doctors were allowed to help a patient only if choking or blindness would result otherwise. No one should carry anything bigger than a fig, or walk any further than the local synagogue.

On this particular sabbath Jesus and his disciples were hungry and, as they walked through a cornfield, they picked some ears of corn, rubbed away the husks and ate the kernels. Some Pharisees saw this and regarded it as reaping and threshing corn, which was forbidden on the sabbath. They reminded the group that they were breaking sabbath rules.

Jesus remarked that it was strange that long ago David had eaten the shewbread, the sacred loaves which only priests were allowed to eat, yet no one had criticized him. I Samuel 21$^{1-6}$ tells how David, escaping from the jealous king, Saul, went to some priests in the mountains. The priests had no food to give to the hungry young captain, but perhaps they knew that their old leader, Samuel, had chosen David to be the the next king. Every sabbath twelve small fresh loaves were set out while the priests prayed. Perhaps the loaves represented the twelve tribes. A week later fresh loaves were set out and the stale ones were eaten by the priests (Lev. 24$^{5-9}$). On this occasion some of the bread was given to David. I Samuel 21^6 (clear in NEB) suggests that it may well have been a sabbath day, too. Jesus seemed to be saying, 'You didn't criticize what David did, and I am a greater person than David,' for he said to them, 'The Son of Man is sovereign, even over the sabbath.' By this he may have meant that he himself, as Messiah, took precedence over sabbath rules, or he may have meant that the needs of ordinary human beings matter more to God that the sabbath observance.

Luke immediately tells another story about sabbath-breaking. On this occasion Jesus had again been invited to teach in the synagogue. He noticed in the congregation a man whose arm was withered. Luke alone mentions that it was the right arm, as if to emphasize that the problem was a serious one for a man trying to earn a living. In the same way he said that Jairus' daughter was an only daughter and the son of the widow at Nain an only son. However, this man was in no imminent danger and any possible treatment could wait until the sabbath ended. No one asked Jesus to help the man, yet Jesus deliberately called him to the front, knowing that there were Pharisees and lawyers there waiting for him to make any false step. Before dealing with the man, Jesus asked, 'Should one do good or evil on the sabbath? Should one save life, or destroy life?' No one replied and he told the man, 'Stretch out your arm.' The man did so and found that he could stretch his arm fully. He was cured.

Jesus' enemies made no comment, but he realized that he had provoked them to further anger. Indeed, it seems almost as if he were going out of his way to annoy them. They got together to discuss what to do about him. All who were present must have been aware that something new and wonderful was happening amongst them. The Pharisees' silence shows that they had taken the point. Whereas Jesus was doing good on the sabbath by helping the man to live his life more fully, the Pharisees were doing evil by plotting to destroy Jesus.

Mark (3^{1-6}) says that it was at this time that the Pharisees got together with the Herodians to work out a way of getting rid of Jesus. It is not certain who the Herodians were. We presume they were influential people, perhaps Sadducees, who were in favour of the administration of Herod Antipas and who saw in Jesus a possible threat to the *status quo*. Perhaps because of the lack of knowledge of their identity Luke has no mention of them.

Jesus chooses twelve disciples (6^{12-19})

Luke marks many of the important events in Jesus' life by saying that Jesus prayed about those events. He now went alone to the hills and prayed all night before returning to the crowds, for he was about to make important decisions, and he would take no decision without God. Jesus was fully aware that he had made enemies who were hoping to destroy him as quickly as they could. He must choose some men who would go on with his work if he were taken from them. He could not afford to choose men who would give up in the face of difficulties, so before making his choice from the many who were now following him, Jesus sought God's guidance.

He chose twelve men. There had been twelve tribes of Israelites, but these had failed to carry out God's purposes in the world. The twelve disciples would be the basis of a new Israel, a new Chosen People, and Luke says that Jesus called them 'apostles'. An apostle is 'one who is sent', a representative given the right to speak on behalf of the one who sent him. To these men Jesus would give intensive teaching for as long as he could. Luke (22^{30}) says that Jesus told them they would eventually sit on thrones to judge the twelve tribes. The twelve were –

1 Simon, whom Jesus nicknamed 'Peter', meaning a rock.
2 Andrew, who was brother to Simon.
3 James, son of Zebedee the fisherman.
4 John, brother to James and son of Zebedee. Jesus nicknamed these two brothers 'Boanerges' meaning 'sons of thunder'.
5 Philip.
6 Bartholomew, meaning 'son of Tolmai'. He may have been the one referred to as 'Nathanael'.
7 Matthew. See Matthew 9^9 and 10^3, where he is referred to again as Matthew, a tax-collector. Mark calls him Levi, son of Alphaeus. Luke calls him Levi.
8 Thomas, or Didymus. Both names mean 'the twin'.
9 James, the son of Alphaeus. Perhaps he was Levi's brother.
10 Simon who was called the Zealot. Matthew and Mark call him the Cananean. There was a Jewish nationalist party called the Zealots, but the names 'Zealot' and 'Cananean' may simply mean that Simon was a zealous, enthusiastic kind of person.
11 Judas, son of James. Matthew and Mark name him Thaddeus, perhaps because this means 'big-hearted'. We cannot tell who is meant by 'James'. Perhaps it meant that he was the son of another of the disciples.
12 Judas Iscariot, who became a traitor. 'Iscariot' may mean 'from Kerioth', which was in S. Judaea. Or 'Iscariot' may mean 'assassin', and perhaps Judas expected Jesus to lead a revolution against the Romans.

Accompanied by these twelve men, Jesus came down from the mountain and taught a great crowd on a level place. Matthew's gospel said that Jesus taught from a mountain. Perhaps, like Matthew, Luke intends us to remember that Moses brought the tablets inscribed with the Ten Commandments from Mount Sinai, having been there in communion with God (Ex. 19). Jesus came as the new and greater law-giver. With his twelve quite ordinary men Jesus set out to preach the good news that the Kingdom of God had come to men. Through them he would change the world.

From far and wide the Jews came, from all over Judaea and its capital city of Jerusalem, and northern areas controlled by Tyre and Sidon. Some came to listen to Jesus, others to be healed of mental or physical illnesses. Sick people struggled forward to touch him, for healing power flowed from him. Such people showed their great faith in Jesus.

Beatitudes and woes (6^{20-26})

In Matthew's gospel, chapters 5, 6 and 7, the writer has collected the teachings of Jesus known as the Sermon on the Mount. Luke chose to scatter the teaching throughout his gospel, and says here that Jesus stood on level ground, having come from the mountain, so Luke's version is usually called the Sermon on the Plain. Each of the two writers begins with the 'Beatitudes', which means 'Blessings'. Matthew gave nine blessings, Luke gave four blessings and four 'woes'. These woe-sayings are not found anywhere else, and, naturally, scholars have wondered why, if Jesus really said them, they are not recorded in the other gospels. Instead of 'blessed' one could write 'Oh, how happy', and instead of 'woe' one might say 'Oh, how unfortunate'.

If, today, we are asked what is necessary for a happy life, we might say security, prosperity, plenty to eat, a comfortable home, peace of mind, popularity. Sometimes we make such an effort to get these things that they cost us our personal and spiritual integrity. Such a cost is too high and cannot bring true happiness. Jesus was turning the standards of the world upside down. True blessedness comes from living according to his standards, even if it means accepting poverty, hunger and being unpopular. We cannot be content to allow anyone in this world to remain in poverty, but if we concentrate on our own wealth and comfort we can easily become complacent and insensitive to the needs of others. So Jesus warns us to consider carefully the true aim of living.

Jesus was being honest and realistic. He knew that his twelve friends would often go hungry, sleep rough, feel tired and depressed and find themselves mocked and unwanted. They would have to live on charity and share the dangers Jesus faced, even perhaps death, but in return they would be citizens of God's Kingdom. During their long history the Jews had experienced hunger and homelessness caused by many foreign invasions. Jesus' disciples would be following in that tradition and struggling to remain true to their belief in God.

Luke's idea of 'weeping' did not mean the shedding of sentimental tears, but a genuine sorrow for what is wrong and tragic in the world. One may be poor in material things but rich in character and having the peace and satisfaction of living as God wants a human being to live. God's rewards are for those who do good without expecting a reward, without thought for themselves.

Luke's version of the Beatitudes is altogether more simple and straightforward than the more spiritual version of Matthew. Luke speaks of the poor, Matthew of the poor in spirit; Luke speaks of the hungry, Matthew of those who hunger for righteousness. Luke doesn't hesitate to condemn riches, not only an obsession for riches. Jesus' teaching was typical of the eastern way – to get a point over he used extreme terms. English people tend to play down incidents. When someone is feeling quite ill we might say they are 'not very well'; we might describe a packed football ground by saying there were quite a few people there. Easterners would be more likely to exaggerate to get their effect. So Jesus could speak of a plank in someone's eye, and a camel going through a needle's eye.

In his condemnation of riches, Luke records in 12^{13-21} a parable about a rich fool, and in 16^{19-31} the parable about the wealthy Dives and the beggar, Lazarus. Luke (16^{14}) criticized the Pharisees' love of money, and 18^{18-30} tells of a wealthy young ruler who could not face life without comfort and security and thus lost the opportunity to go with Jesus. The Magnificat championed the poor (1^{46-55}). Zacchaeus had to part with his money before he could receive salvation (19^{1-10}). Here, Luke describes Jesus as saying, 'Woe to you who are rich, for you've had all you are going to get!' The same applies to those who have full stomachs, who can laugh because they are insensitive to others' suffering and who are popular because they bow to the standards of the selfish world. In fulfilling the idea of God's Suffering Servant, Jesus was setting the example he wanted his disciples to follow.

True happiness is not always seen in a smiling face. It is the inward peace of knowing that one is right with God and that the world is finally in His control. Such happiness can be known by people who have little to eat, who live in poor conditions and who are crippled with pain. Sometimes we can learn a lot by seeing the great faith and courage of such people who, despite their condition, cheerfully serve God and other people.

Real love (6^{27-38})

Luke's gospel shows Jesus as the perfect example upon whom we should model our own lives. Here Jesus reminded his hearers that even the worst people love those who love them, give to those who give something in return and are prepared to lend to those who will return the loan with interest. Real giving only happens when the giver knows he will get nothing back, perhaps not even a 'Thank you' or any kind of acknowledgement. To do good out of a sense of duty isn't enough. Love cannot be limited by rules.

Jesus told the people 'Love your enemies'. Jewish people were prepared to love their neighbours as long as those neighbours were Jews. How could they be expected to love the Roman invaders who bullied them and had taken their freedom and their country? Our English word 'love' describes various emotions. We may say we love ice-cream, sunshine, certain T.V. programmes, friends, parents, boy-friends or girl-friends, pets, certain sports or hobbies, but these emotions are all of different kinds. The Greeks had separate words for different emotions; 'eros' meant the love between the sexes, and 'philia' was the affection one might feel for a relative or close friend. The love that Jesus talked about was best expressed as 'agapē', something too practical to depend upon mere emotions. 'Agapē' means acting towards all other people in accordance with what we honestly believe to be their true welfare, no matter how they act towards us. It necessitates a completely unselfish and limitless concern for all other people. They may be total strangers, they may be people we find we cannot like, they may have treated us badly. In his first letter to the Christians at Corinth (13⁴⁻⁷), St Paul described such love. It is a love which came first from God to man, offered by Jesus whose life and death were his way of showing us that love. When we have that same kind of love and concern for all other people we have come a little nearer to sharing and understanding the nature of God.

Jesus said we should pray for our enemies and offer good in return for evil. Sometimes we might be afraid that we will be considered as 'weak' and that we are being 'taken for a ride'. It isn't easy, but then Jesus didn't pretend that it was!

Many religions teach their followers to avoid harming other people. The famous Rabbi Hillel (first century A.D.), was asked to sum up the Law in the time in which one could stand on one leg. He replied, 'Don't do to others what you wouldn't like them to do to you. That sums up the Law and any commentary on it!' Five hundred years before the time of Jesus the Chinese philosopher Confucius had said much the same. Jesus gave the saying a more positive sense for he said, 'Treat others as you would like them to treat you.' We call this the Golden Rule of life. Jesus also taught, 'If someone takes away your coat, offer him your shirt, too. If someone slaps one side of your face, offer the other side to be slapped.' All this seems to beyond what one can expect of a human being, yet so many will vouch for the fact that it works.

God in His compassion gives the riches of this world to good and bad alike. If we hope to receive tolerance and compassion from God we must treat other people in this way. If we judge people harshly, saying that this is what they deserve, we have no right to expect lenient judgement from God. Acts 7[60] tells us that as Stephen died he prayed for the men who were stoning him, 'Lord, do not hold this sin against them.' He showed himself as a true disciple by following the example of Jesus who prayed for those who crucified him.

Leo Tolstoy and Albert Schweizer were among many who regarded Jesus' teaching as 'an impossible ethic', but no Christian can be content with anything less than the highest standards. It is better to be too generous than too harsh. Love makes less mistakes than hatred does.

As human beings we are constantly judging the merits of the people and things we see around us, but we need to consider our own faults before we criticize the faults of other people. We should be generous in our judgement of others, and hope that God is judging us generously. If someone does something to hurt us and we react by hurting them then evil is controlling both of us. Only by offering love and forgiveness can we allow God to overcome evil. Whatever kindness we show to others, it cannot compare with all that God does for us.

In eastern markets flour was not pre-packed or weighed. A pottery bucket-shape, called a bushel, was used to measure it. The bushel was filled, then tapped lightly on the ground allowing the level of flour to drop, then more flour was heaped on to fill it. A generous shopkeeper served it overflowing, to give good measure. Jesus said that we should show kindness in the same generous way.

Teaching about discipleship; Building on a sure foundation (6[39-49])

At first this section seems to consist of several sayings of Jesus which have no connection between them. The style was typical of the rabbis, and was called 'charaz', which means 'stringing beads'. To keep people's interest and to avoid boredom, they moved quickly from one topic to another.

Looking at the section we see that the sayings have a common theme, for they all say that we can teach best what we know best; that good results can be expected only from a good source; we must put ourselves right before we try to put others right.

So Jesus says that it is silly for a blind person to follow someone who is also blind. One must choose a guide who knows and can see the way. Jesus' sense of humour is seen when he says that someone with a great plank of wood in his eye can hardly be able to remove a speck of dust from someone else's eye!

Then Jesus says that one can tell a good person by what he says and does. One cannot expect good fruit from a poor tree. One cannot expect thistles to produce figs, nor a bramble bush to produce grapes. The words and deeds of a man are conditioned by what kind of man he is. As the disciples hear Jesus' words and see what he does they must decide for themselves whether or not he is a fit guide to follow and an example worth imitating. It is so easy to say that Jesus is our Lord, but we can show that we really mean it by doing what he has told us to do. If we do this we are like a man who digs down to find a solid foundation on which to build a house. Any flooding of a nearby river will be unable to disturb such strong foundations. The man who does not base his life on Jesus' teaching is like a man who built his house on the soft surface soil without bothering to find the rock. Such a house would collapse when a flood came.

Later Jesus was to nickname Simon 'the rock' (Greek – 'petra'), for he was the kind of person whose life was securely based on Jesus' teaching. Troubles and problems come into the lives of all people but we are more prepared to cope with them if we are guided by a sane, sound Christian faith.

The centurion's servant (7^{1-10})

The busy fish-market town of Capernaum was the scene of much of Jesus' ministry. Its synagogue had been built for the Jewish community by a Roman centurion. Romans sometimes found it easier to govern religious people, and many of them respected Judaism because it taught monotheism (belief in only one God), and because it demanded high moral standards in daily life. Here the centurion must have been deeply impressed by the Jews' religion to go to the trouble and expense of building a synagogue. He was admirable, too, because he showed great concern for one of his slaves who was seriously ill. Some slaves, especially those with particular skills, were regarded as valuable and were often well-treated, but some slave-owners regarded their slaves as less than human and treated them brutally. Roman farmers were advised to inspect their equipment regularly and throw away any which was old and worn. The equipment included slaves!

Some Jewish elders wishing to show gratitude to this centurion went at his request to ask Jesus to cure the dying slave (whom Matthew's gospel tells us was paralysed and in pain), and Jesus set out towards the centurion's house.

Someone must have hurried ahead to say that Jesus and the elders were on their way, for the centurion sent to tell Jesus that there was no need to come to the house. He said that as an officer with authority over a hundred soldiers he himself could give various orders and the soldiers would obey, just as he would obey a superior officer. In the same way he believed that Jesus had authority over demons which caused illness and the demons would leave if Jesus sent such orders.

The New Testament seems to speak with respect of centurions. They were like the company-commanders of a modern army. They had to be reliable, sensible, courageous leaders, who wouldn't panic in a crisis and wouldn't lead men into unnecessary danger.

The centurion knew that the Jewish religious authorities expected Jews to keep right away from foreigners who might have a bad influence on them. He didn't want to embarrass Jesus by expecting him to come into a Gentile home. This may be the reason that he didn't go personally to Jesus (though Matt. 8^5 and John 4^{47} say he did). Luke, perhaps, told the story this way to show that the Jews should be bringing Gentiles to God. The Jews had failed to do this, despite frequent reminders. Luke's story shows that some Gentiles were ready to accept Jesus.

Jesus understood and admired the tremendous faith of this man. To those around him, probably Jews themselves, Jesus said, 'Nowhere amongst the Jews have I found such faith.' The messengers returned to the centurion's house and found the servant restored to good health.

When writing an account of this story one should remember the points of importance: (a) it shows Jesus' concern for non-Jews, (b) Jesus marvelled at the faith of the centurion, who received the highest praise Jesus gave, and (c) the servant was healed from a distance.

Luke, a Gentile himself, must have enjoyed writing this story.

The son of a widow at Nain (7^{11-17})

A day's journey from Capernaum was the beautiful city of Nain, situated on a hill. Nain means 'fair'. Jesus and his disciples, accompanied by a great crowd, were climbing the rocky pathway to Nain when a funeral procession came out from the city-gate. (The dead were always buried outside the city-walls.) On the bier (or stretcher), was the body of a man, pathetically young. Luke emphasizes the tragedy by saying that the young man was an only child (like Jairus' daughter and the epileptic boy, 8^{40-56} and 9^{37-45}) and the son of a widowed mother. A large crowd had joined the procession, in sympathy for the woman who was now bereft of anyone to provide and care for her. A further tragedy was that many would see her predicament as God's judgement for some sin she had committed.

Jesus' eyes summed up the situation and the Greek word used to express the compassion he felt for the widow is the strongest one available in that language. He was moved to the depths of his being. In Luke's time there were some philosophers known as the Stoics. They believed it weak to show emotion of any kind and taught that God's superiority lay in His ability to remain detached from any feelings of joy or sorrow. Here, however, Jesus, the man of God, felt a deep sadness for this widow.

No one asked Jesus to help, for surely nothing could help now, but Jesus told the woman, 'Stop crying'. Then he touched the bier to signify that the bearers should put it down. Touching a funeral bier made one ritually unclean as far as the Jewish religious authorities were concerned. Then Jesus spoke to the corpse: 'Young man, sit up!' The Greek word used here was familiar to the doctor, Luke, for it meant 'sit up in bed' as a cured patient would.

The young man sat up and began to speak, and Jesus 'gave him back to his mother'. This last phrase was used in I Kings 17^{17-24} when the great prophet, Elijah, had restored to life the child of a widow at Zarephath. II Kings 4^{18-37} tells how the prophet Elisha brought back to life the son of a widow at Shunem, which was only four miles from Nain. It was understandable that the overawed onlookers should say now of Jesus, 'A great prophet has come amongst us. God is showing that He cares about His people.' The news spread all over Judaea and the surrounding countryside.

Ten minutes walk from Nain brings one to an ancient cemetery which may have been the one in this story, but naturally this episode has been questioned by many people. Some suggest that the boy wasn't dead, but in a trance, from which Jesus disturbed him, thus saving him from being buried alive. Others see the story as an allegory, a parable with several points of meaning. They suggest that the widow stands for 'Mother Israel', the nation to whose children, the Jews, Jesus was offering real life.

The gospels have three stories about Jesus restoring life to the dead and it is possible to see a development from one to another: (a) Jairus' daughter died while Jesus was on his way to her (Luke 8^{40ff}), (b) the widow's son was about to be buried and (c) Lazarus' body was four days in the tomb (John 11^{17}). Some readers have suggested that Jesus cured these people of illnesses and that time and gossip exaggerated the facts. Luke 7^{18-35} will show, however, that the Jews expected their Messiah to be able to raise the dead, and since the Messiah was expected to overthrow the power of the Devil, he must be able to overcome death which was the work of Evil.

The story of the son of the widow of Nain is found only in Luke's gospel.

The importance of John the Baptist (7^{18-35})

Luke 3^{19-20} told how Herod Antipas, son of Herod the Great, imprisoned John the Baptist who had criticized Herod's marriage to Herodias and 'his other misdeeds'. (Luke does not include the detail found in Mark 6^{14-29} and Matt. 14^{1-12}.) John had preached that God's Messiah would soon arrive. John's own disciples visited him at his prison in the Machaerus fortress and the things he heard about his cousin Jesus made him anxious to know the truth about him, so he sent two of his own disciples to ask Jesus, 'Are you the One who is supposed to come, or are we to expect someone else?'

Jesus did not answer their question directly, for he preferred to leave people to decide for themselves about him. He went on with his usual work of healing and preaching, both of which were signs of the presence of God, the arrival of God's Kingdom. Perhaps John's friends were around when Jesus cured the centurion's servant and the widow's son. Jesus then told John's disciples to report to John what they had seen and heard, how Jesus gave sight to the blind, strength to the crippled, cleansing to lepers, hearing to the deaf, life to the dead, and how he brought good news to the poor. Jesus said that he hoped there would be some who wouldn't find all this a stumbling-block to their faith. Now, John had told the people that they would be punished when the Messiah came; he had not envisaged a loving Messiah who would lead them to God with kindness, and love them so much that he would willingly die to express that love. Yet when John heard the report from his disciples he would recognize the words of Isaiah 29^{18-19}, 35^{5-6}, 58^6 and especially 61^{1-2}, the words that Jesus had read in the Nazareth synagogue (Luke 4^{18}), and which many Jews regarded as a prophecy about the One who was to be sent by God. Certainly the prophecy had not mentioned the restoration of lepers and dead people, but the report was enough to assure John of Jesus' identity, and he would be comforted that his work and his present suffering in prison had not been in vain.

When John's disciples left, Jesus went on thinking about John. Jesus' own home had been at Nazareth of Galilee, a long way north of John's home in Judah.

Jesus now spoke highly of John and his words were a rebuke to the Pharisees who were present. Crowds had gone to John despite the heat of the empty and forbidding desert, and Jesus asked why they had gone. Had they gone to look at the ordinary sight of the reeds swaying in the breeze at the edge of the Dead Sea? The stern and courageous John was no swaying reed! Had they gone to see someone dressed in silks and satins from the royal palace? John's rough tunic of camel-skin didn't fit that description either! Surely the crowds had gone to John because they believed he was a prophet sent with a message from God!

Jesus went on to describe John as a very special prophet, unique in fact, because nobody else had been given the job as herald to the Messiah. The angel Gabriel had told Zechariah that his son, John, would be full of the spirit and power of Elijah. Malachi 4[5] said that Elijah would return before the day of the Lord arrived. The report of John's disciples must have assured John that he had done the work expected of Elijah. Jesus now told the people that this was so, and that no human being was greater than John, yet even the least of them could enjoy a privilege that John could never experience, because they would live to benefit from the great change that came from the life and teaching of Jesus. They would know the joy of being in God's Kingdom which was starting then.

The common people, even sinners like tax-gatherers, who had been baptized by John, were thrilled when Jesus spoke so highly of John, but there were some who were not so pleased. These were the Pharisees and scribes who had taken no notice of John. They had refused God's invitation offered by John. Jesus said they reminded him of children playing in a market-place, quarrelling about what game they would play. Neither wedding-music nor the wailing of the professional mourners pleased some children. Nothing is right for some people! The Pharisees said that John was crazy because he fasted and lived an ascetic life in the desert. Jesus lived a more normal life, but the Pharisees said that *he* was a glutton and a drunkard who went around with sinners! They changed as it suited them, and we see more of their lack of understanding in the next section. Jesus commented, 'And yet God's wisdom is proved right by all who are her children.' Perhaps this means that the wise people are those who realize the genuineness of both Jesus and John, for different though they were, they were both working to fulfil God's plan for people.

A sinful woman at a Pharisee's dinner-party (7$^{36-50}$)

A Pharisee named Simon invited Jesus to dine at his home. Usually, the houses of well-to-do people were built around open courtyards where meals were taken in warm weather. When a distinguished guest was present the local people often gathered in the doorways and around the courtyard to listen to the table-conversation. Beggars sometimes came hoping to get the leftovers. Fashionable Jews were now copying the Roman-Greek custom of reclining on low couches at the table, supporting themselves on one elbow, uncovered feet spread out behind them.

A well-mannered host would always greet a respected guest with the kiss of peace. One of the lower servants would be called to bathe the guest's feet with cool water, for sandals gave little protection on the hot, dusty roads. A drop of perfumed oil was put on the guest's head. The etiquette of the times demanded such courtesies, but Simon failed to provide any of these when Jesus arrived.

As the group reclined at table, a woman of bad reputation came in and stood behind Jesus. Obviously she had been deeply moved by his words and knew that he offered forgiveness for sins, even sins as bad as hers. She could begin a new and better life. Her tears began to drop on to Jesus' feet and she used her long flowing hair to dry them. Respectable women bound up their hair and would not dream of appearing in public with the loosely flowing hair which marked this woman as a prostitute. Most Jewish women hung little phials of expensive perfumed oil around their necks. These were called 'alabasters'. The woman, not knowing how to express her gratitude, kissed Jesus' feet and poured the precious oil over them.

Simon's strict religious code was offended. He thought, 'If this man really were a prophet, he would realize what type of woman this is who is touching him!'

Perhaps Jesus saw the disdain on Simon's face, but instead of reproaching him directly, Jesus said, 'Simon, I have something to tell you', and he told a story about gratitude and forgiveness, the story of two debtors.

Two men owed money to a money-lender. One owed five hundred denarii, the other fifty. (A denarius, or Roman silver penny, was the average daily wage of a working man.) Realizing that neither man could pay, the money-lender forgave them both, cancelling the debts.

Then Jesus asked Simon which of the two men would love the lender most, and Simon replied, 'I suppose the one who was forgiven most.' Jesus agreed.

Then Jesus compared the woman's action with Simon's. She had made up for the courtesies that Simon had deliberately neglected. She had washed Jesus' travel-stained feet with tears and had applied oil, not to his head, but to his feet. Simon had given no kiss of greeting, but this woman had kissed Jesus' feet. She was overwhelmed with gratitude, for, like the first debtor, she had been forgiven so much.

Pharisees, or 'separated ones', kept strictly to each detail of the Jewish religious laws. Perhaps the self-righteous and self-sufficient Simon wasn't aware that he also had sins to be forgiven! We wonder why he invited Jesus to his home. Perhaps he was concerned only to have an entertaining guest to dinner. To provide hospitality for a travelling preacher was believed to please God, and to entertain the day's preacher on the sabbath was considered especially good, so perhaps this was what Simon had in mind.

Jesus told him, 'Where little has been forgiven, little love is shown.' To the woman he said, 'Your sins are forgiven.' The guests wondered at this man who took upon himself the right to forgive sins, but Jesus did not explain. He simply told the woman to go in peace, for her faith had saved her.

Mark (14^{3-9}) and Matthew (26^{6-13}) put a similar story at the house of 'Simon the leper' at Bethany, a village near Jerusalem, towards the end of Jesus' life. In their stories the disciples criticized the waste of perfume which could have been sold and the money given to the poor. They wrote that Jesus regarded the woman's action as anointing him ready for burial. John (12^{1-8}) also puts a similar story at Bethany, saying that the perfumed ointment was applied by Mary, sister of Martha and Lazarus.

It has been suggested that the woman in the story was Mary of Magdala, a town in Galilee, and Mary Magdalene is named in Luke's next verses. There is no sound reason, however, for thinking that she was Mary Magdalene or Mary of Bethany.

Jesus travels and teaches; Parable of the Sower (8^{1-21})

Jesus now toured the towns and villages of Galilee, teaching the people. Luke portrays him as constantly on the move, 'preaching the good news about the Kingdom of God'. He was accompanied by the twelve men he had chosen and also a group of women. One of these was Mary Magdalene, from whom Jesus 'had driven seven devils'. We do not know whether this means she had been mentally or physically ill, or that she had been a particularly sinful person. She is mentioned at Mark 16^{1-10} (though the verses from 9 onwards are thought to have been an addition by a writer other than Mark), and John 19^{25}, 20^{11-18}. Another of the women, Joanna, was the wife of Herod Antipas' business manager, Chuza. Another is named as Susanna. Such travelling groups did not normally include women and this story shows that Jesus did not discriminate between the sexes. Jesus' friendship with women is particularly noted by Luke. It is one of the characteristics of his gospel. People considered it an act of piety to help a travelling preacher, and we are told, too, that these women were grateful to Jesus because he had healed them. The story also shows that his followers were not confined to any particular social class, for some were working people and some came from the royal court. (From 6^{11} Luke has been using his own material, but here at 8^4 he is again making use of information from Mark's gospel. Luke re-ordered the information taken from Mark. The parable at Mark 4^{30-32} occurs in Luke 13^{18-19}.)

The Galileans of Nazareth had rejected Jesus, but now there is an account of success and rapid growth for the Kingdom. No longer welcome in the synagogues, Jesus taught by the lake and on the hillsides, wherever the 'great crowd' could gather. The section describes how people listened and the gospel spread. It begins with a parable known as 'the Sower', though really it is better described as a parable about different kinds of soil.

Eastern farmers usually broadcast seed on ground which had not been properly prepared. They walked along hard-trodden paths between the long cultivated strips, scattering seeds to right and left from an apron-bag. Some seeds were bound to drop near their feet and these would remain on the surface of the ground, unable to penetrate it, until the birds snatched them up. Other seeds fell on to the thin layer of soil overlying limestone rock. Unable to draw moisture and nourishment the young plants soon withered in the hot sun. Tough weeds, growing side by side with other plants, took the nourishment the grain needed. Fortunately there was some deep soil without obstacles or weeds, and here the seeds grew, producing the excellent crop on which the farmer relied. Mark and Matthew compared the rate of success as thirty, sixty and a hundredfold, but Luke makes no such comparisons. Any realistic farmer expects some wastage of seeds but still expects a crop.

Having told the story Jesus called out, 'If you have ears to hear, then hear!' A teacher today might tell a class, 'You've got ears, use them!', and the pupils are expected to think out the meaning of the lesson as far as they are able.

On this occasion the disciples themselves were unsure of Jesus' meaning and asked him to explain. Jesus told them that whereas they were able to understand when he spoke about God's Kingdom, some people found the subject difficult to understand, and parables might help these people. We are not all made exactly the same; a friend may find easy something that we find difficult, and something else difficult when we consider it easy. It was not this that bothered Jesus so much, but those who rejected his teaching because they were selfish or obstinate, and who did not want to understand. Perhaps this is what Jesus meant when he quoted some difficult words from Isaiah 6$^{9-10}$ '. . . so that they may look but see nothing, hear but understand nothing'.

Jesus realized that some of the things he said would be more easily understood after his death and Resurrection, but on this occasion he explained to his disciples the parable of the Sower thus:

1 The seeds represent the gospel message, Jesus' teaching. This does not say that the Sower was Jesus alone, for the message has been spread by so many ordinary people.
2 The pathway represents people whose minds are so hard and closed to the message that it cannot begin to germinate. 'Birds' often signified 'evil'.
3 The stony soil represents people who accept the teaching with enthusiasm but give up when they meet any difficulties.
4 The soil with weeds or thorns is like people who begin well but who cannot persevere against the temptations of wealth and pleasure-seeking.
5 The good soil is like those who listen and consider carefully, who clear from their lives any obstacles and temptations which could hinder them from serving God. They have the insight and depth of character needed to apply the gospel to their own lives and they persevere in living according to its guidance.

A parable is a story or short saying which draws a comparison or parallel. It helps one to understand unfamiliar things by comparing them with familiar things. Everyone appreciates a good story and Jesus left people to work out for themselves, as far as they were able, what the story meant for them within the plan of God. They then needed courage and discipline to live accordingly.

Here the interpretation makes several comparisons, for the seed and the soils all have meanings. This makes the story an allegory.

Jesus' stories did not usually need explaining and many scholars think that it was not Jesus but early Christian teachers who added the allegorical interpretation here. Perhaps it began as a straightforward parable teaching that despite apparent failures along the way, the harvest is sure.

In parts of Galilee Jesus had been rejected and eventually he would be put to death, but this would not prevent the success of the Kingdom which had already begun and was spreading rapidly (cf. Luke 10^2). The harvest was there as a result of the work of the prophets and John the Baptist, even before Jesus' ministry had begun. Nothing could stop it now. Harvest-labourers were needed immediately. The disciples no doubt became anxious and discouraged to see their master rejected, especially when they saw the opposition of the Jewish religious leaders. By the time of Luke's writing Jesus' followers were suffering severe persecution. The parable of the Sower was needed to give them courage and hope and thus the detailed interpretation may well have developed during persecution.

Verse 14 is one of several examples in Luke's gospel where Jesus roundly condemns riches (cf. 6^{24}, 12^{13-21}, 12^{33}, 16^{13}, 16^{19-31}, 18^{24} and 19^8). Verses 16 to 18 show that Jesus' message was never intended to be kept secret; it must be made public and spread. The light of an oil-lamp benefited most people when it was high up on a stand. Its very purpose was defeated when hidden under a jar or bed. The very purpose of Christianity requires it to be shared as much as possible, not hidden as if one were ashamed of it. The knowledge given to the Twelve was meant for the whole world. Verse 18 suggests that the more one practises living according to Jesus' teaching, the greater one's ability for it becomes. The body and mind increase in power as they are exercised; they deteriorate if we neglect to use them. Unless one constantly practises Christian living, one's standards deteriorate.

Verses 19 to 21 tell how Jesus' mother and brothers were unable to get through the crowd to see Jesus. Someone spoke of this to him, but he could no longer be restricted by his relatives. He had duties to the larger family of mankind, God-given duties which became more urgent as his enemies became more opposed to him. Mark (3^{21}) tells us that his family, like other people, thought he must be out of his mind. Perhaps they were embarrassed, for they tried to stop his work. Perhaps Jesus was remembering this, for Matthew (10^{36}) says that he warned his followers that their nearest relatives could become their greatest enemies. Discipleship creates a new 'family' with responsibilities and ties. Loyalty to one's new family may come into conflict with loyalty to one's natural family and Jesus' work demands that, if this happens, then the new family must take priority.

The brothers mentioned here may have been later children of Mary or they may have been Joseph's children by a previous marriage. Jesus' brother, James, later became a leader or 'elder' of the Christian church at Jerusalem, and eventually other members of the family joined his followers (Acts 1^{14}, 12^{17} and 15^{13}).

The section ends as it began by emphasizing the importance of listening to and obeying God's message.

The lake storm and the Gergesene madman (8^{22-39})

In this section Jesus is shown as bringing calm into chaos, first in nature and then in a human mind.

Jesus had suggested that he and the disciples should sail over to the other side of Lake Galilee. Obviously he was exhausted, as any human might be, for he fell soundly asleep in the boat. One of the sudden squalls for which Galilee is renowned blew up high waves on the lake. Cold winds, rushing from the north, are forced through the hills and they toss up the waters in a terrifying manner, swamping small boats and hurling tents along the shore into the air.

The fishermen-disciples knew this lake and its storms, and they were frightened. Jesus lay serene and asleep, seemingly oblivious of the danger and the water filling the boat. They roused him shouting, 'Master! Master! We are sinking!' Luke omits the words, 'Don't you care?' found at Mark 4^{38}, and does not report that Jesus asked the disciples why they were afraid, for by the time he was writing there was a tendency to tone down Mark's blunt words about Jesus and the Twelve.

Jesus rebuked the wind and waves, saying, 'Be muzzled!' as if speaking to violent demons, and the storm abated and the sea became calm. Jesus asked his friends, 'Where is your faith?' Their leader's power gave the men a new sense of fear. God alone could control nature and the incident seemed to show that Jesus had God's power. Jesus spoke as if he expected them to understand this.

The lake storms die down as suddenly as they begin and it has been suggested that this is what happened here, but this does not explain why fishermen, familiar with this lake and its storms, turned to Jesus for comfort in their anxiety. This story probably helped to calm the

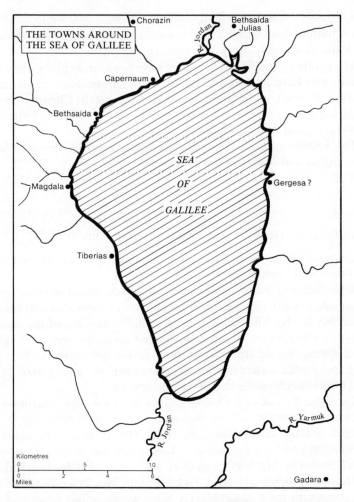

THE TOWNS AROUND
THE SEA OF GALILEE

Chorazin

Bethsaida
Julias

R. Jordan

Capernaum

Bethsaida

SEA

OF

Gergesa?

Magdala

GALILEE

Tiberias

R. Jordan

R. Yarmuk

Kilometres
0   5   10
0   2   4   6
Miles

Gadara

fears of many early Christians who were being persecuted for their beliefs at the time when the gospels were being written.

The boat landed somewhere on the eastern side of the lake, but exactly where we cannot tell, for various manuscripts of the Synoptics suggest Gerasa, Gadara, and Gergesa. Gergesa is unknown. Matthew (8²⁸) spoke of the country of the Gadarenes. Um Qeis, several miles from the lake, is all that now remains of ancient Gadara which may in those days have extended to the lake. We shall see as the story develops that it involves a herd of pigs, which the Jews did not keep as they regarded them as unclean animals. We can deduce from this that the site was one inhabited by a non-Jewish population. According to

Josephus, in *The Antiquities of the Jews* 17.11.4 and *The Wars of the Jews* 2.6.3 (Penguin Classics), Gadara had a mainly Greek population. The best manuscripts seem to show that both Mark 5[1] and Luke named the place as Gerasa, which, like Gadara, belonged to the area known as the Decapolis, or Ten Towns, but Gerasa was even further away, being about thirty miles from the lake. It is thought that a well-meaning scribe, realizing this, altered Luke's 'Gerasa' to 'Gergesa'. There are ruins known today as 'Khersa' or 'Gerga', just off-shore with an overhanging precipice falling steeply to the lake and caves which contain old Gentile graves. The name may once have been 'Gergesa' or even a second town by the name of 'Gerasa'. The site suits this story admirably.

As Jesus stepped ashore he was met by a man who was said to be devil-possessed. The man spent his time amongst the graves, perhaps believing that the spirits in him belonged with those spirits said to hover around the dead. The man was dangerously strong and had torn off the chains used to secure him. On seeing Jesus he fell to the ground and it seemed that the demons were shouting from within him, 'What do you want with me, Jesus, son of the Most High God? I beg of you, do not torment me.' This is one of the very few occasions when Jesus was addressed by his name. Foreigners often referred to the God of the Jews as 'Most High God'. Despite his mental sickness the man seemed to have an insight lacked by Jesus' own countrymen.

Jesus was already ordering the demons to leave the man. He asked the man's name. Adult Jews were often given additional names to suit their characters, and knowing someone's name could tell one much about the person. In the Old Testament book of Ruth old Naomi said her name should be changed to Mara, meaning 'Bitterness', for her husband and sons had died. To know someone's name was said to give one power over that person. The man told Jesus that he was called Legion because so many demons lived in him. (A legion of soldiers numbered up to six thousand.)

The demons begged Jesus not to banish them to the Abyss, to which it was believed the powers of evil would be banished at the end of time (Rev. 20[1-3]). People believed that the earth was flat and supported on great pillars. Around it were bottomless waters often described as the Abyss and there one was beyond the help of God and man. Perhaps the lake itself seemed part of it, giving rise to the belief that demons could be destroyed only by drowning (NEB Genesis 1[2]).

Nearby grazed a large herd of swine, or pigs (Mark said there were about two thousand) and the demons asked to be allowed to enter these animals, so that they could survive there. Jesus agreed, whereupon the pigs rushed over the cliff, falling to their deaths in the lake below. The men who had been looking after the pigs ran off to the town to report what had happened. It has been suggested that perhaps the pigs stampeded in fright at the shouting of the madman, and their keepers, scared of getting blamed for the loss of the herd, ran off to their employers with a story that shifted the blame to Jesus. Modern readers sometimes wonder whether Jesus deliberately caused the death of these animals. Others would argue that the life of a human being must come before the life of an animal. Such concern for animals is a modern one and the concern at that time would be only for the financial loss.

When the townspeople came to look for themselves, they were amazed to see Legion, dressed and calm, sitting at Jesus' feet, no doubt convinced that the drowned demons had left him and could no longer hurt him. The local people, however, were scared of Jesus' powers and asked him to go away. Perhaps they were angry about losing their pigs and did not realize that Jesus had so much more to give them. Legion was keen to go with Jesus, but Jesus told him to stay and tell the local people what God had done for him. Legion obeyed. This meant that Gentiles were being shown God's supremacy over evil.

Some scholars suggest that the story of Legion is not one to be taken literally, but understood as a parable showing that uncleanness was being destroyed. It contains many items which to Jews symbolized uncleanness – e.g. tombs, demons, swine, Gentiles. Legion was involved with uncleanness in all these ways, but his fears were dispelled by Jesus. The symptoms of Legion's violent insanity sound authentic, however, and if someone invented this story one would expect him to end with Jesus being acclaimed by the townspeople rather than driven away. Most would regard it as similar to the story about the storm in that Jesus was bringing peace and calm into chaos. He was taking the Kingdom out of Evil's control.

Jairus' daughter; A woman suffering from haemorrhages (8⁴⁰⁻⁵⁶)

Back on the more familiar side of the lake great crowds waited eagerly for Jesus to return. Out of this crowd came Jairus, a man obviously respected by the local people for they had elected him to organize the work of their synagogue. Dignity and status mattered little to Jairus at this moment for his only child, a twelve-year-old girl, was dying. (As in the story of the widow of Nain, Luke mentions the tragedy of the loss of an only child. The death of the child would mean the loss of continuity of family in each case. Jesus knew this and felt compassion for the bereaved parents.) Jairus threw himself down before Jesus begging him to come before it was too late. Jesus did not hesitate, but it was difficult to move quickly because of the crowd around him.

Many would sympathize with the broken-hearted parents. At the age of twelve an eastern girl was on the threshold of womanhood and preparing for marriage. To die without giving birth was thought of as the failure of a woman's life. Would this girl's life be taken just as it might be about to be fulfilled?

As they were struggling through the crowd Jesus suddenly asked, 'Who touched me?' Peter and the others thought this a strange thing to ask when so many people were pushing and clamouring, but Jesus knew that someone had touched him hoping to be healed, for he said, 'I know that power has gone out of me.' The fact that Jesus knew he had been touched by someone considered to be 'unclean' would be regarded as a sign of his being an authentic prophet.

A trembling woman threw herself at his feet and confessed. For twelve years she had suffered from haemorrhages, and Luke, a doctor himself, says that she had spent all her money on doctors who had failed to cure her. Perhaps his professional pride made him leave out Mark's comment that instead of getting better she had grown worse (Mark 5^{26}). Leviticus $15^{19\text{-}33}$ tells us that the law regarded any woman with a discharge of blood as unclean for seven days. Anyone who touched her at that time was also unclean, so the woman would be expected to stay indoors away from other people. This woman must have felt so desperate at seeing Jesus go off with Jairus that she touched the fringed edge of his robe and felt immediately that she was cured. Deuteronomy 22^{12} and Numbers $15^{38\text{-}41}$ had instructed the Israelites to put blue-corded tassels, or fringes, on the corners of their cloaks as reminders of their duty to obey the Commandments. The tassels also showed everyone that these people belonged to God. Today the tassels usually appear on the talith, or shawl, worn for prayers. Risking a rebuke from those around her she told Jesus why she had touched him and he turned to speak to her, despite the need to hurry to Jairus' house. He told her, 'Daughter, your faith has cured you. Go in peace.' Jesus could have ignored what had happened, but later the woman might feel a sense of guilt. She might have been left with a belief in superstition and magic, as if she had touched a lucky charm! Perhaps Jesus wanted to make sure that she realized that the help came from God. By bringing the matter out into the open Jesus gave peace to her mind as well as healing her body.

Jews wearing Taliths during a festival in modern Israel

A church historian named Eusebius, writing about 300A.D., claimed that the woman was a Gentile from Caesarea-Philippi, and that a statue, put there to commemorate her, was destroyed by the pagan emperor Julian, who replaced it with his own statue. Shortly afterward a thunderbolt destroyed his statue. Of course this may well be a legend.

The group continued towards Jairus' house, but soon they were met by someone who told Jairus, 'Your daughter is dead. Don't bother the Master further.'

Jesus heard this and said to Jairus, 'Don't be afraid. Just have faith and she will be cured.' At the house the wailing women, the professional mourners, had already arrived. Such a custom may horrify us, but failing to hire these women was seen as lack of respect for the dead, just as some people still regard the necessity of flowers or black clothes at a funeral today. Jesus said, 'Stop weeping. She is not dead, but asleep.' It has been suggested that Jesus meant that the girl was unconscious, or in a coma, in which case he could save her from being buried alive. (In the east the corpse was buried immediately.) Verse 53, however, stresses the fact that those around laughed at him, knowing the girl was dead.

Jesus allowed only the parents and Peter, James and John into the child's room with him. He took her hand and said, 'Get up, my child', just as if she really were asleep. (Luke, writing for Gentiles, leaves out the Aramaic words found in Mark 5[41].) The girl was seen to begin to breathe and she got up.

The gospel stories are restrained, simply stating such events without comment, but one can imagine the tremendously emotional scene which might have followed had not Jesus sent off the astounded parents to get some food, perhaps to restore the child's strength, perhaps giving them an opportunity for tears of relief without frightening the child.

It would be impossible to hide the story from neighbours who were already aware of part of it, but Jesus asked that no attention should be drawn to it, no fuss made. He was anxious, no doubt, to avoid the kind of public acclaim which might try to set him up as a national leader against the Romans.

By now Jesus had been rejected in the synagogues. It must have been rather an embarrassment for the synagogue president, Jairus, to pocket his pride and ask help from a rejected man, but results left him in no doubt that he had done the right thing. His little daughter had been returned to life to fulfil her full term of years.

The girl was twelve years old, the woman with the haemorrhage had suffered for twelve years. For some reason Jesus had chosen twelve disciples. One wonders at this point if Luke, concerned as he was for fellow-Gentiles, were also emphasizing Jesus' concern for the Jews, the descendants of the twelve tribes of Israel. The twelve disciples may well have symbolized the New Israel (meaning Christians) who would serve God faithfully.

In the stories from 8^{22-56} Jesus has triumphed over a storm, over demons, over incurable illness and over death. Luke seems to be preparing his readers for the final triumph, the Resurrection of Jesus. The promise of 4^{18} is being fulfilled in the way that Jesus is freeing people imprisoned in various ways, by anxiety, evil powers, social customs, pain and even death. Through him God is taking over, the Kingdom of God has already begun.

Jesus commissions his disciples (9^{1-9})

Disciples are pupils or followers. Jesus now sent out his disciples to preach and heal, to do what they had seen Jesus himself doing, so Luke refers to them as apostles, meaning 'people sent out as messengers'. Their task, preaching and healing, showed that God was concerned about people's physical well-being as well as their souls. Jairus' daughter had just been raised from death when Jesus sent the Twelve out to the towns and villages as apostles. After Jesus' Resurrection they were to be sent out to all nations. Between these times Luke reverts to calling them again 'disciples'.

The great crowds surrounding Jesus made it difficult for him to move quickly from one place to another. The synagogues no longer welcomed him and there was growing opposition from the Jewish leaders. Mark 6^{14-28} also puts John's death at this point in the story, cf. Luke 9^7, and Jesus knew that his own turn to die must come soon. There was a sense of urgency and haste as Jesus sent out the Twelve to spread his message.

He gave them power to cure physical illnesses and to drive out the demons believed to cause mental illness. They must tell people that God's Kingdom had come to them, but they must not waste time with anyone who wouldn't listen. When strict Jews were leaving Gentile areas they shook away every speck of 'heathen' dust before re-entering Jewish territory. In the same way the apostles must 'shake off the dust' when leaving those who had rejected God's invitation to become His people. They must not carry any luggage which would slow them down. They must travel as Josephus tells us the Essene monks did, with no extra clothes, food or money (Wars, 2.8.4.). Luke had little regard for money or possessions and shows that Jesus saw luxuries as something which could hinder a man's devotion to God's work. Mark (6^{8-9}) says that they were allowed sandals and a stick, which seems to echo the way the Israelites set out on the Exodus journey (Ex. 12^{11}). Jesus' life was like a journey taking him to his destiny at Jerusalem. Luke emphasizes that lack of possessions left the Twelve free to concentrate on their task. Eastern people usually shared the burden of providing hospitality for a guest staying any length of time, but Jesus advised his men to make their headquarters at one home if possible, content to accept whatever hospitality was offered.

The Twelve must have been successful on their preaching tour, for news of their doings soon began to worry Herod Antipas, tetrarch of Galilee. A tetrarch was a prince who governed one fourth of a Roman province. Herod Antipas was a son of Herod the Great who was king at the time of the birth of Jesus (cf. 1^5). The name 'Herod' had become a dynastic name like the Roman name 'Caesar'.

Some Jews were wondering if Jesus could be Elijah returned to life. (They believed that the great prophet Elijah would return to help them in times of crisis. It was also thought that Elijah would come back to herald the arrival of the Messiah.) Other Jews were suggesting that Jesus was one of the other great prophets. Still others were suggesting that he was John the Baptist returned to life. Mark (6^{16}) suggests that Herod himself began this tale, but Luke describes Herod as contemptuous of the superstitious idea, for Herod knew that John was very much dead, but was concerned that now he had another religious troublemaker, Jesus, to deal with. He was curious to see Jesus, but did not manage this until Jesus was being tried before Pilate. Later, when some friendly Pharisees went to warn Jesus that Herod was plotting to kill him (Luke 13^{31-32}), Jesus seemed unconcerned, knowing that his end would come only in Jerusalem.

The return of the Twelve; The feeding of the crowd (9^{10-17})

The tour of preaching and healing had been a great success and the Twelve returned anxious to tell Jesus all that had happened, but, as Mark, (6^{31}) tells us, the group found it difficult to get away from the crowds even to eat or sleep, let alone have any private conversation. Jesus took them to a quiet place. Luke says they went to Bethsaida, but this was a new sizeable busy town. Probably they went to nearby grassy slopes. This territory belonged to Philip and was therefore a safe distance from Herod Antipas.

The crowds soon discovered where they were, however, and, perhaps afraid that Jesus had left Galilee for good, they followed. He could not be angry with these people. He welcomed them, talking to them again about God's Kingdom and healing many. Towards the close of the long and tiring day the people were still there and the disciples suggested that Jesus should send them away to nearby villages to find food and lodging. They were astonished when Jesus answered, 'You give them something to eat!', and they told him that all they had was five little loaves and two fishes, unless he imagined that they could go and buy food for this crowd! (Only in John's gospel is there mention of a boy bringing the bread and fish.) Luke says there were about 5000 men. Some commentators suggest that Jews counted only the adult males in any crowd. Others remind us that in a Semitic environment such crowds often consisted only of men, for the women and children were usually at home.

Jesus told them to sit the people down in groups of fifty. Then taking the bread and fish he 'looked up into heaven' and blessed the food. When the Jews prayed they looked up, arms stretched out, palms facing upwards. Jesus made it obvious to the crowd that he was praying. He broke up the food and gave it to the disciples to distribute. Everyone had plenty to eat and the disciples gathered up twelve basketsful of leftovers.

This story is the only miracle story recorded in all four gospels. Mark described it as happening in an unnamed lonely spot before the group went to Bethsaida. Luke leaves out here many of Mark's details, condensing the story. Mark said the people sat on green grass, which suggests that it was springtime, when grass is green for only a few weeks.

Various opinions have been expressed about this story:

1 Some regard it as a miracle in which Jesus multiplied food for a hungry crowd, though no gospel says in so many words that Jesus miraculously multiplied the food, nor do they mention any astonishment on the part of the crowd. John (6^{15}) says that after this event the people wanted to make Jesus their king, but that he went away by himself into the hills. The other gospels follow the event with Peter expressing the disciples' conviction that Jesus was God's Messiah.

2 Other interpreters suggest that the people had sensibly brought some food with them but were reluctant to produce it until they were shamed at the disciples' willingness to share the little they had. When they all shared their food there was more than enough for everyone, just as there would be if the affluent nations of our modern world were more willing to share the world's resources with the under-developed countries.

3 The Jews saw themselves as God's Chosen People who would be welcomed into His Kingdom with a great banquet. Some readers suggest that here Jesus was providing them with a banquet to show

that the Kingdom had arrived, and no matter what the nationality of those present, his followers were God's new chosen people who would take on the task that the Jews had failed to accomplish.

4 Just as God had provided manna for the people on the Exodus journey, so He was providing now for people setting out on a journey as God's new people.

5 The story shows that Jesus was certainly as great as Elisha who had provided food enough and to spare (2 Kings 4^{42-44}).

6 The way Jesus took, blessed, broke and gave the food reminds one of the special meaning he gave to those same actions at the Last Supper, which is remembered every time Christians are present at the service of Holy Communion (also called the Eucharist), when the words of I Corinthians 11^{23-28} are read.

Whatever one's ideas, at the very least the story shows Jesus' concern for people. Some people feel it was a farewell meal for the Galilean followers of Jesus, for it certainly seemed now that his ministry in Galilee was over and he was preparing for the journey to Jerusalem (see verse 51), the place of conflict and death.

Who was Jesus? Peter confesses his belief (9^{18-22})

At this point for some reason Luke has left out the material found in Mark 6^{45} to 8^{26}, stories about Jesus' work in Galilee, Tyre and Sidon, and the Decapolis, areas to the north near Mount Hermon. G.H. Streeter wondered if the section were missing from Luke's copy of Mark's gospel, but other readers realized that Luke had already included some of the material elsewhere and that much of it would not be of great interest to Luke's Gentile readers. By leaving out the section Luke was able to continue writing on the subject of Jesus' identity.

Verse 51 makes it clear that Jesus was preparing for his last visit to Jerusalem. One can be sure that something of importance is about to happen because Luke says that Jesus was praying. Then Jesus asked his disciples, 'Whom do the people say I am?' They had just returned from a tour of preaching and healing in towns and villages, and would therefore know what people were saying about him. They told him, 'Some think you are John the Baptist, some say Elijah, or one of the other prophets returned to life.' Then Jesus asked a far more difficult and personal question, 'Whom do you think I am?' If they gave the wrong answer now, it would mean that his work with the Twelve had been in vain and Jesus was conscious that he had little time left with them. Until now the only ones to recognize openly his true identity had been the demons in sick people!

It was Peter, speaking for the others, who answered, 'God's Messiah!' Mark and Matthew say that all this happened near Caesarea Philippi and Matthew's version shows that Jesus was relieved and grateful for Peter's answer (Matt. 16^{17}). The event marks a definite turning point in the ministry. Jesus must have felt that his friends were now ready to be prepared for what would happen to him at Jerusalem. From now on Jesus was to concentrate on teaching his disciples so that they would be equipped to take over the work when he had left them.

The Jews hoped that God would give to them a Messiah from the descendants of King David. Like David, this Messiah would lead the Jews to victory against the nation's enemies, who at this time were the Romans. He would make himself king and would bring in a time of peace, plenty and national importance to the Jewish people. The world would respect them as the Chosen People of the Most High God.

Jesus emphasized that his disciples should not declare publicly that they believed he was the Messiah. Such a declaration would encourage people to prepare for rebellion against Rome. First he must turn upside-down the idea the disciples had about what to expect of the Messiah, and here and at 22$^{67-69}$ Jesus used for himself a title which might give them a clearer idea of his purpose, the 'Son of Man' (see pp. 77–8). He told them that the Son of Man must suffer many things. He would be rejected by the Jewish leaders (like those in the Sanhedrin), by the chief priests and the scribes, who were the professional rabbis or teachers. He must be killed and must rise again on the third day. Mark and Matthew show that Peter could not understand or accept all this and rebuked Jesus, receiving in turn a counter-rebuke from Jesus, who was going to find it difficult enough to face trials and death without Peter tempting him to run away from them. Peter could not understand that all this was the only way to bring about God's plans. Luke leaves out this conversation between Jesus and Peter, but stresses that all these things MUST happen. At 7^8, a centurion realized that Jesus was under the command of someone higher, as he himself was, and Jesus accepted his destiny saying, 'I must be', (2^{49}), 'I must preach', (4^{43}), 'I must go', (13^{33}), and here he says that he must suffer, be rejected, put to death and be raised again. From now on Jesus often warned his friends of what would happen (9^{44}, 17^{25}, 24^7).

Jesus' words show us what he thought of himself and his work, ideas he must have worked out at the time of the Temptations. Isaiah (53$^{2-9}$) described the coming of the servant of God who would be rejected by the people, would suffer and even die in order to bring the nations to

God. Then God would exalt that servant who would return to judge the people and rule over them for ever. The passage seems to be a remarkably accurate description of the way taken by Jesus, who obviously saw himself more as a Suffering Servant than a militant Messiah.

Various people speculated as to whom Jesus might be. Herod wondered about him. The crowd, fed by Jesus, concluded that he was certainly someone special. When Jesus asked directly, Peter confessed to the belief that Jesus was the long-awaited Messiah. In verses 28–36, the story of the Transfiguration, we are told that God Himself identified Jesus by saying, 'This is my beloved Son'. Yet, to the Jews, the idea of their Messiah suffering was unthinkable. They had grown to understand suffering as the surest sign that a man was being punished by God for some sin he had committed. How could a man be the Messiah, the one specially chosen by God, and also be punished by God? When Jesus brought together the ideas about the Messiah and the Suffering Servant as one person it was such a new suggestion that the Jews of his time found it difficult to accept. (See again notes on 4^{31-44}.)

Some people have suggested that the words about being raised again were put in by the writers after the resurrection of Jesus. The prophet Hosea had said that, after disaster and destruction, the nation of Israel would be restored on the third day. (Three days usually signified a short time.) If Jesus spoke about being raised on the third day, some people wonder if he were quoting from Hosea 6^2, intending this to encourage his followers, the New Israel, who, despite persecution, would emerge triumphant. History has since shown that Christianity survived and spread despite many periods of despair and persecution.

General note on title 'Son of Man'

The words 'son of man' often simply meant 'man'. The prophet Ezekiel said he was often addressed by God in this way, e.g. Ezek. 2^1 – 'Son of man, stand on your feet and I will speak with you.' The writer of Psalm 8 marvelled that God should give honour, importance and care to an ordinary human being, a son of man. In about 164 B.C., the Jews, under the leadership of the Maccabees, were fighting the Seleucid invaders. Wishing to encourage them to stand firm someone wrote about a wise man named Daniel who was helped by God to stand firm while exiled in Babylon. Daniel 7^{1-14} tells of the defeat of four enemy powers (the four beasts) then 'one like a son of man' came with the clouds of heaven, invested by God with power and glory to rule the nations of the world for ever. In Daniel 7$^{13-18}$ 'son of man' seems to symbolize 'the saints of the Most High', which then meant the Jewish nation whose task was to bring the world's people to God. Jesus had now taken over this task and the title he chose for himself stated that he had God's authority (e.g. Mark 2^{10,28}, 14^{62}), and that his suffering would be followed by glory. Sometimes Jesus' words and actions made it clear that he had God's authority (see p. 44, also Luke 22^{69}). The Similitudes of Enoch, a strange apocalyptic writing from the time between the Testaments (the only existing version, however, is one made by Christians for Christians), described the Son of Man as an individual, man-like yet angel-like too, who was with God before Creation. At the time of Judgement he would be enthroned in glory to judge all nations and rulers, angels and evil spirits, after which he would live for ever with the righteous close to God's presence. 'Son of man' may also have expressed the ancient belief that one day there would come a perfect man, all that God intended every man to be.

It is difficult now to know how much the early Church was really responsible for identifying the term 'Son of Man' with the title 'Messiah'.

The cost of being a Christian (9$^{23-27}$)

Jesus told the people that anyone wanting to be one of his followers must leave behind all self-concern, must deny himself and take up his cross daily. People who are only concerned about themselves lose something of great value in life. One can get everything available in a material sense, comfort, security, popularity, but lose one's soul and character in doing so. Such a cost is too high.

The Jews believed that angels would collect people from all corners of the earth for judgement. Jesus told the people that anyone ashamed now to declare his allegiance to him must be prepared for the Son of Man to disown him when he came 'with the glory of God and His angels'. The follower of Jesus has to be prepared to take risks, forgetting himself in the service of others, prepared to sacrifice even his life itself if the need arises. Jesus knew what 'carrying a cross' meant. The Roman way of executing foreign criminals was by crucifixion. There had been a mass crucifixion of about two thousand rebel Jews when Jesus was about eleven years old. Prisoners were forced to carry the cross-pieces of their own crosses to the place of execution. Jesus realized that some of his followers might have to do this, and he knew that every day could bring its own problems for them. It would not do for them to become his followers, thinking of what they could get out of it for themselves. They must join him thinking only of what they could give. Their loyalty to Jesus and his work would bring its own kind of reward. To reject him brought judgement upon themselves and punishment.

Jesus said that some of the people who were standing near him would see the Kingdom of God before they died. Jesus seemed to expect the Kingdom to come within the lifetime of some of his followers. Either he was mistaken in this, or his followers misunderstood his meaning. They interpreted his words in this way. Later, after many of his followers had died, they believed the coming of the Kingdom would be delayed for a great many years. Today some Christians still believe the Kingdom will come some time in the future. Others believe that the true interpretation of Jesus' words is that Christians would experience the presence of God with them. Events like the resurrection and the Day of Pentecost (Acts 2) made them aware of God's power amongst them. Jesus taught that the Kingdom was not something in the far-distant future, it had begun already for those with the insight to understand and accept it. The miracles were signs that God had already arrived to help His people.

The Transfiguration (9^{28-36})

Luke tells us that 'eight days later' Jesus took Peter, James and John up into a mountain. Obviously he wants us to recall the last story, which told of Peter's declaration that Jesus was the Messiah and how Jesus warned the disciples that soon he must die at Jerusalem.

Mark and Matthew had described the last event as happening near Caesarea Philippi, so the mountain may have been Mount Hermon which was about fourteen miles north of that town. They say this story happened 'six days later'.

Throughout the story there is much symbolism which would have meant more to the Jew of that time than it does to us today. Jesus took his friends to a mountain. A mountain would immediately signify that they were going to meet with God. Moses met with God at Mount Sinai, or Mount Horeb, as did Elijah, in Jerusalem the people met with God on the Temple Mount. Now Jesus and his friends go to meet with God.

Jesus must have felt the need of the companionship of his three friends, the three who were at the raising of Jairus' daughter and would be nearest to him at Gethsemane some time later. Luke emphasizes the sense of crisis by telling us that Jesus went to pray. The three disciples must have dropped off to sleep but when they were wide awake they realized that Jesus looked different – his face looked different and his clothes seemed to be brilliantly white – and he was talking to two men. Luke did not say, as Mark and Matthew did, that Jesus was 'transfigured'. The word might make Luke's Gentile readers think that Jesus was like their pagan gods who changed their shapes in a magical way. Exodus 34²⁹⁻³⁵ says that Moses' face shone whenever he had been speaking with God, and great saints, artists and writers have been known to look transformed when their minds were completely engrossed by their work.

The disciples somehow recognized the two men talking with Jesus as Elijah, considered by Jews to be the greatest of their prophets, and Moses, the great law-giver who took the enslaved Israelites on the Exodus journey to the land promised by God. Jesus was to free people enslaved by sin so that they could enter God's Kingdom. Elijah and Moses were talking to Jesus about the way in which he would make his departure in Jerusalem, and for 'departure' Luke uses the same Greek word 'exodus'. Moses and Elijah had prepared the work that Jesus was about to complete. Moses and Elijah symbolized the religious authority of Law and Prophecy, the means by which God had chosen to reveal Himself to His people. Now Jesus was following in the work these had begun. He had fulfilled all they had said and had superseded them.

When it looked as if Moses and Elijah were about to leave, Peter, anxious to prolong this wonderful mountain-top experience, suggested that they should put up tabernacles, one each for Moses, Elijah and Jesus. A tabernacle was a shelter of branches, used by the Jews when they camped out, as they had on the Exodus journey, during which time they had been most faithful to God. A special tabernacle of curtains had served as a shelter for God along the way. Luke excuses Peter by saying that he spoke without understanding the situation.

A cloud cast its shadow over the scene. Luke uses the Jewish word 'shekinah' which described a cloud that symbolized God's presence. The shekinah as a pillar had guided the people of the Exodus, had been seen over Mount Sinai as Moses wrote the Commandments, had hovered at the special tabernacle in the wilderness and was seen at the dedication of Solomon's temple. It would later be present at the Ascension of Jesus. Naturally, the disciples were frightened. God was present.

Having patterned his life on the description of the Suffering Servant,

Jesus knew that the way was leading rapidly to his execution. He must be sure that this was what God wanted.

At his baptism, as Jesus was about to begin his ministry, God's voice had assured him, 'You are my Son, my Beloved, on whom my favour rests.' Eight days before the Transfiguration Peter had stated the belief of the disciples, 'You are God's Messiah!', and now on the mountain these disciples heard for themselves God's voice (the 'Bath Qol') saying, 'This is my Son, my Chosen; listen to him.' Their belief was confirmed. Only from this important place in the story could Jesus know that his disciples, the nucleus of his future followers, were ready to understand and continue his work. From this point there seemed to be a new beginning to his ministry, the journey towards Jerusalem when they would be learning the true meaning of his Messiahship. Later, when they faced doubts and danger, and even death, the memory of this experience would strengthen them, assuring them that their work was for God. Jesus himself must have felt reassured that he was following God's plan for him, and that in the difficult years ahead Peter, James and John would stand firm and encourage the other disciples. Jesus had been seen with the representatives of Law and Prophecy. Synagogue readings worked systematically through the first five books of the Old Testament (the Pentateuch, the books of the Law attributed to Moses), and the writings of the prophets. Law and Prophecy formed the basis of Judaism and now it was clear that Jesus was fulfilling the aims of both. He was linked with these men who had taken a great part in God's plan for the Jews, yet he went beyond them both, completely transforming the relationship between God and people. The death he chose in order to show how much God loved mankind made him unique. When Moses and Elijah had disappeared, the disciples were left with Jesus who was the fulfilment of all their work. Peter had wanted to hold on to the three, but he had the one who mattered most.

For a long time the three disciples told no one of their experience. Mark (9^{9-13}) and Matthew (17^{9-13}) say that as Jesus walked with them back down the mountain he asked them not to mention it to anyone until after his Resurrection. Malachi had prophesied that Elijah would return to the earth to announce the arrival of the Messiah, but now Jesus told the three that Elijah had already been and was not recognized, he had suffered as the Son of Man would now suffer (Mark 9^{13} and Matt. 17^{12}), from which they understood him to be referring to John the Baptist.

This strange story has been much discussed by modern readers. Some wonder if it describes a post-resurrection appearance of Jesus which was misplaced in time, or perhaps an exaggerated account of an experience shared by Jesus and the three disciples, when a discussion about Moses and Elijah became presented as an actual meeting with them. Certainly the later lives of Peter, James and John and their willingness to face persecution and death, showed that they had experienced the transcendence of Jesus.

The epileptic boy (9^{37-45})

The experience of witnessing the Transfiguration of Jesus must have strengthened the ability of Peter, James and John to face the problems that had become a part of their lives. Such a problem faced them now, for on the plain below a great crowd awaited them.

From the crowd came a distressed father begging Jesus to cure his son. Like Jairus' daughter and the son of the widow at Nain this was an only child. The father said that a demon inside the boy would sometimes scream and strike the boy to the ground. The child would then writhe about, foaming at the mouth. The disciples had proved unable to cure the boy, whose symptoms suggest that he was having epileptic fits.

This report distressed Jesus. Only a little while before the disciples had been out preaching and curing all kinds of illnesses. How would they manage when Jesus was no longer with them? Time was so short now, and they still had much to learn. Mark (9^{14-29}) gives a longer account which says that before Jesus arrived an argument had begun between the disciples and some lawyers. Matthew's account says that Jesus told the disciples they lacked the necessary faith to cure the boy. Luke leaves out these rather blunt and critical comments, also omitting the father's confession that he himself needed more faith. Jesus said, 'What an unbelieving and awkward generation! How much longer must I put up with you! Bring your son here!' How much of this was intended for the disciples, the crowd or the father is difficult to decide. Jesus' words are reminiscent of Numbers 14^{11} and Deuteronomy 32^5 where Moses also had despaired of the people's lack of faith.

As the epileptic boy approached Jesus he had another attack, falling on the ground in a convulsion. Jesus 'rebuked the demon', cured the boy and gave him back to his father.

The onlookers were awestruck, amazed at 'the majesty of God'. Again it was a triumph for Jesus and perhaps the disciples began to feel that he was fast becoming a popular hero. They themselves would gain popularity and power if this happened. Perhaps Jesus saw their reaction. On the mountain three of them had been told, 'This is my Son, listen to him!' Jesus told them now that they should be more concerned about the things he said and, in the middle of this triumph, he warned them for a second time that soon he would be arrested. Perhaps, with the admiring people around, they could not believe that it could all change, for Luke says they couldn't understand Jesus' warning and were afraid to question him about it. Only when it was all over would they be able to look back and understand.

The wonder and admiration of the people may also have been to Jesus one of those times when it seemed the Devil was tempting him to seek worldly power.

The strength and radiance of Jesus as seen in the Transfiguration story contrasts greatly with the weakness and dullness of the disciples in the story of the epileptic boy, and the events of the next three sections, as far as verse 56, again illustrate the disciples' imperfections.

Who is greatest? (9^{46-48})

It was obvious that the disciples were still thinking that Jesus was going to assume worldly power, because now they began to argue about which of them was greatest. They were probably wondering which would get the important positions when Jesus took over the Jewish kingdom. Perhaps there had been some jealousy and resentment because on certain occasions Jesus took only Peter, James and John with him.

To Jesus greatness was seen in the way one served other people, even people who didn't seem to deserve help and those, especially, who could not in any way return the kindness. The disciples were human enough to think that greatness necessitated being recognized by other people; they wanted the reward of men's praise and admiration and this self-interest was bound to bring jealousy between them.

Jesus took the hand of a child and drew him to his side, telling the disciples, 'Whoever receives this child in my name, receives me. And whoever receives me, receives the One who sent me. The least amongst you is really the greatest.' They must serve others in humility without expecting praise or reward.

Tolerance (9^{49-50})

Many people in the east claimed to be able to exorcize demons. John came and told Jesus that they had heard someone using Jesus' name to drive out demons, so they had forbidden him to do this again because he wasn't one of their company. Jesus told John, 'Don't try to stop him. If he is not against you, he is on your side.' The man about whom John complained must have believed in Jesus' power. Having failed to cure the epileptic boy, the disciples should have been grateful to see that someone had faith in Jesus' name. No one has the monopoly of God's truth. In the short time that he had left, Jesus welcomed the support of everyone, and to him no one was an outsider.

These recent stories have not attempted to hide the weaknesses of the disciples. They had failed to cure the epileptic, and to understand Jesus' warning about coming arrest; they argued amongst themselves about their individual importance, and they showed resentment towards an 'outsider'. The next section again shows their intolerance when things don't go their way.

Jesus Journeys Towards Jerusalem (9^{51} to 19^{27})

Journeying south through Samaria (9^{51-56})

Jesus now 'set his face like a flint' to go to Jerusalem for the Passover, knowing that he would die there, but equally sure that he would be going to God. His crucifixion needed courage and determination, but it would be followed by Resurrection and Ascension. The words remind us of the story of Elijah (II Kings 2^{9-11}) who also looked beyond death to the glory of being with God.

Elijah and Jesus taught different concepts about God, however, for Elijah had called on God to destroy his enemies with fire (II Kings 1^{9-12}) as the disciples John and James wanted to do here, but Jesus showed love and forgiveness for his enemies and even willingness to die for them. This was something the Jews certainly did not expect of their Messiah.

To make a direct journey from Galilee to Jerusalem necessitated travelling through Samaria (see map facing p. 1). For centuries the Jews and Samaritans had nursed a grievance against each other (see p. 93), and the Samaritans worshipped God in their own temple built on Mount Gerizim.

Rather than travel through Samaria many Jews preferred to cross over to the east side of the Jordan river and travel south through Peraea until they could cross the river straight into Judaea, but Jesus had no intention of doing this. He travelled by the quickest route, sending some of the disciples ahead to arrange lodgings for the night. Perhaps he was making a gesture of friendship towards the Samaritans.

The Samaritans of one village were reluctant to help pilgrims travelling to the Jerusalem Temple and the Zebedee brothers, John and James, suggested that they should command lightning to strike the village. Little wonder that Jesus nicknamed these two the 'Boanerges' – 'sons of thunder' (Mark 3^{17})! He rebuked their quick tempers and intolerant attitude and said that they would travel on to another village. The prophet Elijah had done spectacular things like calling down 'fire from heaven' but this was not the way of Jesus.

Luke presents the story of Jesus as one great journey towards Jerusalem, a journey that ends only when Jesus returns to God in the story of the Ascension (chapter 24^{50-51}). Luke's second volume, the Acts of the Apostles, tells how the spirit of Jesus guided his followers as they journeyed, taking his message to Rome, the heart of the Empire.

Luke's account of the journey between Galilee and Jerusalem seems to move backwards and forwards in a most illogical way. The scholar, Conzelmann, suggests that Luke who was not a Jew didn't know the geography of Palestine very well. At Luke 8^{22} Jesus sails across the Sea of Galilee, at 9^{51-56} he is in Samaritan villages heading for Jerusalem, 10^{38} finds him at Bethany, 13^{31-35} Pharisees warn him to leave Galilee, 17^{11} he is on the borders between Samaria and Galilee, 18^{35} he is at Jericho. It has been suggested that Luke, having found stories not included in Mark's gospel, fitted them into his account of Jesus' journey to Jerusalem without concern for keeping to a logical route.

From 9^{51} to 18^{14} Luke uses material not found in Mark's gospel. He has used material of his own and material from Q (see pp. 4, 10–11).

Following Jesus (9^{57-62})

There were many who wanted to become disciples of Jesus. He was honest and did not try to minimize the difficulties of such a life. He did not expect anyone to follow him until they had considered the matter carefully and counted the cost.

To one man who wished to go with him, Jesus warned, 'Foxes have holes, the birds have nests, but the Son of Man has nowhere to lay his head.' The disciples must have lived and slept in the open quite often. On another occasion Jesus invited a man to accompany him, but the man said he wanted to be allowed to bury his father first. Probably the father wasn't dead or even dying, but the man considered it his duty to care for his father as long as he lived. Afterwards he would feel free to go with Jesus. He had not realized that the call of God comes even before the most sacred family commitments. At first it seems that Jesus did not understand family responsibilities, for he answered, 'Leave the dead to the burier of the dead. Your job is with the living.' It has been suggested that perhaps Jesus was thinking of those who were 'dead' in a spiritual way, but it seems more likely that here his words could be taken more literally.

Another man who wanted to accompany Jesus first wished to have time to say goodbye to his family and friends. Jesus told him that anyone who begins to plough and keeps looking backwards is of no use for the Kingdom of God. There was now a sense of urgency in the work. The man had to be prepared to break with the past and work for the present and future. The work was too urgent and important to be postponed. Often postponement means a job never gets done, and a good decision is best put into practice immediately. If the work did not matter enough for the man to leave everything else it was doubtful whether he would survive the pace later.

It is not always easy to make rigid interpretations of Jesus' sayings however, for eastern people often used hyperbole, or extreme exaggeration, to get over their meaning. English people, who are prone to understate rather than exaggerate, have to allow for this (see p. 52).

Seventy helpers commissioned; Workers for God's harvest (10¹⁻¹⁶)

There was little time left and still so much to be done. From the crowds that followed him Jesus chose seventy men and sent them to preach and heal in the towns and villages he still hoped to visit. They worked in pairs as they did afterwards in the early Church (Acts 13², 15⁴⁰). The number seventy had been important in various ways. Moses had chosen seventy elders to help him govern the Israelites (Numbers 11²⁴) though some versions give the number as seventy-two. The translating of the Hebrew scriptures into Greek had been done by seventy-two scholars (a translation known as the 'Septuagint' meaning 'work of the seventy'). The Jews had a belief, based on Genesis 10, that there were seventy or possibly seventy-two nations in the world.

Originally Jesus had sent his twelve disciples on a mission to the Jews, a nation comprised of the twelve tribes of Israel. Perhaps now he deliberately sent out a further seventy-two disciples to symbolize the wider mission to the other nations of the world.

The story of the sending out of the Twelve in 9¹⁻¹⁰ is so similar to this account of the sending out of the seventy-two that many people feel that they are two versions of the same incident. Luke is the only writer to mention the seventy-two, perhaps because as a Gentile he wanted to make it clear that Jesus came not only to the Jews but to all the world. However, we will refer to them as 'Seventy'.

Jesus told the seventy disciples, 'The crop is heavy, but labourers are scarce. You must ask the owner to send more labourers to harvest his crop. Now listen, I am sending you like lambs among wolves.' The Jews often referred to themselves as the lambs of God's flock. 'Wolves' often referred to foreigners. Isaiah (11^6) had said that one day lambs and wolves would sit down together in peace. Perhaps Jesus thought of the seventy as going into great danger amongst foreign people.

Jesus gave them instructions. They need not take money nor luggage. They should not carry an extra pair of shoes (cf. 9^3 and 22^{35}). Travellers might consider such things necessary, but these travellers should travel light, avoiding the long preamble of polite conversation which went on between eastern people before they got down to discussing their real business. Nothing must delay nor distract them. Their needs would be supplied. The Jewish Talmud, a great collection of laws and teachings, said that no one should go on the Temple Mount with staff, shoes, scrip or money in his purse. Jesus' disciples are told to go out to their task in the same spirit as they would go to the worship of God at the Temple.

Wherever they are welcomed they should say, 'Peace to this house!' It was the everyday eastern greeting, but was to gain a deeper meaning in Christian use. (It had become casually used, much as we say 'Good morning'.) Wherever peace was deserved, it really would remain. If possible the preachers should stay in one home without feeling guilty about accepting the hospitality of one family, for their work earned them their keep. Villagers usually shared the burden of providing hospitality for a guest who stayed any length of time. Jesus' work often sapped his strength (see $8^{23,46}$). These men would need quiet, rest and peace of mind after a day's work and moving around to different families might be a strain. One lodging place would enable people to find them easily. They were told to be content with whatever food was offered. Perhaps Jesus meant they should not expect luxuries, perhaps he meant them to accept the food which was not always 'kosher' (prepared according to Jewish rules). Their preaching and healing should be signs that God had come amongst His people, the Kingdom had begun. Wherever people did not welcome them they should shake off the dust of that town and warn the people that they had rejected the invitation of God. Such people would fare worse than Sodom on Judgement Day. (Sodom and Gomorrah were cities well-known for wickedness, believed to have been the reason for their destruction in an earthquake (Gen. 19).)

Then Jesus continued, 'Woe to Chorazin and Bethsaida! If Tyre and Sidon had seen the signs that you have seen, they would have repented in dust and ashes' (cf. Matt. 11^{21-24}). Perhaps Jesus had been at

Chorazin at some time, though we have no record of the visit. The gospels were not intended as biographies and did not record everything Jesus did. The Gentile cities of Tyre and Sidon had always been known for heathen worship and many evils. Capernaum had been Jesus' main centre of work, but obviously the people of that town did not come up to his expectations either! They would find themselves in Sheol, the land of the dead. Everyone was to be judged according to the opportunity they had to hear and accept the gospel.

Wherever the seventy were welcomed it was as if Jesus himself were welcomed. Whoever rejected them was rejecting Jesus and God Himself. If civilized, adult, responsible people rejected the message, they would be judged accordingly. They were condemning themselves. Again there is a feeling of urgency.

The story of the mission of the seventy is like a miniature of Luke's second volume, for in the Acts of the Apostles we are told how salvation was offered to the other nations of the world.

The seventy return; What is success? (10^{17-20})

The seventy men returned thrilled because they had been able to heal the sick and 'drive out demons'. Jesus told them that he had seen Satan fall like lightning from the skies. Jewish mythology thought of Satan as an ex-angel banned from Heaven because of his pride. Sometimes he was described as a counsel for the prosecution, who brought to the attention of God the wrongs he found in men (Job 1 and 2, Zech. 3^{1-2}). Now people did not need to fear the condemnations of Satan because the seventy proclaimed God's love and mercy even for wrongdoers. Perhaps Jesus was using the words of the old myth to say he was pleased that the seventy had been successful, perhaps he was warning the seventy against feeling proud. They had received power to keep them from any harm that 'snakes and scorpions' (evil forces), could do to them, but this was God's power and not of their doing. What should please them more was the fact that they belonged to God's Kingdom.

Jesus thanks God (10^{21-24})

Mention of Jesus being filled with the Holy Spirit and praying tells us again that Luke considers the event described here as important to Jesus. This story is found only in Luke's gospel. It sounds like one which has found its way in from John's gospel where Jesus often claims a unique relationship with God. Jesus was filled with joy and gratitude because many of his disciples had shown that they understood and accepted his teaching. Jesus' knowledge had been entrusted to him by God his Father. The one who can best appreciate the qualities of a good father is his son: no one understands the full meaning of son-ship more than a father. Of human relationships the closest is marriage; a well-married couple know each other better than anyone else knows them. The prophet Hosea had compared the closeness of God and a human being with that of husband and wife, one of understanding, loyalty and concern. Jesus was close to God yet wanted to share that closeness with humanity. God was great and powerful, the Lord of all Creation, yet Jesus called Him Father. Although the disciples were mainly uneducated simple men they seemed to understand these things, whereas the learned religious leaders did not. Others knew about God, but his disciples knew God. The Greeks claimed that one could not know God and it was impossible to describe Him to others. As the early Church developed there were some who claimed that their learning and intelligence gave them a special knowledge of God. They were called Gnostics ('gnosis' – knowledge). Jesus makes it clear here that God is gracious enough to help simple folk to know him. The sincerity, faith and humility of his disciples enabled them to accept instruction from the Heavenly Father and to become like Him. There was no need of special cleverness. In the east the term 'son' meant 'taking after one's father'. A peace-loving person may be called a 'son of Peace'. Evil people were described as 'sons of Satan'. God's sons are those who live according to His will. When Jesus thought of himself as the son of God, it does not necessarily mean that he was claiming to be God.

Jesus told his disciples that they were fortunate to see and hear things that many kings and prophets had longed to experience. He was conscious of his own privilege, but also of the responsibility it brought. His work of introducing the Kingdom to people was beginning to seem worthwhile. Men were coming to know God through knowing Jesus.

The parable of the good Samaritan (10^{25-37})

The Scribes, who made handwritten copies of the Jewish scriptures and interpreted them for the people, were considered to know the religious laws better than most people. Luke, writing for non-Jews like himself, calls them lawyers. Here, in a story only told by Luke, we hear of a lawyer coming to Jesus to try him out. He asked, 'Teacher, what must I do to be sure of eternal life?'

Jesus quickly sized up the situation, and realizing that the lawyer considered himself already able to answer such questions for himself, he replied, 'What does the Law tell you?' The lawyer gave his answer from Deuteronomy 6$^{4-5}$ and 11^{13} – 'You must love the Lord your God with all your heart and soul and strength', (Luke adds 'and mind') – and from Leviticus 19^{18}, 'You shall love your neighbour as yourself.' Jesus told the lawyer 'That's right. Do that and you will live.' (cf. Mark 12^{28}, Matt. 22^{34}).

Orthodox Jews wore tiny leather boxes, called phylacteries, strapped to forearm and forehead. They contained little rolls of paper on which were written laws that Jews must obey. Jesus may well have been pointing to such a roll. Almost certainly Deuteronomy 6$^{4-5}$ was included, but probably not the Leviticus quote. Jesus was giving a new and greater significance to the quotation from Deuteronomy.

Everyone knew these laws, and perhaps the lawyer was annoyed because Jesus dealt with him briefly, knowing he was hoping to stir up an intellectual argument. The lawyer would be thinking of eternal life as something which God would give as a reward to people who kept all the Jewish rules. There were 613 of these rules, describing in detail how one should interpret the Ten Commandments.

The lawyer, determined not to let the argument end so quickly, asked Jesus, 'And who is my neighbour?' According to the Jews' understanding of their Law one's neighbour was a fellow-Jew, but no one else.

Jesus told the lawyer a parable. Parables left the listeners to ponder out the meaning, and in doing this they often found out the answer to a problem for themselves.

A man was travelling alone between Jerusalem and Jericho, when he was attacked by robbers, who stripped and beat and robbed him then went away, leaving the man to die. By chance a Jewish priest came along that way and saw the injured man, but continued on his way on the other side of the road. Later a Levite came along and looked at the wounded man, but he too passed by on the other side. Then a Samaritan came and looked. He felt great pity for the man. He put wine and oil on his wounds. (Wine and oil were antiseptic and soothing.) He bandaged the wounds, lifted the man on to his own animal (a donkey, perhaps), and took him to an inn. There he cared for the man until next day when he himself had to leave. He gave to the innkeeper two silver denarii (about two days' wages), and asked him to care for the man, promising that when he came that way again he would pay any further expenses needed.

The old road from Jericho to Jerusalem

Jesus then asked the lawyer, 'Which of these three men was a neighbour to the one who was attacked by robbers?' Seeming reluctant to mention the despised name of 'Samaritan', the lawyer replied, 'The one who showed him kindness.' Then Jesus told him, 'Now, you go and do the same.'

The seventeen-mile road between Jerusalem and Jericho has always been frightening and dangerous. It descends steeply through rocky passes and has sudden turnings. Even in the last century travellers had to bribe the local sheikhs to get through in safety and the road used to be known as the Way of Blood. No sensible person travelled that way after sunset and certainly not without company! The man in the story was either a fool or he had a very urgent reason to travel.

If the priest had touched the injured man then discovered that he was dead, the priest would be unable to perform any ceremony in the Temple for seven days, being considered ritually unclean. The Levite, an assistant in the Temple, may have avoided the body for the same reason. There was also the risk that perhaps the man was lying there to attract an unsuspecting traveller who would be set upon by the man's bandit-friends. Either way these men, the priest and Levite, had a wrong sense of values. They placed the duty of leading worship before a concern for suffering humanity.

In 701 B.C. the armies of Assyria invaded Israel and deported thousands of Israelites, settling other foreign captives in Israel. The few Israelites who survived and remained often married these foreigners. In 597 and 586 B.C. the armies of Babylon invaded the southern kingdom, Judah, and took away any Jews who were educated or skilled in some way. In Babylon, however, these Jews lived together, keeping their old customs and avoiding marriage with other races. When, eventually, they were allowed to return to Judah, they rebuilt the ruined Temple at Jerusalem, refusing the help of the people of Israel whom they regarded as inferior and of mixed race. The population in Israel lived close to their old capital of Samaria, so became known as Samaritans. Their resentment caused them to hamper the rebuilding work in Judah as much as possible. They built a temple of their own on Mount Gerizim.

The Jews to whom Jesus spoke would not appreciate his suggestion that a Samaritan could behave in a more humane way than two religious Jews! Jesus wanted to show that human need matters more than religious ceremony. He dared to tell the Jewish lawyer to go away and behave like the Samaritan!

Such a parable would have appealed to Luke who was the only Gentile amongst the gospel writers. It tells us that God expects us to help people who are in need whatever their nationality, social class or religious beliefs may be.

Mary and Martha (10^{38-42})

Luke alone tells this story of Jesus receiving hospitality at the home of two sisters, Martha and Mary. According to John (12^1), they were the sisters of Lazarus whom Jesus raised from the dead, and they lived at Bethany, a village near to Jerusalem.

The practical Martha busied herself preparing an elaborate meal for Jesus, but Mary sat at Jesus' feet listening to him. Eventually, the harassed Martha said to Jesus, 'Lord, don't you think it's wrong that Mary should leave me to do all the work? Tell her to come and help me!' Jesus told Martha, 'You are being too fussy, Martha. I need only one thing. Mary has chosen a good thing and no one should prevent her from doing this.'

The trials and Crucifixion of Jesus were not far away and perhaps Jesus found it helpful to be able to pour out his thoughts to someone who cared enough to listen. At such a time he hadn't much concern about food. Probably Martha was a responsible, unselfish woman anxious to please Jesus, but her good intentions were spoiled by self-pity.

Sometimes we try to be helpful in the wrong way, helping as we think best instead of considering what the person concerned thinks. Jesus needed all kinds of helpers, practical types like Martha and thoughtful listeners like Mary.

Jesus teaches about prayer (11^{1-4})

Luke again marks the importance of an event by telling us that Jesus was praying. The place of this story is not mentioned.

As Jesus finished praying, one of the disciples said, 'Lord, teach us to pray. John the Baptist taught his followers.'

Rabbis often taught their pupils a simple prayer for daily use. The prayer Jesus gave is probably repeated more frequently than any other prayer in the world and one has to guard against reciting it without due thought. Matthew (6^{9-13}) gives a longer version of the Lord's Prayer, one which perhaps developed rhythmically as the first Christians chanted it together. Luke's shorter version may be nearer to the original words of Jesus, who said:

'When you pray, say,
Father, Thy name be hallowed
Thy Kingdom come.
Give to us each day our daily bread,
And forgive us our sins for we too forgive
   all who have done us wrong,
And do not bring us to the test.'

This short and simple prayer has in it all that one needs to say and is a model on which we can base our own prayers.

Father   The Jews usually addressed God formally as 'Father of our nation', but Jesus used the Aramaic word 'Abba', an affectionate word used by Jewish children to their fathers, similar to our word 'Dad', Luke does not even say 'Our Father' as Matthew did, because it might sound more formal and distant than 'Abba' intends. This familiar word reminds us that God, as a loving father, wants to help His children wisely and carefully, providing only what is good for us. A wise father does not always give what a child asks.

Thy name   Eastern people were given names appropriate to their characters. To know God's name meant knowing what He was like and what He expected, and doing one's best to obey His purposes. God should be first in one's life as He is in this prayer. This is what is meant by 'be hallowed'.

Thy Kingdom come   The time when all the world's people are guided by God. Scholars such as Streeter and Lampe regard the alternative 'Let your Holy Spirit come and cleanse us' (used early on by Gregory of Nyssa and others), as more likely to be Luke's original words. The alternative was used perhaps particularly at baptism, Holy Communion and the 'laying on of hands' when someone was being blessed for a task ahead.
   Eventually the alternative died out giving way to the more widely used words, 'Thy Kingdom come'.

Daily bread   We ask for simple necessities, not luxuries; bread enough for the immediate future, not to be hoarded. The word for bread was one used when referring to the daily rations of a soldier or slave. Soldiers knew they would get these rations and had no need to worry about them. When we become unduly worried it is like saying that we don't trust God. On the Exodus journey the Israelites received manna sufficient for only one day at a time.

As we forgive   We have no right to ask God to forgive us unless we have forgiven those who have wronged us. No one is perfect, and each of us needs to be forgiven.

The test (or temptation)   Some manuscripts follow this with 'but save us from the evil one'. The meaning of 'test' has been discussed frequently. Some regard it as meaning the ordinary temptations of daily living; others say that God tests us to see what we can do; others say it means that we should not put God to the test. The first Christians believed that their time of judgement before God would come very soon (see notes on Luke 9^{27}), in which case they were asking for an extension of time before the end came. (James (1^{13-17}) said that no one should claim that they are tempted by God.) Jesus received strength to overcome temptation. In Gethsemane he asked to be excused the test of crucifixion, but when faced with it he did not give way.

Asking of God (11^{5-13})

This parable is usually known as the story of the Friend at Midnight. Because people travelled in the cool of the evening they often arrived very late and unexpectedly, making things awkward for their host. Bread was freshly made every day because it went stale quickly. It was considered a sacred duty to provide a traveller with hospitality and if one ran out of bread one would borrow some rather than allow a guest to go without food.

Doors were left open all day. Unless the matter were very urgent no one would knock on a closed door at night, knowing the inconvenience it would cause. Most houses consisted of only one room with a raised platform at one end. Underneath the platform a fire burned during the day. At night the family slept on the still-warm platform and all the domestic animals slept on the floor. To answer the neighbour's knock the householder would have to step over members of his family in the darkness as well as disturbing chickens, goats and perhaps a donkey! At first he might call, 'Go away. I cannot disturb my family. The door is shut for the night.' Persistent knocking would awaken everyone, however, and eventually the householder would get up and open the door, giving his neighbour some bread just to get some peace.

The parable says that if a reluctant man will help out his neighbour who is in need, then surely a loving God will willingly help those who ask. God does not have to be pestered, because He wants to help us. The same idea is found at 18^{1-8}, the parable of the Unjust Judge.

Jesus' words, 'Ask and receive, seek and find, knock and it will be opened', are in the style of typical Hebrew poetry, repetition of similar ideas stated in different words. They tell us to have faith that God will answer prayer. One must persevere and never give up praying.

Jesus continues the analogy by saying that no human father would give a snake to his son who asked for fish, nor a scorpion when asked for an egg. An ordinary human father will give what is good, not something harmful. How much more so will the Heavenly Father, who is perfect, give the Holy Spirit to those who ask. The parallel section in Matthew 7^{7-11} says 'good things' instead of Holy Spirit. By the time that Luke was writing the gift of the Holy Spirit was the greatest thing a Christian could ask and one that perhaps Luke felt God would not deny.

Jesus is slandered (11^{14-23})

Jesus cured a man who was dumb. Regarding this as the driving out of a dumb demon the people began to wonder where Jesus got his power, and some of them (Mark 3^{22}: 'lawyers', Matt. 12^{24}: 'Pharisees'), suggested that he got the power from Beelzebub. Beelzebub had been a Philistine god, known by the Jews as Lord of flies, or dung-heaps, or Lord of the dwelling-places of demons. Here he is synonymous with evil.

The people asked Jesus to prove that his power came from God by showing them a sign from Heaven. In Palestine at that time there were people who could exorcize demons. The historian, Josephus, wrote that they chanted words which had been known by Solomon. Jesus offered three arguments:

1 Just as a kingdom can be destroyed by civil war, so surely Satan would be destroyed if he gave someone power to drive out his own evil!
2 What about their fellow-Jews who were driving out demons? Must one conclude that their power came from Satan, too?
3 In the time of Moses, Pharoah's magicians had proved unable to cope with the plagues (Ex. 8^{19}), and they said that the plagues were caused by the 'finger of God'. The finger of God was the only power that could drive out evil and this itself was a sign from Heaven, a sign that God's Kingdom was beginning amongst them, for God was defeating the powers of evil. Satan's strength was being overcome by the greater strength of God. Jesus said that when a strong man guarded his castle it was safe, but only until a stronger man came. Then even the strong man was defeated and robbed of the property and armour on which he had relied.

The war between God and Satan was on! At this time no one could remain neutral. One must side with Jesus or stand against him.

Empty places are likely to be filled with evil (11²⁴⁻²⁸)

Jesus used a story to emphasize the need to make a decision for good or evil.

It was believed that when a demon was driven out of a person it would try to settle inside someone else (as demons settled in the swine at Gergesa, Luke 8³³). If this failed, it would go back and try to get into its first home again. If this were empty it would return, and perhaps bring its friends! Jesus was pointing out that driving out evil isn't enough. One has to fill the space with something good and worthwhile, otherwise evil will take over again, perhaps even worse than before. (A similar section is found at Matthew 12⁴³⁻⁴⁵.) We have a saying, 'The Devil finds work for idle hands to do'.

As Jesus was speaking a woman in the crowd called out to him, 'Happy the womb that carried you and the breasts that fed you!' Some versions of the Bible used the word 'blessed' instead of 'happy'. True happiness comes from knowing that one is doing what God would want, knowing that the relationship between God and oneself is a happy one. No doubt the woman in the crowd had been carried away by emotion. Emotion can be a fine thing, but Jesus realized that it was more important to be realistic and practical about what needed to be done, and he replied, 'No! Happy are those who hear and obey God.' The same idea is expressed at Mark 3³²⁻³⁵, when Jesus felt that his place was with the people rather than with his own family.

The Jews asking for signs; Privilege brings responsibility (11²⁹⁻³²)

Jesus was still speaking to the people who had asked for a sign to prove that he had been sent by God (see verse 16). Mark's gospel said it was the Pharisees who asked for a sign, Matthew's gospel says that Jesus was speaking to Pharisees and lawyers (Mark 8¹¹, Matt. 12³⁸).

We ask for a sign to prove something only when we haven't the faith to believe. Jesus expected his followers to have faith. If they had faith they would not need proof. Jesus told them that they would receive only 'the sign of Jonah'. The pagan people of Nineveh, capital of

Assyria, had believed Jonah when he told them they should repent. Their faith in his words made them change their way of living (Jonah ch. 3). The Queen of Sheba had made a long and difficult journey to Jerusalem to hear the wise teaching of King Solomon and was deeply impressed when she heard him (I Kings 10$^{1-10}$). The queen and the Ninevites had been Gentiles, yet these Jews, who were God's special people taught by His prophets, were rejecting the words of someone greater and wiser than either Jonah or Solomon, and were daring to ask for signs before they would believe him! On the Day of Judgement the example of the Queen of Sheba and the Ninevites would condemn the failure of the Jews who were unwilling to change.

Matthew 12^{40} favours a different interpretation of the words 'sign of Jonah', pointing out that as Jonah was inside the sea-monster for three days and nights, so the Son of Man would be in the bowels of the earth for three days and nights. The experience had not finished Jonah, who lived on to do his work. Neither would death finish Jesus. If this was Jesus' meaning he foresaw his resurrection.

A further possible suggestion comes from the teaching of Judaism prophesying that the generation of the Messiah's time would be a particularly evil lot. Perhaps Jesus meant that the people around him were so evil that this must be the time of the Messiah!

The lamp of the body; The importance of light (11$^{33-36}$)

The Jews wanted signs from God, but Jesus told them they lacked the insight and understanding to recognize the signs that already were being given.

A light is not meant to be hidden in a cellar or under a bushel-measure, but should be put up on a stand to give maximum benefit to everyone. A light can guide one's way, but someone with poor eyesight is unable to see the light properly, even though they imagine they are seeing properly. Jesus was God's light in the world, but many Jews lacked the insight and understanding to recognize him, though they imagined they knew all such things. Without spiritual vision they could not see clearly enough to understand God's ways. One's attitude to life can only be sound when one is guided by what is good.

The Greeks thought of wisdom as being divine light; ignorance was darkness. The Jews seemed to be 'in the dark' about Jesus! God had chosen the Jews to take His light to other nations, but they covered the light with prejudices and petty rules, so that no one could see the light properly. If the Jews did not see that Jesus himself was a sign from

God, it was because of their own lack of vision. (At that time the eye was believed to be the means of allowing light into the body.)

Jesus criticizes the Pharisees (11$^{37-44}$)

A Pharisee who invited Jesus home for a meal was astonished to find that his guest did not wash his hands before eating. This handwashing had nothing to do with hygiene, it was to do with religious ritual. A firkin (about 1½ eggshells) of water was poured over fingertips to wrist, then vice-versa. Another ceremonial rule stated how many times cooking-pots and dishes should be scoured first in one direction then the other. Thus they cleaned their dishes carefully because they could be seen. Jesus said that if the Pharisees were as particular about the way they cleansed their hearts they would be much better people. Verse 41 is difficult to understand and various suggestions have been made. It seems to mean, 'Give alms from within yourself, rather than from your surplus'. Matthew (23^{26}) is probably nearer to Jesus' original Aramaic words, 'Clean the inside of the cup first, then the outside will be clean also!' One who has an inner purity will not go far wrong in what he says and does.

The Pharisees were meticulous in their keeping of the laws. For instance the laws said that one should give a tithe (tenth) of one's agricultural produce. To be on the safe side the Pharisees gave a tenth of everything grown in their gardens too. These tithes were given to the priests, the male descendants of Jacob's son Levi, who assisted in the Temple and were thus unable to earn a living in more usual ways. The Pharisees kept the rule to the tiniest detail. They gave dutifully, but without love.

To make sure that graves could be seen, and thus avoided, the Jews whitewashed the gravestones. Jesus told the Pharisees that they themselves were like unmarked graves whose inside decay polluted any unsuspecting people who came into contact with them. They were proud and self-righteous, lacking charity and mercy. They expected to be greeted with respect in streets and market-places, and considered that they had a right to the few seats in the synagogue. The rigidity of the Pharisaic approach to the externals of religion made them harsh and inhuman in relationship with people. Jesus said they were fools, concerned about their outward appearance to men, neglecting to put their innermost beings right with God. Jesus said, 'Alas for you, Pharisees!' He was sorry that such well-intentioned people could be so misguided. (General Note on Pharisees, p. 41.)

The scribes, or lawyers (11$^{45-54}$)

The scribes interpreted and copied out the Jewish scriptures, so they were considered to have expert knowledge of the contents and were often consulted about the meanings of the laws. The scribes decided how the laws should be carried out, so thought of themselves as more distinguished than most Pharisees, who obeyed their instructions. Many of the scribes *were* Pharisees, keen to keep every minute detail of the Law. For the sake of his non-Jewish readers Luke refers to the scribes as 'lawyers'.

One such lawyer heard Jesus' criticism of the Pharisees and said to him, 'Master, when you say things like this you are insulting us, too.' (Again Luke may simply be setting Jesus' teaching into a narrative situation.) Jesus agreed, saying that the lawyers were no better, for their interpretations of the law had become a burden to ordinary, simple people and the lawyers gave them no help to carry the burden. Surely this was not what God intended life to be! The lawyers were helping to put up fine memorials over the tombs of dead prophets, prophets who had been rejected and killed by the intolerant fore-fathers of the lawyers. Now those same lawyers were showing intolerance towards the prophets of their own time! The fine memorials seemed to Jesus like signs of approval for the murders that had been committed! God in His wisdom had known what would happen to His messengers the prophets, but His purposes would not be defeated. This generation would take the blame for the deaths of all martyred prophets, from Abel the first one to Zechariah the last one.

Genesis 4$^{1-11}$ tells how Cain and Abel, the sons of Adam and Eve, offered sacrifices. God approved of the gift offered by Abel, who was then murdered by the jealous Cain. In the Jewish scriptures Chronicles is the last book, and II Chron. 24$^{20-22}$ tells how a prophet, Zechariah, was stoned to death in the Temple in 772 B.C., because he said that God would forsake the wicked Jewish people.

The lawyers were now rejecting Jesus, the prophet of their own time, and they were doing all they could to persuade the people to reject him, too. They were supposed to open out a knowledge of the scriptures for the people; instead they had locked such knowledge from the people and had taken away the key. Luke (20$^{46-47}$) makes further reference to Jesus' remarks about these lawyers.

Infuriated by such words from Jesus, the lawyers and Pharisees tried all ways of provoking Jesus, hoping he would say something which they could use as evidence against him.

A similar section is found in Matthew 23$^{1-36}$, but there the event does

Scribe (note that the script is written from right to left). This picture was taken in the Yemen

not take place in a Pharisee's home. Some people think it unlikely that Jesus gave these criticisms in a Pharisee's home where he was a guest. Luke may have collected together remarks Jesus made on various occasions and introduced them by saying that Jesus went to a Pharisee's house for a meal. Other readers think it unlikely that Jesus himself made these remarks and suggest that they came from the early Church which suffered much opposition from Judaism.

The evil of the Pharisees; Body and soul (12^{1-12})

This section corresponds to Matthew 10^{19-20} and 10^{26-33}. Thousands of people were now following Jesus so closely that they were treading on one another. Apparently he was still thinking about the Pharisees, for he told his closest friends, the disciples, to be on their guard against the 'leaven' of the Pharisees, meaning their hypocrisy. 'Hypocrite' is a Greek word which came to mean 'actor'. The Pharisees were like play-actors pretending to be good. 'Leaven' was the name given to the little piece of dough saved from the day's breadmaking. When this little piece was beginning to ferment it was added to newly-made dough. It caused the new dough to rise, thus making yeast unnecessary. As the leaven influenced the dough so a corrupt person could influence other people, leading them from the best ways of life. In Jesus' time 'leaven' often referred to something which had a widespread influence, sometimes good, sometimes bad (cf. Mark 8^{15}, I Cor. 5^6, Luke 13^{21}). The Pharisees' hypocrisy, their obsession with petty rules, their harsh condemnation of the ordinary people made them a dangerous and evil influence.

Jesus went on to say that things now being kept secret would one day be shouted from the housetops. In the Messianic Age everything would be seen clearly as it really was and judged accordingly. Neither the Pharisees, nor anyone else, would be able to put on a pretence. Things now whispered in dark corners would be brought to light and made public. Perhaps Jesus wanted to encourage the disciples to speak out without fear. Their message must go through the world. The disciples must have been well aware of the danger that could come from the religious authorities whom Jesus had so bluntly criticized. There might be times when they would feel tempted to play-act, to hide their true identities. Jesus told them not to be worried about people who could destroy their bodies, but to be concerned about God who had the power to send their souls to Gehenna. Gehenna, or Hinnom Valley, was south of the city of Jerusalem and was an ever-smouldering rubbish dump. Centuries before, in the reigns of kings like Ahaz and Manasseh, children had been burnt there as sacrifices to the pagan god, Molech (II Kings 16^3, 17^{17}, 21^6, 23^{10}). The Jews thought that Hell would be an ever-burning fire like Gehenna.

Jesus reassured his disciples of God's personal concern for each of them. Sparrows were sold, five for twopence, in the market place. Men had little concern for them, yet every sparrow mattered to God. God knows the number of hairs on each man's head. Jesus, addressing his disciples as his friends, told them that each of them was of more value to God than many sparrows. If they were not afraid to be loyal to Jesus, the Son of Man would be loyal to them when they were being finally judged in the court of angels. If they did not stand loyally now they would have no one to stand by them in the heavenly courts. Jesus said that people might be forgiven for speaking against the Son of Man. Perhaps he meant that it was understandable that many would misunderstand him. They would not be forgiven if they spoke against the Holy Spirit. Mark (3^{28}) may have a more correct version of this, for he says that all sins of the 'sons of men' may be forgiven except the sin of speaking against the Holy Spirit. Perhaps Jesus was remembering the time when the Pharisees had said that his power came not from the Holy Spirit but from Satan (11^{14-26}). Some scholars think it means that people can become so used to sin that they become impervious to the influence of God's Spirit. In verse 8 the term 'Son of Man' seems to mean Jesus himself, and in verse 10, although it could mean ordinary people, it seems more likely that again it refers to Jesus.

Perhaps Jesus sensed the anxiety of his disciples, for he told them not to worry about preparing their defence if they were tried before religious or State authorities, for the Holy Spirit would guide them in what to say. At his own trial Jesus proved that he could put this advice into practice.

In Matthew 16^{5-12} 'leaven' seems to represent the teaching of the Pharisees. In Mark 8^{15} it seems to mean their political behaviour.

The dangers of wealth (12^{13-34})

Jewish rabbis were often asked for legal advice. A man in the crowd obviously took Jesus to be a rabbi and said to him, 'Master, tell my brother to divide the family property with me.' There were definite rules about the sharing of property; on the father's death, the eldest son got the greater share. Perhaps this man was dissatisfied with the system. Certainly he was concerned only with his own gain.

Jesus asked, 'My good man, who made me a judge over you?' John (3^{17}) makes it clear that Jesus had no intention of judging people, his job was to save them. He was concerned with spiritual not material wealth, and warned the people against greed, for there are limitations to the things money can buy.

He told the parable of the Rich Fool, a man whose lands produced so much that he hadn't enough storage space for the crop, so he decided to build bigger barns. With so much hoarded he felt he didn't need to work any more; he could take life easy, eating, drinking, enjoying a life of merriment. Then God said to him, 'You fool, you are going to die tonight! What good is your wealth now?' Jesus concluded the story, 'A man can amass wealth yet still be a pauper in the sight of God.' This parable is found only in Luke's gospel which frequently condemns wealth itself, whereas Matthew's gospel condemned the love of wealth, meaning an obsession for wealth.

The parable is not intended to illustrate that death can strike suddenly, nor does it say that it is wrong to take reasonable steps to provide oneself with food and clothing. The trouble was that here were men who thought that riches alone could provide a good life, and could be concerned about money and property when Jesus was offering them the Kingdom of God. Jesus saw that the real secret of a successful life lies in loving God and one's neighbour.

Jesus then spoke about birds and flowers which are completely dependent upon God. His words were spoken as poetry, which made them easy to remember. (Matthew includes these sayings in his Sermon on the Mount.) He said that ravens do not plant nor harvest corn nor build granaries, yet God provides their needs. Surely these human beings who followed Jesus meant more to God than the birds did! Worrying could not make one a cubit taller in height (or 'add to one's span of life') and it certainly couldn't change other circumstances. He spoke of the field-lilies probably meaning the wild anemones whose colours brightened the hillsides after rain. They were more splendid than all the glory of the wealthy Solomon had been, yet they didn't spin nor weave. After one brief day they dried up and were collected with the dry grass to serve as fuel for ovens, for wood was scarce.

People who worried about wealth were those who didn't know God. The people to whom Jesus was speaking knew God, and surely knew that He could be trusted to provide their basic needs, so they could give their time and effort to the more important task of working for God's Kingdom.

Money soon dwindles away and moths (also meaning 'rust') destroy material goods. Jesus spoke to the group that had become closest to him, 'Have no fear, little flock, for your Father has chosen to give you the Kingdom.' He told them to sell their possessions and give the money to charity, to find purses that wouldn't wear out and treasure in Heaven which couldn't be spent nor stolen. 'Treasure in heaven' meant a right relationship with God and eternal and indestructable treasures would be qualities of character like honesty, goodness, generosity, purity, humility. No material goods can be guaranteed to last for ever. ('Today we have a saying, 'You cannot take it with you when you die.') This teaching of Jesus uses hyperbole, or exaggeration, a typical Eastern way of getting over ideas, and one that was not usually to be taken literally.

The people of the early Church carried out the advice of Jesus about material wealth (Acts 2$^{44-45}$).

Be prepared (12$^{35-48}$)

Jesus warned his listeners to be prepared and ready for action in any crisis. He spoke of servants 'with belts fastened and lamps alight' (NEB), alert and waiting up in the second or third watch of the night for their master to return home from a wedding reception.

When an eastern man was working he tucked up his long loose robes into his belt. To keep an oil-lamp alight one had to top up the oil and trim the floating cotton wick frequently. (The story reminds one of the ten bridesmaids in Matthew 25$^{1-13}$.) Between 6p.m. and 6a.m. there were guards on night duty. The Jewish night-watch men had three duties, each of four hours. The Romans did four duties, each of three hours. The second and third watches would be the most difficult for servants trying to stay awake. Wedding-parties could go on for a week. One never knew when the guests would go home, but the servants were expected to be up and ready to serve a meal whatever time their master arrived, even in the middle of the night or just before dawn. We might describe these servants as waiting 'with their coats off and sleeves rolled up', ready to work as soon as the opportunity came.

Jesus said that the master who found his servants awaiting his arrival in the early hours of the morning would be so pleased with them that he himself would wait on them and they would be given promotion to higher positions. One feels that this serving master represents Jesus. Luke 22$^{26-27}$, and particularly John 13$^{3-11}$, with its account of the washing of the disciples' feet, show Jesus' readiness to wait on others. When he died he was serving mankind by showing that nothing could stop God loving the world. The mention of a wedding-party would make the Jews think of the great banquet to which they as God's people would be invited, at the end of time when the world is finished.

Jesus went on to say that anyone who expected a burglar to call would make sure that his house was securely protected so that the burglar would be unable to break in. Unfortunately one doesn't know when a burglar might come! Verse 40 sounds like a sentence put in by an early Christian scribe, reminding people to be ready and not caught napping when the Son of Man arrived.

No one knows exactly for what crisis Jesus' listeners are asked to be prepared:

1 Some Christians believe that Jesus will come a second time to this world, and they refer to this coming by the Greek word 'parousia'. Matthew obviously thought that Jesus was warning his followers to be ready for the parousia, for he puts this event with other material about Jesus' second coming.

2 Some people feel that Jesus meant his followers to be alert and ready, not knowing when God might call them to some task for Him.

3 By the time Luke was writing it was becoming increasingly clear that Jesus' return was not imminent and that his followers should concentrate on their own work for the Kingdom. Some readers feel that Jesus would not have asked his disciples to watch constantly for his second coming if it wasn't going to happen in their lifetime. Some would say that Jesus returned on the Day of Pentecost giving his followers the gifts of the Spirit (Acts 2). Perhaps Jesus, realizing the imminent danger of his arrest, trials, scourging and crucifixion, meant his followers to be alert and prepared, for the events that follow show Jesus being watched and warned as the plot against him thickens. Long after the Crucifixion the early Church remembered these words of Jesus and applied them more generally to a second coming in the future.

Peter asked whether Jesus intended his words just for the disciples or for everyone present. As he often did, Jesus told a parable in which Peter could find his own answer:

While a master was away he would leave a steward in charge of the other servants and property. Knowing that the master might return at any time a wise steward would work conscientiously and honestly. If the steward was a fool he might console himself that the master wouldn't be back for a while. His master, returning suddenly, might catch him drunk and bullying the other servants, and then the steward would be severely flogged. Servants who had not received the Master's instructions would also be flogged for doing wrong, but less severely.

From this, Peter and the rest of the Twelve would realize that in Jesus' absence they were left in charge. Having received more of Jesus' teaching than anyone else, more would be expected of them than of people who had not heard Jesus. Throughout their long history as God's Chosen People, the Jews had received instruction, yet even now they were not obeying Him. They must prepare to be judged more severely than people who had not received God's messages. They thought of God's Judgement as something to come in the far distant future, but it was already happening. God was judging them according to their response to Jesus.

Signs of the times (12⁴⁹⁻⁵⁹)

Verses 49–53 are a series of parallel sayings, typical of Hebrew poetry. Each saying is repeated in a different way. Jesus said, 'I came to start a fire on earth, and I wish it were burning already! I have a terrible ordeal to face and I wish it were over! Did you imagine I would bring you peace and quiet? Indeed not; I bring trouble and division. Members of a family will hate each other. Children and parents will turn against one another; in-laws will be against in-laws.'

The ordeal, or 'baptism', in his immediate future was crucifixion, the hurt of betrayal and the humiliation of trials, an ordeal which could submerge him in tension and pain. It would be a time when those around him would be forced to make a decision for him or against him, and their decision could bring about differences of opinion with close relatives and friends. This was certainly true for the first Christians, but can apply in any age.

The 'fire' of which Jesus spoke may refer to God's judgement, or may mean that Jesus' ideas would set the world ablaze with new ideals. Matthew (10³⁴⁻³⁶) said that Jesus was putting a sword amongst the people. Micah (7⁵⁻⁶) prophesied that family loyalties would be made difficult when the Messianic Age began. For people looking back on the Crucifixion and Resurrection the decision is more straightforward than for Jesus' listeners who had no idea what the future held for him.

The Palestinians understood the signs of the weather. When they saw clouds forming in the west over the Great Sea (Mediterranean) they knew it would rain soon. When the sirocco wind, or simoom, blew from the deserts in the south they could expect a heatwave. Jesus told the people they understood the weather-signs but not the signs of the times. They seemed unable to assess the present situation and decide the right action to take.

Jesus advised, 'Before you get taken to the debtor's court try to settle your debt privately, otherwise you may get put in the debtor's prison where you will be kept until you have paid the last farthing' (cf. Matt. 5²⁵⁻²⁶). Again readers have interpreted this in two ways. Firstly, the Jews had heard so often what God wanted of them, and they had fallen short of it. They would be wise to put things right before Judgement Day. Secondly, perhaps Jesus was advising the Jews to come to terms with the Romans before it was too late.

Suffering, sin and a last chance (13^{1-9})

This section continues the idea begun at 12^{54}, where Jesus was warning the people to put themselves right with God. Some of his listeners were still more concerned with other people's sins than with their own. They came to ask Jesus what he thought about some Galileans who had been killed, on Pilate's orders, while they were offering sacrifices to God in the Temple. We know nothing further of the incident to which they referred, but the historians of the time tell us that groups of Jews frequently rebelled against the occupying Roman troops and Pontius Pilate, the Roman governor, had brutal ways of dealing with rebels. The historian Josephus says that Pilate wanted to make improvements to Siloam, the water-system of Jerusalem. Pilate demanded money from the Temple treasury towards the cost of an aqueduct. The Jews were horrified at the idea and crowds gathered to protest. Soldiers, wearing cloaks to hide their armour, were sent by Pilate to mingle with the crowds. It is said that they were told to disperse the crowds, but at a given signal they drew out cudgels and struck out so savagely that many Jews were killed. Josephus says that Galileans had the reputation of being amongst any rebels, so the incident mentioned to Jesus was typical of what happened at the time.

The Jews had been taught that suffering was a punishment for sin and perhaps they found it difficult to understand why God punished the Galileans who were worshipping Him. They probably felt that God would approve of their fighting the pagan Romans, and of their protest at the use of Temple funds. Jesus made it clear that he did not necessarily link sin with suffering and said that they must not assume that the dead Galileans had sinned more than other people. Then he told his listeners that unless they altered their ways they would die as the Galileans had died. He knew that Rome would not tolerate rebellion much longer and he was right, for from A.D. 66–70 the Romans struck without mercy until Jerusalem was besieged and destroyed and its inhabitants suffered famine, misery and death. Had they listened to Jesus they would have realized the futility of struggling against Roman power and would have avoided the terrible suffering they brought upon themselves.

History has made many attempts at explaining why good people sometimes suffer. The Old Testament tells of a good man named Job who suffered one thing after another – robbery, bereavement, desertion and illness. One of his friends told him, 'You must have sinned, otherwise God would not make you suffer like this' (Job 4^7), but Job did not agree with them. There were always some who were not satisfied with such an explanation. Sometimes Jesus himself seemed to regard an illness as the result of sin (e.g. the paralysed man, Luke 5^{20}), but here he wants to show that those who have come to discuss the matter see others' misfortunes as punishment, but cannot see what will result from their own foolishness. If only they were more concerned about God and His Kingdom they could make a more positive and lasting impact than by revolt against Rome. Jesus was offering them a last chance to save themselves, in more ways than one. He reminded them of how a tower at Siloam had fallen and killed eighteen people. Pilate could be held responsible for the deaths of the Galileans, but the Siloam case had not been caused by a human hand and many must have explained it as attributable to God. (Perhaps the eighteen had been Jewish workmen, in which case they would be criticized for taking part in a Roman construction, and their deaths would be seen as well-deserved.) Jesus rejected the idea saying that they were no worse than anybody else living at Jerusalem, no worse than those who were here discussing the matter.

He continued this teaching by telling a parable about a fig-tree planted amongst grape-vines. Farmers sometimes planted fig-trees and apple trees in vineyards in the hope that at least one crop would be successful. (The Scriptures often referred to Israel as a vine or fig-tree, e.g. Isaiah 5, Hosea 9^{10}, Luke 20^{9-18}.) Fig-trees are fully mature in three years, but after three years this one still bore no fruit. The owner said it should be cut down, but the man working in the vineyard asked that it should be given another chance, one more year in which he would do all he could to help it to bear fruit. If it still failed, it should be cut down since it was taking goodness from the soil and giving nothing in return.

In the same way Jesus was doing all he could to help the Jews to serve God. They had been in a favoured position throughout their history but had shown no return for God's love and concern. They were being offered a last chance, a short time to show what they could do. If they failed now their privilege and responsibility would be taken from them.

Privilege gives people a responsibility. People who have knowledge and material wealth have a responsibility to help their poorer neighbours. The Jews should have been sharing their knowledge of God with other nations.

A Jewish woman with a crippled back (13^{10-17})

One sabbath when Jesus was teaching in a synagogue he saw a woman who could not stand up straight because of a crippled back with which she had suffered for eighteen years. The people believed the deformity to be caused by a demon. Some Bibles describe her as the woman with a spirit of infirmity (weakness). The story, found only in Luke's gospel, again reflects his interest as a doctor.

Work of any kind was forbidden on a sabbath day, and this included healing unless a life was in imminent danger, but Jesus called the woman and told her, 'You are rid of your trouble.' He laid his hands on her, an action associated with healing or blessing, and she was able to stand up straight, praising God as she did so.

Each synagogue had a president, chosen by the congregation to organize the services. The president here was most annoyed with Jesus, but addressed his criticism to the people: 'You have six days in which to come for healing. Come then, and not on the sabbath.'

Jesus reminded him that people took their farm animals out to water on the sabbath rather than allow them to go without water for twenty-four hours, but they expected this Jewess, one of their own people, one of God's Chosen, to put up with her suffering on the sabbath. She had suffered for eighteen years and surely she should not be left in the Devil's power for one moment longer. The Law itself was humanitarian, but the Pharisees' interpretation of the Law was not humanitarian. Jesus was calling them to keep God's Law in its true interpretation (cf. 6^{6-11}, 14^{1-7}).

No one had asked Jesus to heal this woman. Perhaps he did so intending to provoke this discussion. The men who had criticized were lost for words, but everyone else in the synagogue was delighted with the wonderful things that Jesus was doing. In driving out the evil spirit that caused her weakness, Jesus was demonstrating that God was defeating Satan's power, but the authorities failed to recognize this as a sign that God's Kingdom had already come to them. They believed that in the Kingdom they would be free from all bondage. What better day than the sabbath could there be for freeing this woman? This, to Jesus, was as much a part of his work as preaching and dying on the cross.

This is the last story that Luke tells of Jesus speaking in a synagogue.

Two parables about God's Kingdom (13^{18-21})

The main theme of Jesus' teaching was, 'Repent, for the Kingdom of God is at hand!' He often used parables to help people to understand the Kingdom. A parable draws a parallel (or comparison) between one thing and another. If we are already familiar with one it will help us to understand the other. We are challenged to think out the deeper meaning of the parable as far as we are able, then apply that meaning to our own way of living.

Jesus told the people, 'God's Kingdom is like a mustard seed growing in a garden. It grows to become a tree in which birds can roost.'

Mark and Matthew (Mark 4^{30-34}, Matt. 13^{31-32}) emphasized the smallness of a mustard seed, obviously meaning that the Kingdom developed from insignificant beginnings to amazing proportions. Luke does not mention the smallness of the seed, but does speak of it growing big enough for birds to roost on it. As a universalist he was concerned to show that from seemingly insignificant beginnings God's Kingdom would become like a mighty empire, giving protection not only to the Jews but to people of all nations (cf. Dan. 4^{10-22}, Ezek. 31^6 but the 'tree' idea is used here in a slightly different way).

A second parable is similar in meaning. A small piece of leaven (kept from previous dough until it was beginning to ferment), would affect new dough made from half a hundredweight of flour. At present the unseen power of the Holy Spirit worked unnoticed in the small group around Jesus, but it would in time affect all the world. In this case the addition of leaven is good (cf. the 'leaven' of the Pharisees, 12^{1-12}).

No doubt these parables suited Luke's purpose well, for when he was writing some people were perhaps bewildered and disappointed because Jesus had not returned. Luke wanted the early Christians to realize that they must follow up the work that Jesus had begun; they must spread his influence in other countries.

Towards the city of Jerusalem; The narrow way (13^{22-30})

Jesus was making his way to Jerusalem for the last time, teaching in towns and villages on the way, when someone asked him, 'Lord, will only a small number be saved?' The Jews often wondered how many and who would enter God's Kingdom. They imagined it as a banquet not open to foreigners.

Jesus answered, 'You must make a determined struggle to get in through the narrow door. Many will try and fail' (cf. II Esdras 7^{6-7}; Matt. 7^{21-23}). In Palestine doors were rarely closed, but when they were the householders were very reluctant to open them. Jesus imagines latecomers knocking at the door of a banqueting room, and the host calling to them, 'Go away, I don't know you!' From outside the latecomers called, 'But we ate together and you taught in our streets', but they were left outside wailing and grinding their teeth. Then Jesus makes his warning clearer, saying that inside the room were Abraham, Isaac, Jacob and the prophets, and people from all four corners of the earth. Those who considered that they would automatically be allowed in would not get in; those who had considered themselves unworthy would be the first to enter.

Jesus was warning his listeners that their place in God's Kingdom was not automatically reserved just because they were Jews. The Kingdom is open to all and God does not judge people as we do. Things we may consider important may not be important to God. The Jews might be surprised to find foreigners in the Kingdom and themselves shut out. Amongst the early Christians the words were a reminder that knowing Jesus and hearing his message were not enough; they had to do something about it in the way they lived. There is far more to being a Christian than claiming to be one.

Jesus laments over Jerusalem (13^{31-35})

Not all of the Pharisees were against Jesus, for some of them came to Jesus to warn him that he should leave Galilee, for Herod Antipas, the ruler of this area, was out to harm him. Jesus told the Pharisees, 'Go and tell that fox that I will cast out devils and go on with my cures today and tomorrow. On the third day I will reach my goal.' The Aramaic phrase 'after three days' usually signified a short time, and a time of crisis. Jesus wasn't going to be intimidated by the crafty and destructive Herod who had no power to harm him. Jesus' work would end only when God chose, and that, Jesus was sure, would be when he reached Jerusalem, where prophets usually met their doom. No one could frustrate God's plans, so here in Galilee Jesus was safe. He was not going to run away.

Jesus' lament for Jerusalem, capital city and religious centre of his countrymen, is poetry typical of a Hebrew dirge. The Jews expected a Messiah who would gather them together as God's nation, but they had rejected Jesus' attempts to do this. He said, 'Oh Jerusalem, Jerusalem, city that murders prophets and stones God's messengers! How often have I longed to gather your children as a hen gathers her chicks under her wing, but you wouldn't let me.' Prophets had sometimes been ill-treated and even killed in Jerusalem (see Hosea 11^{1-7}, Is. 30^{10}, 31^6, Jer. 6^8, $8^{13,19}$, 20^{1-2}, 22^5, 26^{7-24}, 37^{15}), but probably the words were intended for the whole nation. The Israelites had often rejected the offer of God's love and care given through their prophets.

Matthew's account puts these words of Jesus much later in the story, after the cleansing of the Temple and before he was arrested (Matt. 23^{37-39}). Some readers think that both Matthew and Luke have misplaced the words, because verse 35 suggests that Jesus said them on a previous occasion when leaving the city. John's gospel describes various occasions when Jesus visited Jerusalem (the Synoptics mention only one, apart from Luke's story of the visit when Jesus was twelve), and it seems that when Jesus had been rejected early on by the Jews of the city he went further north for some time. He avoided Jerusalem until he returned now for the Passover, when he was greeted, as all Passover pilgrims were, with the words of Psalm 118, 'Blessings on him who comes in the name of the Lord!' (Luke 19^{38}). However, Psalm 118 was often regarded as one of the psalms which looked forward to the coming of the Jews' Messiah. If Jesus really did speak these words on this last visit to the city he must mean that God would not be with His people, the Jews, until they were ready to accept Jesus as their Messiah. Verse 35 speaks of '*your* Temple' as if telling the Jews that God wants no more to do with it (cf. Jer. 12^{7}).

Luke (9^{51}) described Jesus travelling south through Samaria on his way to Jerusalem, yet here he seems to be back again in Galilee in the north (13^{31}). Luke alone mentions the Pharisees' warning about Herod Antipas and seems to suggest that this started Jesus thinking about Jerusalem.

Jesus at a Pharisee's house (14^{1-24})

Chapter 14 contains material mainly found in this form only in Luke's gospel. The sayings of Jesus must have become separated from the stories surrounding them, for the gospel-writers seem to give different background-events to many of the things Jesus said. Here, Luke seems to have collected together some of Jesus' conversations with Pharisees and attached them to a story of his dining at the home of a leading Pharisee.

The man suffering from dropsy (14^{1-6})

Religious Jews considered it an act of merit to provide hospitality for wandering teachers, especially one who had just addressed the local congregation. On this occasion, however, the invitation seemed only to provide the scribes and Pharisees with an opportunity to watch Jesus closely to find fault with him.

Often a meal was served in a courtyard and the local people gathered around to listen to the conversation while the meal was in progress. Right in front of Jesus was a man suffering from dropsy, a painful illness in which fluid collects in the body and causes swelling. One wonders whether he was a casual onlooker or whether the Pharisees had brought him in deliberately. Jesus was well aware of being watched, so he asked, 'May one heal on the sabbath, or not?'

No one answered. If they answered 'No', it would seem they were brutally callous about the man's suffering. If they said 'yes', it would seem they were ignoring the law which allowed healing on a sabbath only if it were necessary to save a life. Jesus cured the man and sent him away.

Then to the scribes and Pharisees he said, 'If one of you has an ass or ox which falls into a well, will you leave it there because it is the sabbath?' They were unable to answer. Uncovered wells were common and such accidents often happened. The Law allowed one to help such an animal, yet it was forbidden to help a human being! Some manuscripts have 'son' instead of 'ass'. This may be because an ass was sometimes called the 'son of a yoke'.

Even under stress Jesus seemed calm and confident. He must have realized that he had been invited to this house for the wrong motives, yet he accepted the invitation. Perhaps some good came of his being there. The story is similar to those of the man with the withered arm (9^{6-11}) and the woman with the crippled back (13^{10-17}).

Lessons in humility and charity (14^{7-14})

As the guests were coming into the Pharisee's house, Jesus noticed how they made for the honoured places near the host. He spoke to them about the embarrassment of being asked to move down the table at a wedding reception because the place is needed for a more important guest, and he pointed out that it is wiser to choose a less important place, for one may be invited to take a more important place. Jesus ended by saying, 'He who exalts himself will be humbled, and he who humbles himself will be exalted.'

Great people often seem quite unconscious of their importance. One way of keeping oneself properly humble is to compare oneself constantly with Jesus. His followers must never be concerned about their own importance. Jesus' words about a banquet may have been intended as a further warning to the Jews that they should not take for granted their status in God's Kingdom.

Jesus then spoke to his host, the Pharisee (14$^{12-14}$), saying, 'When you give a lunch- or supper-party, don't invite your relatives and friends and rich neighbours who can repay you by inviting you to their parties. When you give a party, invite the poor, crippled, lame and blind. This will give you greater happiness, for such people cannot repay you, but you will be rewarded on the day when men rise from death.' The mission of Jesus himself was to the poor, crippled, lame and blind (4$^{18-19}$).

When we give something it can be for various reasons. Sometimes we are hoping to get something in return; sometimes we are showing off to someone who isn't as well-off as we are; sometimes we give out of a sense of duty. Sometimes we give out of genuine love and concern and nobody knows that we have given. Charity is love and does not require praise or thanks.

The parable of the great feast (14$^{15-24}$)

Jesus had been talking about banquets and invitations and someone at the Pharisee's table commented in a pious way, 'Anyone who sits at the feast in God's Kingdom really will be happy and blessed.' Perhaps the man expected all Jews would be in God's Kingdom and thought that everyone present would agree.

Jesus answered him in a parable. (In this case, since it makes several parallels rather than one, it is an allegory.) The Jews believed that God's Kingdom would begin with a great banquet to which they, as God's Chosen People, were specially invited. In the east one might be invited to a party months before it took place. No date or time was mentioned but when the arrangements were complete a messenger was sent to collect the guests, saying, 'It's time to come now. Everything is ready.'

In Jesus' story, the host became angry when, one after another, the guests who had agreed to come made excuses not to come. One was busy inspecting some land he had just bought. A second was busy matching up five pairs of oxen so that the yoke would lie evenly on each neck. A third guest had just got married. In Deuteronomy 24^5 a newly-married man was excused military service and other public duties for a year. This was to allow time for the wife to conceive a child. The host sent servants to the streets and alleys to compel the poor, crippled, lame and blind to come to the feast he had prepared. (Unfortunately in the Middle Ages and times of the Inquisition etc. the word 'compel' was used as authority to force people to make statements of Christian belief.) Still there were empty places, so the servant was sent to fetch the tramps and beggars from the wayside to fill the places. Those who had received the early invitations were not among the guests present.

The Jews had received God's invitation in Abraham's time. The covenant, or agreement, between God and the Jews had been repeated many times since then and was established particularly in Moses' time. The prophets frequently reminded the Jews of their responsibilities as God's Chosen People, and at last Jesus came to tell them, 'Come, everything is now ready', but they rejected the invitation for their own trivial reasons, thus excluding themselves from the Kingdom. The parable was Jesus' way of telling the Jews that Gentiles and outcasts would be brought in to take their places. Being invited out brings pleasure and enjoyment and reminds us that Christians should enjoy their lives, trying to ensure at the same time that other people are happy too.

Counting the cost of becoming a Christian (14^{25-35})

Great crowds were following Jesus as he travelled towards Jerusalem, for they expected that soon he would become a popular and victorious leader who would give them freedom from the Romans. Jesus knew he was on the way to a cross.

Here, as at Mark 8^{34} and Matthew 10^{37-38}, Jesus warned that if they went on following him they too must be prepared to carry a cross. Perhaps he meant this literally at the time, for his immediate friends were going to be in serious danger. For everyone the future might bring hardship and suffering. Unless they were ready to face opposition and even separation from parents, wives, children, brothers and sisters, they should not set out to be his disciples.

Christianity can cause tension and division, even within one's own family, and for a disciple everything and everyone must take second place to Christ. The Semitic language was vivid and used exaggerated terms to make the point clear. Jesus' call to 'hate' one's family should not be taken literally; here it means 'to love less'. To decide to be Christ's follower is the most important decision one can make. It should not be made impulsively or in a rush of emotion, for it concerns a whole lifetime. One has to count the cost, considering carefully whether one can see it through despite all difficulties and demands.

Only Luke's gospel records the two little parables which illustrate this:

1 Before a man sets out to build a tower, he should consider whether or not he has enough money and materials to complete it. People seeing a foundation without a tower would rightly assume that the builder was a bit of a fool! The 'tower' may have been a watch-tower in a vineyard.

2 A king with 10,000 soldiers should consider his chances carefully before he goes to war against a king who has 20,000 soldiers. It might be wiser to send ambassadors to discuss peace terms!

Jesus said that a worthless disciple was like tasteless salt. In the east salt was used to give taste to foods but was also valuable for preserving foods, and as an antiseptic and fertilizer. Without its essential saltiness it was useless for any of these purposes and fit only to be thrown away with other rubbish. In the same way a follower of Jesus was useless unless he could give himself immediately and completely to the tasks required of a disciple. Before deciding to be a disciple of Jesus one has to work out one's priorities (cf. 9^{23}, 9^{57-62}, 10^{25-28}). Jesus may also have been thinking again of those Jews who had not been the good salt to flavour life, to preserve what was good, to destroy evil and have a generally good life-giving effect on mankind's progress.

Jesus hoped that his listeners were taking in what he said, and he emphasized again the advice he had given previously: 'If you have ears to hear, then hear.'

The parables of the lost (15^{1-32})

Chapter 15 is made up of the three well-known 'parables of the lost', a lost sheep, a lost coin and a lost son. Luke emphasized the fact that Jesus' mission was to people who were lost in some way or another.

The notes about the Good Samaritan (10^{25-37}) explained how the people of Judah were taken away to Babylon. There they had no Temple and were not able to offer animal sacrifices, but met in groups to read and discuss their Scriptures, and they managed to edit the ancient scrolls. By the time they were allowed to return to Judah their way of religion had benefited, rather than deteriorated, from their time in exile. Back at home their continued zeal for holiness made them keep away from the influences of any kind of paganism or low standards which might defile them or their worship of God.

Some Jews did not or could not keep all the detailed rules of the religious system. These included people like shepherds, tax-collectors, tanners, pedlars, donkey-drivers, whose work rendered them ritually unclean. They were unable to attend the synagogue, were not allowed to hold public office nor act as witnesses in a court of law. Although religious Jews mixed with such people in everyday situations they kept themselves separate from them in a spiritual sense, and this separateness was maintained particularly by the Pharisees. The Pharisees, and those scribes who belonged to the Pharisaic group, could not understand Jesus consorting with these, the 'people of the land'. Jesus, in fact, demanded an even higher moral code than they did, one which came from an attitude of heart and mind. By these standards all were sinners, Pharisees included. All needed love and forgiveness, the grace of God offered even when one could not earn it by one's own merits. Jesus claimed that God had sent him to seek and save the lost people of Israel. He even said that he had not come to virtuous people, but to call sinners to repent (5^{32}), whereas the Pharisees had a saying, 'There is joy before God when those who provoke him perish from the world'.

Jesus addresses himself to the scribes and Pharisees in these parables, not only justifying his behaviour and teaching, but challenging them to make their decision for or against his work, and to accept, with everyone else, the grace of God.

The lost sheep (15^{1-7})

An eastern shepherd would risk his safety and even his life to bring in one sheep which had wandered off from the rest of the flock. The flock often belonged to a town or village and each shepherd was responsible for a group of sheep and would be expected to explain the loss of a sheep, providing proof of what had happened to it. Sheep were counted into the fold, and the number 'ninety-nine' suggests that this had just been done. The shepherd left the others safely in the fold, perhaps watched over by the other shepherds, while he searched for any missing sheep. His friends would be relieved and happy to see him returning safely with the sheep.

Jesus must have thought of himself as being like a shepherd for in 12^{32} he told the people, 'Have no fear, little flock . . .'

The lost coin (15^{8-10})

A woman might have ten silver pieces, and if she lost one she would light a lamp and sweep until it was found. Then she would call her friends and neighbours to rejoice because she had found it. In the same way there is rejoicing amongst the angels when one sinner returns to God's family.

The silver piece, or drachma (a quarter of a shekel), was worth more than a day's wage. The little dark eastern houses had beaten-earth floors covered with rushes. To search for a coin there would be like looking for a needle in a haystack! In Palestine most people lived in poverty and the loss of a drachma could mean hunger for a family. Another possibility is that the coin was one which made up the woman's marriage headdress. Its loss would be like the loss of a wedding ring to us.

In the story of the lost sheep the sheep was lost through its own fault, because it wandered away. The coin was lost through the carelessness of the woman. Some people deliberately wander away from God and are lost because of their own foolishness and disobedience. Sometimes they can be 'lost' because of the carelessness of others who hinder someone who only needs a chance or a little help. The point is made that no one is beyond recovery no matter what the circumstances.

The lost (or prodigal) son (15^{11-32})

This superb short story is probably the most loved of all the parables of Jesus. Because it clearly illustrates God's love for his children as it speaks of the love of an ordinary father, it could be called the 'Parable of the Loving Father'. It could also be called the 'Parable of the Elder Brother', because Jesus was addressing scribes and Pharisees who were like the elder brother in the story. The story is usually known as the 'Parable of the Prodigal Son'. 'Prodigal' means 'wasteful' or 'extravagant'.

When an eastern father died his property was divided so that the eldest son was given a double share and each of the other sons received a single share. Knowing that the bulk of the property would remain with the eldest, the younger sons sometimes asked for their inheritance, converted it into cash and went off to make their own way in the world. Often a father was glad to hand over the responsibility of managing the business to the eldest son who made sure that his father still received the profits and produce due to an owner.

In this story there were just two sons. The younger one asked for his share, sold the property and left home. In the time of Jesus many young Jews went away to try their luck in foreign countries. Unfortunately the younger son did not invest his money wisely but spent it recklessly until it was all gone. When a famine hit the land he found things particularly difficult, for food then rose in price. Forced to take any job available, he found himself looking after a herd of pigs, a job which Jews considered degrading and rendered one unfit to keep the sabbath. Jews regarded pigs as unclean animals and did not keep or eat them. The situation worsened so that he came near to eating the pods given to the pigs (usually the pods of the carob tree).

When he considered his predicament he realized that, back at home, the workmen hired on a day-to-day basis were better off than he was. He was well aware that he had only himself to blame. He decided to go home. He worked out the speech he would make on arrival: 'Father, I have sinned against Heaven (meaning 'God') and against you. I am no longer fit to be known as your son, so will you take me on as a casual labourer?'

The young man set off for home. His father must have been on the watch constantly in the hope that one day his younger son would come home. He spotted him when he was still a long way off and, 'moved to the depths of his being', he ran to meet him. It was most unusual for an eastern man to be so undignified as to run and this in itself suggests the father's emotion and joy. He flung his arms around his son and kissed him, showing that past foolishness was forgiven and forgotten. The son began to say the words he had practised, apologizing and confessing that he was no longer fit to be considered as a son; but the father broke in, telling his servants to fetch the robe that was usually kept for the use of honoured guests, and a ring and shoes for his son. A ring was the sign of status and authority and shoes were never worn by anyone as low as a hired servant. Meat was a rare luxury but the father ordered that the calf, kept specially fattened ready for any celebration, should be prepared as meat. It had been just as if his son were dead, but here he was alive and safe at home.

The elder son, arriving home from his work on the farm, heard the merry-making and asked a servant what was going on. When he was told, he was resentful and refused to go in. His father came out hoping to persuade him to join in the rejoicing, but he replied, 'I have slaved for you all these years. I have never disobeyed you, but you never gave me so much as a kid for a party with my friends. Yet when your son turns up after wasting your money on his women, you kill the fatted calf for him!' No mention had been made previously of 'women', but the elder brother was ready to assume the worst. He spoke of 'your son' for he was too angry to speak of the prodigal as 'my brother'.

The father loved both his sons and seemed to understand, for he affectionately reminded his elder son that the property had been his to use as he wished. He begged him to join in the celebration, saying, 'My boy, you are always with me, and everything I have is yours. How can we help being happy? Your brother was as good as dead and has come back to life. He was lost but is found.'

When one considers the situation in which Jesus found himself with the resentful, self-righteous scribes and Pharisees, it is easy to see how much they were like the elder brother in the story and the importance of the last part of the parable is appreciated. The story does not tell us whether the elder brother finally went in or stayed outside. It ends as a challenge to the religious leaders, 'Will you, as God's friends, join in the rejoicing when a sinner returns to God's fold, or will you stay outside?'

By sending Jesus to seek and save sinners and outcasts, God was taking the initiative, offering forgiveness and reconciliation even before it was asked. The younger son, who had himself chosen to leave home, represented sinners, outcasts and Gentiles.

The dishonest steward (16^{1-13})

Luke probably received much of Jesus' teachings as isolated sayings. Here he seems to have collected into a common background some of the things Jesus said about wealth.

Jesus told his disciples a parable about a steward who was mismanaging his employer's business. When the employer got complaints about the steward he demanded to see his accounts. In this crisis, realizing that he was about to get the sack, the steward hurried around to the customers, getting them to alter their account books, so that one who owed for 1000 gallons of oil was marked down as owing for only 500 gallons. Another, who owed for 1000 bushels of wheat, was written down as owing for only 800 bushels.

The steward realized that he couldn't face a future of manual work or begging and hoped that the grateful customers would provide a home for him when he had lost his job. Verse 8a says that the master applauded the steward's action. One cannot be sure whether 'the master' refers to the employer or to Jesus himself. One can be sure, however, that the dishonesty was not applauded, but that the master could not help but admire the astute way in which the steward made use of his opportunities. The steward was 'worldly-wise'. The followers of Jesus should be alert for opportunities of serving and pleasing God, giving as much thought, care and enthusiasm to spiritual matters as worldly people do to business matters. Verse 9 said that his followers should use their worldly wealth (Authorized Version has 'unrighteous mammon'), to make friends for themselves so that when money was a thing of the past they would be received into God's Kingdom. Perhaps this means that the best use of wealth is to provide help for the needy. Some readers suggest that verse 9 was Jesus' ironic way of telling the Pharisees that they wrongly imagined that they could buy their way into God's favour. H.A. Guy suggests that it should be translated to mean 'Make true friendships apart from wealth because when there is no money such friends will still be loyal to you'. Other commentaries suggest that Jesus was telling the Jewish leaders that their Employer, God, was calling them to account for the way they were mismanaging their work for Him. Faced with this crisis, they should use every opportunity of making friends with outcasts and Gentiles otherwise they would find themselves outside God's Kingdom.

Normally stewards received no wages, but took commission from the profits they obtained from the business. In this story the steward may have been reducing the customers' bills by forfeiting his own commission.

Jesus said that one's attitude towards unimportant things shows how one will deal with important matters. The wealth of this world is temporary, simply on loan to us for a while, but if we are irresponsible about its use, how can we be trusted with spiritual and permanent matters?

No one can be equally devoted to two masters; one is bound to get better service than the other. Concern for money and selfish interests can get in the way of one's devotion to work done for God. Jesus' original parable probably ended at verse 8. It is thought that verses 9–13 were the attempts of the early Church to provide an interpretation.

Various sayings of Jesus (16^{14-18})

Jesus told the parable of the Dishonest Steward and then made the statement, 'You cannot serve God and mammon (money).'

Luke's next verses contain some sayings of Jesus taken from Q, probably said on various occasions, but brought together here by Luke because they are about the Jewish laws and the Pharisees who lived so strictly by them. Many well-known Pharisees were poor men and it is only Luke who claims that they loved money (16^{14}). Perhaps some of them, like many of the Jews, thought of wealth and success as signs of God's favour.

Some Pharisees, hearing Jesus' words about money, jeered at his claim that money was unimportant. These were men who considered that obedience to the Mosaic Law was all-important. Their devotion to it unfortunately gave many of them a sense of superiority and self-righteousness. Jesus told them that although ordinary people might be persuaded that they were good, God could see through the pretence and knew what they were really like. Things which impress people may not impress God.

Jesus said that before John the Baptist came, the Jews had been right to be guided by the Law and the Prophets, scriptures which were the foundations of Judaism. Now, however, a new era had begun for they had received the good news of God's Kingdom and 'everyone enters it violently' (RSV) or 'everyone forces his way in'. The meaning of these words is difficult to decide. The Jews had regarded Judaism as the way by which they could enter the Kingdom, but now the gospel of love and forgiveness opened the way for Jew and Gentile alike – anyone could enter. It has been suggested that 'force' and 'violence' may mean that Jesus was regretting the way that some people, like the Zealots, imagined that God's Kingdom would come about when they had driven out the Romans and set up a free Jewish nation. A zealot is someone passionately devoted to a cause. In A.D. 6 the territory which had belonged to Archelaus, son of Herod the Great, came under the direct rule of a Roman governor. He was answerable to Quirinius who had oversight of Syria and Palestine. Many Jews hated the power of Rome and rebelled, particularly when Quirinius demanded a census. Among these was a resistance party known in later years as the Zealots, men with great zeal for the Temple and the Law. They believed that God would help them to drive out the Romans from their holy land. The historian, Josephus, called them 'sicarii' (assassins).

The Mosaic Laws would lose none of their permanent value. Jesus said, 'Heaven and earth will come to an end before one dot or stroke disappears from the Law.' The teaching of Jesus did not cancel out Moses' Laws, but gave them greater meaning by demanding even higher moral standards. (Some scholars, however, suggest that Jesus was being sarcastic, suggesting that when the world was ending, the scribes, who copied and interpreted the laws, would still be more concerned with the horns or elaborations added to the tops of some Hebrew letters to distinguish them from others.)

Jesus felt that, despite their so-called love for Moses' Laws, the scribes and Pharisees were the ones who were misusing them. The seventh commandment said, 'You shall not commit adultery.' Adultery means sexual relations of a married person other than with the marriage partner. Moses had allowed divorce because it was better than the previous standards of the Israelites. Deuteronomy 24$^{1-4}$ laid down that a man could divorce his wife if he found 'something shameful in her'. Many Jews understood this to mean unchastity or adultery, but some rabbis were prepared to interpret it as shouting so that the neighbours heard her, burning the dinner, or merely being no longer as attractive as other women! A man need only give his wife a letter stating that she was divorced and free to marry someone else. Conversely a woman could divorce her husband only if he had become a leper, had forsaken Judaism or had raped a virgin.

Obviously Jesus considered that marriage vows, made before God, really were to be kept until death parted the two people who had become one by marriage. He considered remarriage after divorce to be nothing better than adultery by anyone involved in it, man or woman. The Commandments, so important to Judaism, forbade adultery; yet divorce, which could lead to adultery, was accepted by the Jewish leaders. Jesus was not advocating change in the civil laws, but stating the high standards he expected of those who wished to be his followers. He was showing that, in truth, he himself was more of an upholder of Moses' laws than the Pharisees were.

Jesus showed courage in speaking this way about divorce and remarriage, for Herod Antipas, the ruler of Galilee, had recently divorced a Nabatean princess in order to marry Herodias, who was herself divorced from Herod's brother.

Luke does not mention divorce anywhere else in his gospel, and even here the subject is remarriage rather than divorce. Mark and Matthew deal with a similar matter but there are differences in approach (cf. Matt. 19$^{1-9}$ and Mark 10$^{2-12}$).

Parable about a rich man and Lazarus the beggar (16$^{19-31}$)

In the last section we read that Jesus said, 'You cannot serve God and money.' He now told a story illustrating how affluence can make someone insensitive to the needs of other people. The story began like a popular old folk-tale, but Jesus gave to it an unexpected ending. This parable is found only in Luke's gospel.

There was a rich man who could afford to dress in clothes of purple and fine linen, clothes usually worn by royalty and Jewish High Priests, made from materials which cost roughly three years' wages for an ordinary working man. At the gate of his residence lay Lazarus, a poor man who didn't have the strength to drive away the street dogs that came to lick at the sores which covered him. Most Jews would see

Lazarus' condition as God's way of punishing him for some sin he had done, so he would get little sympathy. He would have been grateful to receive the leftovers from the rich man's table, the pieces of bread thrown away when people had wiped greasy fingers on them after eating. The rich man, sometimes called Dives (Latin for 'rich'), did not ill-treat Lazarus; the trouble was that he made no effort to help him. He couldn't make the excuse that he didn't know him, because later in the story he asks for Lazarus. Having so much, he gave no thought to the suffering which poverty, illness and hunger could cause.

Eventually Lazarus died and went to be with Abraham. The rich man also died but found himself in Hades. 'Hades' was the Greek name used to translate the Hebrew 'Sheol'. Originally Sheol was thought of as the shadowy dwelling-place of departed spirits. The idea developed in various ways and by the time of Jesus there were many theories and beliefs about an after-life. Sheol became thought of as a place of waiting until the time of Judgement after which good spirits went to Paradise to live comfortably in God's Presence. Wicked spirits went to Gehenna, an ever-burning fire in which they suffered torment for ever. Some descriptions of Sheol picture it as having two compartments, separated by a gulf, but visible one from the other, as it seems to be in this parable. It is important, however, that we realize that Jesus' parable was not intended to provide a description of life after death. Jesus was using folk-belief in a parable intended to show how wealth can be misused and how it is wrong for people who have plenty to ignore the needs of the poor.

Dives, used to privileged treatment, still seemed to expect it even in Hades and called to Abraham asking him to send Lazarus to moisten his burning tongue with cool water. Abraham showed compassion, addressing Dives as 'my son', but reminded him that he had had his share of comfort in his lifetime and now it was Lazarus' turn to be comfortable. Anyway, no one could get across the great gulf which lay between them.

Jesus could have ended the parable there and he must have had good reason for adding the unusual ending. He said that the formerly rich man asked that Lazarus should be sent to warn his five brothers who were still living, so that they could change their way of living and avoid the torments of Hell. Abraham reminded him that warnings had already been sent in the laws of Moses and the message of the prophets. The rich man said he thought that people would be more inclined to take a warning from someone returning from the dead, but Abraham thought this was unlikely.

Like the rich man the Jews often expected spectacular signs from

God, but ignored the signs already there. By the time Luke was writing this it was obvious that Jesus' own return from death was being ignored by many people. The Pharisees had failed to understand the Mosaic Laws, and in the same way they would fail to understand the Resurrection. Luke seems to be offering this as an explanation of why the Jews of the time rejected Jesus' claims.

The name Lazarus was a common name at that time, but appropriate here because it meant 'God is my help'. (John's gospel, chapter 11, contains a story of Jesus bringing back to life a man called Lazarus, the brother of Martha and Mary. John tells how the event served only to make some Jews more hostile to Jesus.)

The rich man, Dives, was typical of the Sadducees, men of status and property, who did not believe in life after death nor in a final Day of Judgement. Jesus' story assumed that there is a life after death, but it did not intend to describe what that life was like. (The ideas were popular beliefs of the time and are found in old Jewish writings like the books of Esdras and Maccabees and particularly 2 Enoch 9^{10} and 12^{8-13}, in a collection called 'The Apocrypha'.) The Jews imagined Hell as an ever-burning fire like their rubbish dump in the Gehenna valley outside Jerusalem.

The parable is characteristic of Luke's gospel, for Luke included many stories to show that the poor are loved and helped by God and that riches have no real or permanent value.

Jesus speaks about forgiveness, faith and service (17^{1-10})

Here again we have a number of separate sayings of Jesus brought together by Luke.

Jesus was well aware of the pitfalls and temptations that make life difficult for people who are struggling to do the right thing, especially if they are young or inexperienced or somewhat weak-willed. It is sometimes easy to think of these people as unimportant, but to Jesus every single person was of great value. He warned his followers that they could expect to be severely punished if ever they were hindrances or stumbling-blocks to these 'little ones', perhaps meaning young in the faith. They would be better off 'thrown into the sea with millstones around their necks'. This was a way of emphasizing that such people had no hope of escaping punishment. Millstones were large, round stones between which corn was ground into flour. Smaller stones were turned by women, the very large ones were turned by donkeys or oxen. (Similar ideas are found in Mark 9^{42-48} and Matthew 18^{6-10}.) Originally,

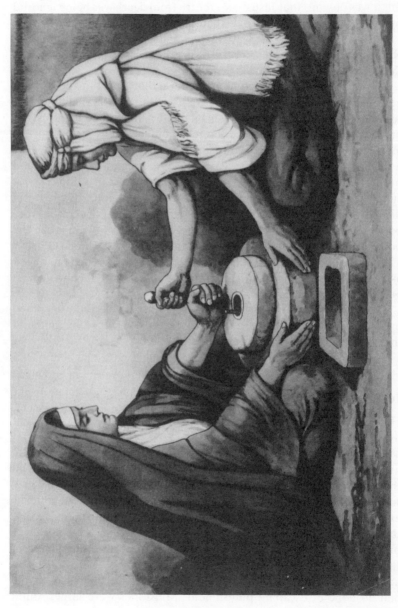

Grinding corn. Grain is fed into the central hole and the upper stone is then turned round

Jesus may have been addressing the warning to the scribes and Pharisees who hindered people's way to God by presenting it as the obeying of burdensome rules.

Jewish rabbis said that a really good person would forgive a wrongdoer three times. Jesus said that a wrongdoer should be reproved and if he were sorry he should be forgiven, but one cannot put a limit on forgiveness. The wrongdoer should be forgiven even if he does wrong and repents seven times a day. To the Jews the number seven signified completeness, and Jesus meant his followers to go on forgiving over and over without limit (cf. Matt. 18^{21-35}).

Perhaps the Twelve were beginning to realize how hard it was to keep up to the standards Jesus expected of them and they asked his help. He told them that if they had faith only as big as the tiny mustard seed they could order a mulberry tree (Mark and Matthew say 'mountain') to uproot itself and plant itself in the sea. Jesus' words are typical of the colourful and imaginative language of eastern people. He was telling his disciples that faith can achieve many things which seem impossible at first.

The Pharisees seemed to think that their good works were making up a kind of credit-balance with God, but Jesus said it is one's duty to serve God without expecting thanks or reward. He illustrated this with a parable about a slave serving his master. The slave would work all day perhaps as a shepherd or ploughman, but expected no thanks or reward from his master at the end of the day. In fact he would probably have to prepare his master's evening meal before thinking of his own. When one has given oneself to serve God the work is a duty and a privilege, and one does not expect rest or reward.

Ten lepers cured (17^{11-19})

Luke says that Jesus, still on his way to Jerusalem, was now on the border between Galilee and Samaria, yet at 9^{52} Luke said that Jesus was leaving Galilee.

As Jesus came into a village ten lepers called to him from an appropriate distance. They addressed him by name, which was unusual, saying, 'Jesus, Master, take pity on us.' Jesus told them to go and be inspected by the priests, for the Law demanded this, and Luke often reminds us how Jesus was obedient to the Jewish Law. As they moved away the ten realized that the leprosy had left them. One of them, a Samaritan, turned back, praising God for his cure. He fell at Jesus' feet and thanked him. Jesus asked where his nine companions were. They had all been cured, yet only this foreigner had come back to say Thank you! Jesus told the man to stand up and go on his way, his faith had cured him. The others had been cured, but perhaps Jesus meant that the Samaritan's cure was more than physical, for he seemed to have recognized in Jesus one who had the healing power of God.

The story should be compared with that of 5[12-16]. Some readers wonder if the two stories are different versions of the same incident. Here, however, Luke shows how a Samaritan, a man belonging to a people despised by Jews, reacted to Jesus in a better way than his Jewish companions (cf. also 10[25-37]). Laws like those of Leviticus 13[45], 14[1-8] and Numbers 5[2], made lepers into lonely outcasts. Jews and Samaritans had no dealings with one another, but their common plight had brought them together here. The story shows that the Kingdom of God was opening to Gentiles.

For more information about Samaritans see notes on 10[25-37] and for leprosy see 5[12-16].

Signs of the coming of God's Kingdom (17[20-37])

A century and a half before Jesus was born, Judas Maccabeus had led the fight to free his country from foreign invaders and foreign religion (see p. 42). Now the Jews were hoping for a God-sent deliverer, or Messiah, to lead them against the Romans. They hoped that he would inaugurate a great kingdom of free Jews, ruled over by God and respected by the other nations, an example for other nations to admire and copy.

From time to time there had been men who claimed to be the Jewish Messiah. They led rebellions against the Romans in an effort to make Palestine a kingdom which could serve God in freedom. The rebellions were crushed and the rebels dealt with severely. Each defeat meant a disappointment and many Jews looked for a true Messiah who would be victorious and who would inaugurate the Kingdom of God.

Some Pharisees asked Jesus how they would know when the Kingdom was about to begin. They were looking for some spectacular happening as a sign of God's intervention in history. Jesus told them this was not a future event, nor something to look for with one's eyes, 'for, in fact, the Kingdom is among you'. There are various meanings suggested for this difficult verse:

1 Jesus may have been saying that the Kingdom of God was an inner experience within each individual, a change of heart rather than an event in a particular time or place.

2 He may have meant that he himself was the Kingdom in embryo, the greatest sign, but one they did not recognize.
3 He may have meant that the Kingdom was already being offered to them by the fact of his being there.

The Jews thought of the Messiah, the Kingdom, the resurrection of all people to be judged and the gift of God's Spirit as things which would mean the approach of the end of the life they knew, the end of Satan's power. The first Christians, being Jews, saw Jesus' Resurrection and their experience of the gifts of preaching and healing as signs of the last days of this world. This is evident in St Paul's earliest letters (I Thess. 4^{13} to 5^{11}). One of Luke's aims was to show that many Christians had now accepted that the parousia might be a long way off, giving time for Christianity to be offered to all the people of the world.

Jesus said that the future would bring many occasions when his followers would long for God's intervention, for the coming of the Son of Man, but they should not chase after every sign and rumour. Before all that he must endure much suffering and be ignored and rejected by the people of his time. However much they looked for signs they would still be caught by surprise when it came, just as the people of Noah's time had been unprepared when the Flood came (Gen. 7^{23}), and just as the earthquake had caught the people of Sodom and Gomorrah unprepared (Gen. 19^{25}). When at last the day of the Son of Man came there would be no doubts, for it would be as obvious to everyone as the lightning which illuminates everything.

The remainder of the section is not easy to understand. (There are similar sections in Matthew 24^{17-18} and Mark 13^{15-16}.) Verses 31–32 seem appropriate to the hurried leaving of home and work on hearing of the approach of foreign invaders. At such a time, to spend time and energy in collecting up one's household goods could slow one down and cost one's life. Such advice certainly applied to the time preceding the Roman destruction of Jerusalem in A.D. 70. Having ignored Jesus' warnings the Jews paid the price of continued resistance and rebellion and thousands were caught unprepared just as they would be when the Day of the Son of Man arrived. Verses 33–37 show that it is this, the time of God's final Judgement, a time of individual assessment, that is uppermost in Jesus' mind. His followers will be known by their single-minded concern for God's Kingdom; and their lack of concern for security and earthly possessions, which they will leave easily and immediately when called to do God's work. This quality distinguishes the true disciple from others, so that one may be taken while the person beside him is not. (Modern translations usually omit verse 36 referring to 'two men in a field' because the words are not found in the Greek manuscript.)

Jesus' listeners, still thinking of the Kingdom as a particular place and arriving at a particular time, asked him, 'Where, Lord?' His answer was probably a well-known saying of the time, 'Where there is a corpse, the vultures [or eagles] will gather.' Vultures do not need to be informed of the presence of a dead body. In the same way people should not expect to be told that God is coming. If we are doing what is right at all times, we need not worry about being caught unprepared.

Some readers have suggested that the alternative translation, 'eagles' rather than vultures, may have been a warning that the Romans, whose symbol was the eagle, would pounce on any Jewish rebels who gave trouble.

The unjust judge (18$^{1-8}$)

Often the disciples must have wondered why God did not bring in His Kingdom for which they prayed and waited. Jesus told them they must not give up, thinking that God was not listening or concerned. The parable of the Friend at Midnight (11$^{5-13}$) and Matthew 7$^{7-11}$ express the same idea.

Jesus told them a parable about a judge who didn't care about people and who had no respect for religion. The judge was being pestered by a local widow who wanted him to take on her case and eventually he agreed to deal with the case, not because he was concerned about her but because it was the only way he could get some peace!

Usually Jews consulted the elders of their town when they required justice, so Jesus must have been thinking of the kind of magistrate appointed by Herod Antipas or the Romans. Such judges were notoriously lazy and had to be bribed or threatened before they would budge to do their work. A poor widow would stand little chance.

Unlike the judge in the story, God is concerned for His people and anxious to help when they ask. Jesus assured his disciples that God would satisfy their longing for the Kingdom when the time was right, but they had to accept that the waiting was in God's plan. Jesus wondered how many of them would be able to wait patiently and humbly for the time when the Son of Man would bring in the Kingdom (a link with 17$^{22-37}$), and how many would lose their faith and give up.

The section is typical of Luke's emphasis on the importance of prayer.

Parable of the Pharisee and the tax-collector (18⁹⁻¹⁴)

Jesus knew that many of his listeners were self-satisfied, regarding themselves as the good people with whom God was pleased, and feeling contempt for anyone who could not match their high standards. This section and the following ones as far as verse 30 deal with the qualities necessary to ensure a right relationship with God.

The parable here is about a Pharisee and a tax-collector, or publican, who were praying in the Temple at the same time. (Refer to notes on 5²⁷⁻³² about tax-collectors, and notes on 5¹⁷⁻³⁹ about Pharisees.) Prayers were said at 9 a.m., 12 noon and 3 p.m., and those said in the Temple at Jerusalem were considered to bring the greatest blessing.

The Pharisee said, 'I thank you, God, that I am not like other men. I am not greedy, dishonest nor adulterous. I am not like that tax-collector over there. I fast twice a week and give tithes [tenths] of all my possessions.'

In many ways this Pharisee was a good man. The Levites, who were workers in the Temple, had no way of earning money to live, so all other Jews were expected to provide for them by giving a tenth of their corn, wine, oil and cattle. There was no need to give a tenth of everything as this Pharisee did. Jews were expected to fast on the annual Day of Atonement, but some chose to fast also on the second and fifth days of the week, the busy market-days when there would be lots of people around to admire their piety, made obvious by whitening their faces, wearing ragged clothes and looking generally miserable. This Pharisee was prepared to do far more than the Law demanded of him, but he trusted in himself instead of trusting in God. His speech was a way of reminding God what a good fellow he was, rather like little Jack Horner! Although he was not aware of it, he needed forgiveness for being proud and for despising his fellow-men.

Meanwhile the tax-collector also prayed, without daring to come too near to the religious Pharisee. He hadn't the nerve to lift his head but he beat his chest in despair and shame and said, 'O God, have mercy on me, sinner that I am!'

Tax-collectors were not good men but this one had realized his faults and was repentant. This brought him closer to God than did the proud behaviour of the Pharisee. The tax-collector asked forgiveness, the Pharisee did not. Jesus said that God would accept the tax-collector's prayer before that of the self-righteous Pharisee. Before God one can come only in humility, aware of one's imperfections.

Be childlike (18$^{15-17}$)

Many modern parents take their babies to church to be blessed. Jewish parents took their infants to the rabbi at the synagogue. Here they came to Jesus asking him to bless the infants.

As they travelled to Jerusalem perhaps the disciples sensed Jesus' tension and weariness. They felt he should not be bothered by little children and told the mothers to take them away. So many people value children only as future adults.

Luke has not made use of Mark's gospel since 9^{50}, but now and until 18^{43} he again follows Mark. However he does not say, as Mark 10^{14} did, that Jesus was very annoyed with the disciples. By the time Luke was writing the Christians held the disciples in such respect that they avoided being critical of them. On several occasions Luke omitted or softened Mark's blunt words (see pp. 4, 65, 167).

Jesus insisted that the children should be brought back to him, saying, 'Allow the little ones to come to me. Don't try to stop them for the Kingdom of God belongs to people like them. I tell you that anyone who does not accept the Kingdom of God like a child will never belong to it.'

While the story shows that Jesus was fond of children, it seems strange to suggest that adults should copy children, who, after all, are not always lovable, well-behaved, obedient or kind! Perhaps Jesus was thinking of other characteristics of tiny children, their eagerness and lack of self-consciousness, their trust and dependence on those who look after them, the fact that when young they are unspoiled by the complicated and cynical ways of adult life with its hypocrisy and prejudice. Children see something new and wonderful in each discovery in the world around them. They are quicker than adults to forgive and forget. Jesus said that his followers should be childlike. This does not suggest that they should be childish.

A rich ruler; The dangers of wealth (18$^{18-30}$)

A man 'of the ruling classes' came to Jesus. He must have been of social or religious importance, perhaps an elder at a synagogue. Matthew's story says he was a 'young man' (Matt. 19$^{16-22}$, cf. Mark 10$^{17-22}$).

He asked Jesus, 'Good Master, what should I do to win eternal life?' Before answering the question Jesus asked, 'Why do you call me good? Only God is good.' It was not usual to address someone as 'good' and perhaps Jesus felt it sounded like flattery or that the man was using the word 'good' in a casual way. It is clear that the gospel-writers thought that Jesus was good, but Jesus was drawing attention to the goodness of God.

Jesus reminded the man of some of the Ten Commandments, fully aware that any law-abiding Jew would know them already. These commandments forbade adultery, murder, stealing, giving false evidence, lack of respect and concern for one's parents. The man broke in, 'I have obeyed all of these since I was a boy.' He must have felt that he could do more than this.

Jesus told him, 'There is one thing you have not done. Go and sell your property and give the money away to the poor. Then come and be one of my followers.' Mark (10^{21}) said that Jesus had taken a liking to the young man. Many would have jumped at the chance of being a disciple, but this man's heart sank, for he was very wealthy and could not face a future without comfort and security. He could not bring himself to do what Jesus asked. Jesus said to those near him, 'It is very difficult for a wealthy person to belong to God's Kingdom! It is easier for a camel to go through the eye of a needle than for a rich man to enter the Kingdom of God!' The Jewish Talmud talks about an elephant passing through the eye of a needle. A well-known saying such as these illustrated the impossibility of such a thing and it seemed to be saying that it was impossible for a rich person to belong to God's Kingdom. Many Jews, however, regarded success and wealth as a sign of God's blessing, and these people must have been puzzled by Jesus' words. Someone nearby asked Jesus, 'Then who can be saved?' and Jesus replied, 'Things which men find impossible are possible to God.' God could break down human selfishness.

It has been suggested that the needle's eye referred to a little postern doorway in the city wall through which an unloaded camel could squeeze with difficulty. It has been suggested also that 'camel' (Greek – Kamelos), should really be 'ship's rope' (Greek – Kamilos), but most scholars agree that there is no evidence for either of these suggestions and that Jesus' words were just an example of typical eastern cxaggeration, or hyperbole, to emphasize his point. It is easy to understand that anyone who keeps wealth while others suffer poverty and starvation cannot be pleasing God.

The disciples, who had left homes, property and security to go with Jesus, no doubt felt self-satisfied for they had done what this rich young ruler had failed to do, and Peter said to Jesus, 'We have left our belongings to become your followers.' Jesus had told them that they could expect to suffer and be persecuted, but they had experienced also the joy of following him, and the thrill and satisfaction of their successful tour of preaching and healing (10^{17-18}). Jesus told them that no matter what or whom they had left – home, wives, brothers, parents or children – for the sake of the Kingdom of God, they belonged already to a much greater family and eventually would gain eternal life itself (cf. Mark 10^{30}).

Matthew (19^{29}) made no mention of leaving wives. I Corinthians 9^5 suggests that Peter and other disciples sometimes took their wives with them.

For a third time Jesus speaks of his death (18^{31-34})

Jesus wished to prepare his friends for what would happen when they reached Jerusalem and now, for a third time, he took them aside to talk, saying that everything the prophet had foretold about the Son of Man would come true. (See Is. 50^6, 53^8.) He would be handed over to a foreign power, obviously meaning the Romans. He would be mocked, ill-treated and spat upon. They would flog and kill him, but on the third day he would rise again. The two previous warnings (9^{22} and 9^{44-45}) made no mention of Jerusalem or the Gentiles.

Again the Twelve were unable to believe or understand what Jesus was telling them. In chapter 22^{24-27} we find them arguing about which of them would get the highest positions in the Kingdom over which they expected Jesus to rule. Mark (10^{33-34}) shows that they were bewildered at Jesus' words, and John and James, expecting that soon Jesus would be proclaimed king, asked if they could be the chief men at his side (Mark 10^{35-45}, Matt. 20^{20-25}). Luke says that 'the meaning was concealed from them' as if he saw this as part of God's plan (24^{27}).

The blind man at Jericho (18^{35-43})

The last story showed how the disciples had been blind to the truth of what would happen at Jerusalem. Their 'blindness' makes a link with this story.

The company was approaching the low-lying fertile valley sixteen miles from Jerusalem where one finds Jericho, 'the city of palms', the most ancient city in the world. A blind man sat begging at the roadside as they entered the city. He probably expected to receive help from the Passover pilgrims as they arrived. The noise and excitement of the crowd made him ask what was happening and he was told, 'Jesus of

Nazareth is passing by.' The unnamed man (Mark 10[46] calls him Bartimeus and says the event happened as they left Jericho) called from behind the crowd, 'Jesus, Son of David, have pity on me.' Jesus had not been addressed as 'Son of David' before. The title shows that Jesus, known to belong to King David's descendants, was being discussed as a possible Messiah, or God-sent deliverer.

The people told the beggar to be quiet, but he shouted all the more until at last Jesus stopped and told the people to bring the beggar to him. Then Jesus asked him, 'What do you want me to do for you?' The man replied, 'Sir, I want my sight back.' Jesus told him, 'Have your sight; your faith has cured you.' The man was able to see immediately and he followed Jesus, praising God. Luke says that the people, seeing what had happened, also praised God. Perhaps they had tried to silence the man in case his shouting alerted the Roman guards of the approach of a man who might be persuaded to lead the Jews in a rebellion. To openly acclaim Jesus as 'Son of David' was to court danger. The pilgrims going to the Passover came from many different places. As they joined other groups they sang old psalms, and nationalistic awareness grew as they approached the capital to remember the time when their people had escaped from the slavery and oppression of Egypt (Exodus chapters 11 and 12). Extra legions were brought to Jerusalem at these times to keep the peace.

Zacchaeus the tax-collector (19[1-10])

Tax-collectors, or publicans, were treated with contempt for the reasons given in the story of Matthew Levi (5[27-39]) and now, in Jericho, Jesus was to meet another tax-collector, Zacchaeus.

Jericho was a rich and fertile oasis on the trade-route between Judaea and the East. It was rich in palm-forests, balsam-groves and rose-gardens, the produce of these was exported and a lot of revenue could be collected in taxes. Zacchaeus was the superintendent of the area's tax-collectors. His success and wealth came at the expense of the local Jews, so they would hate this man particularly. His only friends would be the other tax-collectors.

The presence of Jesus of Nazareth, rumoured to be the Messiah who would free the country, perhaps made the pilgrims even more excited than usual as they were leaving Jericho to begin the last stage of the journey to Jerusalem. It was a time for hating all traitors!

No one would be likely to help Zacchaeus to the front where he might catch a glimpse of Jesus, who was said to befriend outcasts and sinners. Being short in stature, the tax-collector knew he would be likely to miss the scene so he ran on ahead and climbed into the branches of a 'sycamore' tree (probably the wild sycamore upon which a fruit similar to figs grew), to get a better view. One wonders who would be more surprised, Zacchaeus or the people, when Jesus stopped by the tree, looked up and called, 'Zacchaeus, be quick and come down, for I must stay with you today.' Note again the 'must' as if Jesus were aware that bringing in outsiders was part of his mission.

The offer of unexpected friendship for one who had few friends must have been enough to bring down Zacchaeus in a hurry to welcome Jesus into his home, but there was a general murmur of disapproval from the crowd, horrified that a man reputed to be good and holy was accepting the hospitality of a money-grabbing traitor whom they would not allow into the synagogue and who was not allowed to take any public position in the Jewish community.

Perhaps they revised their opinions when they heard what effect Jesus' visit had made on Zacchaeus, a much greater effect than that achieved when the rich, law-abiding young ruler had found himself unable to give up his money (18^{18-30}), for the little official stood up and announced, 'Here and now, sir, I give half of my possessions to charity; and if I have cheated anyone, I am ready to pay him back four times the amount.'

Zacchaeus was prepared to pay back what the law demanded of a criminal, a thief. In a case like his, Jewish law would have asked him to return the amount wrongfully claimed plus one fifth (Lev. 6^5). His generosity must have left him with no money for himself, but Jesus had promised that no one would regret what they had given up to become his follower. Jesus told the Jews, 'Salvation has come to this house today. Zacchaeus is a descendant of Abraham. The Son of Man has come to seek and save what is lost.' As soon as Zacchaeus had paid what he promised he would be accepted back into the Jewish community. Perhaps his conscience had been troubling him for some time. He needed only the chance to reform, but the attitude of his neighbours had been a barrier to this.

The story of Zacchaeus is found only in Luke's gospel. In many ways it is a miniature of Luke's gospel for it shows how Jesus fulfilled the prophecies which spoke of one who would care for outcasts and oppressed, who would come to the lost people of Israel. It also emphasizes those things which are more valuable than money and status and shows that there is no sin too great to keep one from God if one is willing to repent (cf. 18^{9-14}).

The parable of the pounds (19¹¹⁻²⁷)

Luke introduces the next section by describing the growing excitement of the pilgrims as they left Jericho and began the last sixteen miles of the journey to Jerusalem. They seemed convinced that God's rule was going to begin there, and, knowing that instead of becoming their king, he was going to die and leave them for a long time, Jesus told them a parable.

A nobleman went to a distant country to receive the title of 'king', intending then to return. He called ten of his servants and gave to each of them one pound, saying, 'Trade with this until I get back.' (The pound is used here instead of the Greek 'mina', which was worth 100 drachmae. Inflation makes it difficult to give the true modern equivalent.) The servants hated the nobleman and sent a deputation to the distant country telling the authorities, 'We do not want this man as our king.' Eventually, however, the nobleman returned as their king.

Up to this point, the story would sound familiar to Jesus' listeners. In 4 B.C., Herod the Great had died and his son, Archelaus, went to Rome hoping to receive the title of King of Judaea. He was followed by a deputation of fifty Jews who told Augustus, the Roman emperor, that they did not want Archelaus to be their king. He returned to rule but without the title of king, and eventually was replaced by a Roman governor. Pontius Pilate was the fifth of these governors.

Jesus developed the story in his own way, saying that, when he returned, the newly-appointed king asked to receive an account of the trading. One servant had done very well, having multiplied his pound ten times. The master said, 'Well done! You are a good servant', and he gave him responsibilities commensurate with his effort and ability, putting him in charge of ten cities. A second servant had increased his one pound to five pounds. He, too, was congratulated and was put in charge of five cities. The next servant said to his master, 'Here is your pound which I kept wrapped safely in a cloth. I was afraid, because I know you are a hard man. You expect to get profit even when you have not invested, you expect to reap when you have not sown.' The servant had been afraid he might lose what he had been given and had kept it tightly to himself, benefiting no one.

The angry master told him, 'Surely, then, you should have put the pound into a deposit-account so that I could claim interest on it!' The master took the pound and gave it to the first servant who had proved that he could make full use of anything entrusted to him. The other servants felt this to be unfair, since this man had ten pounds already. The master told them, 'The man who has will always get more, but the man who has not will lose even the little he has.' Then Jesus ended his story by saying that the new king ordered the destruction of those who were not prepared to accept him.

Luke's story seems to be a combination of two stories: (a) a nobleman leaves to get a title as king and (b) a trader entrusts work to his servants. This certainly seems so when one compares this with the somewhat different version in Matthew 25$^{14-30}$, where no mention is made of a nobleman becoming king. Each of the gospel-writers adapted the common material according to his own purposes. Luke's version of this parable tells his readers:

1 Jesus received his title of King from God and those who did not accept him as their King would be punished;

2 There was no need to feel disillusioned because Jesus had not yet returned. The delayed parousia was in God's plan, allowing Jesus' followers time to make use of the gospel he had left with them. They must not keep it for themselves but spread it in the world, thus multiplying their number. The Jews had failed to make proper use of what God had given to them, like the man in the story who had not used his pound. The New Israel (Christians) must not fail.

Jesus' Last Visit to Jerusalem (19^{28} to 24^{53})

Jesus rides into Jerusalem (19^{28-44})

Leaving Jericho, the Passover pilgrims began the long climb towards Jerusalem. Many Jews had rejected Jesus as the servants rejected the king in the Parable of the Pounds. Some, however, seemed to think that Jesus would be proclaimed Messiah when they reached Jerusalem, and that he would bring in the reign of God by first taking over from the Romans.

The pilgrims came at last to the villages of Bethphage and Bethany, near the Mount of Olives, on the outskirts of Jerusalem. From here it is obvious that nothing is left to chance, for Jesus must have made previous plans for a dramatic and meaningful entry into the city. Two disciples were sent ahead, having been told where they could find the foal of a donkey on which 'no one has yet ridden'. Somehow it did not seem fitting to use for such an important event something which had been used before (cf. I Sam. 6^7, II Sam. 6^3). If anyone queried their borrowing the foal they were to answer with a prearranged password, 'Our master needs it'.

When the foal arrived Jesus' friends put their coats on its back for him to ride, and some even spread coats on the ground as the procession went down the tree-covered hillside.

According to John's gospel Jesus paid several visits to Jerusalem during his ministry. The Synoptic Gospels describe only the final visit (apart from his visit as a boy, Luke 2^{41-52}), saying that Jesus stayed in the north away from Jerusalem and the Jewish authorities, often asking people to keep quiet about his healing miracles and discouraging any public recognition of him. He wished to avoid a reputation as a military Messiah, a reputation which could bring about an early arrest before his work was established and his disciples were ready to continue without him. Now he seemed to be drawing attention to himself deliberately, setting out to fulfil the prophecy of Zechariah 9^9, 'Rejoice! Rejoice, daughter of Zion. Shout aloud, daughter of

Jerusalem. See, your king is coming to you. He has won his cause and gained his victory. He is humble and mounted on the foal of an ass.' An eastern king might ride a horse in battle, but in peacetime he would ride a donkey. Jesus' ride into Jerusalem was his public claim to kingship there, the first great symbolic act of Holy Week, one which fulfilled the ancient prophecy. There are earlier parallels: (a) II Kings 9^{13} tells of Jehu, an army commander, who set out to become king of Israel. His officer-friends spread their cloaks before him in greeting. (b) In 141 B.C. Jerusalem was free from pagan Greek invaders and Simon, brother of the Jewish hero Judas 'Maccabeus' (the Hammerer), was greeted with songs and the waving of palm branches when he rode in peace into the freed city to cleanse it of everything left by the Greeks (I Maccabees 13^{51}).

As they went down over the Mount of Olives the Passover pilgrims would see the south-eastern part of the 'City of David' about a mile away. The disciples began to sing part of Psalm 118^{26}, with which the priests welcomed pilgrims to the Temple, but Luke changes the words so that they welcome 'the King' who comes, and he follows these with 'Peace in heaven, glory in highest heaven', reminding us of the angels' song at Jesus' birth (2^{14}).

Some Pharisees, who, perhaps, were amongst the pilgrims going to keep the Passover, asked Jesus to reprimand his friends. Probably they were afraid that the outburst would bring reprisals on the crowd, for Roman legions, brought in to keep peace at festival-times, were always alert for national uprisings. Jesus told the Pharisees, 'If they are silent, the stones will cry out!' It was a time of great emotion; too late now to ask people to keep quiet about what was happening. Jesus' life had been a journey leading to this climax at Jerusalem.

Jerusalem has great importance in Luke's writings. It was the place of Jesus' death and Resurrection. Luke's gospel began and ended at Jerusalem; his Acts of the Apostles began there and showed how Jesus' message spread from the city to Rome itself, the heart of the empire. Ironically the name Jerusalem meant 'foundation of peace'. As the full expanse of the city he loved came into view, tears came into Jesus' eyes and he said, 'If only now, today, you would realize which things could bring you peace! As it is they seem hidden from your eyes. The day is coming when your enemies will set up siege-works against you. They will surround you and shut you in at every point. They will dash you and your children to the ground. They will not leave one stone standing on another, because you did not recognize God's moment when it came.' He felt great sorrow knowing that the Jews were bringing upon themselves the anger of the Romans. Eventually

Pilgrims going down the Mount of Olives on Palm Sunday. Jerusalem is on the hill ahead

the inevitable would happen, as indeed it did, for in A.D. 70 General Titus brought in the Roman legions to besiege Jerusalem. The suffering of the Jews was so horrible that many Romans were sorry for them.

Cleansing of the Temple (19$^{45-48}$)

In 141 B.C. Simon, brother of Judas Maccabeus, had cleansed the Temple after its use by the Greeks, and re-dedicated it to God (I Maccabees 13^{50}). Perhaps Jesus had the same idea in mind for he went now straight to the Temple. (Luke's version of this event is less detailed than those found in Mark 11$^{15-19}$ and Matthew 21$^{12-17}$.) Malachi 3$^{1-3}$ may also have been in Jesus' mind. The people thought of the Temple as God's dwelling place, the place where they could come to meet with God. Perhaps Luke's main concern in this section was to show that people meet with God in Jesus. Jesus himself becomes the true temple and no building, great or small, is necessary.

Foreigners were allowed to worship God in the first courtyard of the Temple (see plan), but beyond this they must not go. In this Gentile court merchants sold birds and animals advertised as perfect and unblemished and therefore acceptable as sacrifices but the prices were extortionate. Adult Jews were also expected to pay an annual Temple tax of half a shekel; about two days' wages. Many Jews lived abroad but tried to attend the Passover festival, the most important one. They needed to exchange their money for the special coins acceptable at the Temple. Ordinary coins might have on them the image of the Roman emperor or a foreign god and were not accepted. There were stalls where money-changers charged high fees for this service. Pilgrims came wanting to give their best to God, but they were cheated and taken full advantage of by the stall-keepers, and the stalls were the property of the High Priest! Back in Judah, after the exile in Babylon, an unknown prophet had spoken of encouraging non-Jews to come to God (Is. 56$^{6-8}$), and said of the Temple, 'My house shall be called a house of prayer for all nations.' Strangely enough, Luke, despite his keenness to write a gospel for all the world, has omitted the words 'for all nations'. Perhaps it was because the Temple had been destroyed by the time Luke was writing and anyway he wanted people to think of Jesus, rather than a building in Jerusalem, as their meeting-place with God. Jesus said that instead of the Temple being a house of prayer it had become more like a robbers' cave. Before the people of Judah were taken as captives to Babylon the prophet Jeremiah had

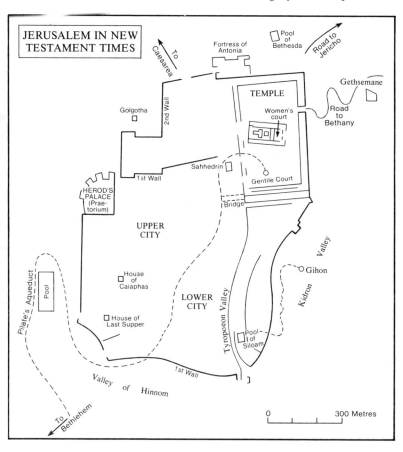

JERUSALEM IN NEW TESTAMENT TIMES

To Caesarea

Fortress of Antonia

Pool of Bethesda

Road to Jericho

Gethsemane

Golgotha

2nd Wall

TEMPLE

Women's court

Road to Bethany

Sanhedrin

1st Wall

Gentile Court

HEROD'S PALACE (Praetorium)

Bridge

UPPER CITY

Gihon

Valley

House of Caiaphas

LOWER CITY

Pilate's Aqueduct

Pool

Tyropoeon Valley

Kidron

House of Last Supper

Pool of Siloam

1st Wall

Valley of Hinnom

To Bethlehem

0   300 Metres

stood in the Temple doorway warning them that they were not living according to God's standards. He told them that the armies of Babylon would come and destroy Jerusalem and the Temple, and that the Temple had become more of a robbers' cave (Jer. 7¹¹). Jesus now reminded the merchants of the words of these two prophets and drove them out of the Gentile court.

One does not think of Jesus as a violent person, yet all four gospels vouch for this incident. By his action Jesus was openly challenging the Jewish religious authorities. He was leaving no doubt about his mission and his own position. His action led to his arrest and crucifixion. During the next days Jesus spoke openly to the Passover pilgrims in the Temple courts, undeterred by the knowledge that the priests, scribes and leading citizens were now anxious to find some way of destroying him. For a while their efforts were frustrated by the crowds who were always there listening attentively to Jesus' words. He was making full use of the little time left to him.

The authority of Jesus (20$^{1-8}$)

Somehow, the authorities decided, Jesus must be trapped. One day, while he was speaking in the Temple courts, a group of priests, lawyers and elders turned up to challenge him, 'Who gave you authority to do these things?' They had every right to ask, since it was their duty to check on all that went on around the Temple. The Sanhedrin, the Jewish court of law, was made up of seventy such men. Jesus knew that if he claimed to come from God he would be accused of blasphemy. The Romans would arrest him as the rebel-leader Messiah. Anyway, Jesus liked people to make up their own minds about his identity. Skilfully he turned the situation, saying, 'First answer a question for me. When John baptized, did his authority come from God or from men?'

The group discussed the question together and soon realized the impossibility of answering it. If they said, 'From God', Jesus would say, 'Well, then why didn't you believe him?' If they said, 'From men', the people might turn on them with violence because the people had loved John and regarded him as a wonderful prophet sent from God.

The priests, lawyers and elders decided to answer that they did not really know. These men were supposed to be the experts, the authorities on any religious matters, yet they were admitting that they could not make up their minds as to whether John had been inspired by God. If this was the best they could manage the Jews needed someone else to guide them! They were hardly the ones to challenge Jesus! Since they were unable to answer him, he told them, 'Then I won't answer your question. I won't tell you who gave me authority.'

If they had not been convinced by John, it was likely that they would not believe Jesus either. If they had believed John they would realize that Jesus' authority came from God, because John's work pointed to Jesus.

The parable of the wicked vine-growers (20$^{9-18}$)

In this section it becomes quite obvious that Jesus knows what is going to happen to him. Luke seems to have chosen to put the story here to prepare his readers for the arrest and death of Jesus. He seems to suggest that Jesus preached in the Temple for several days (see 19⁴⁷). He had claimed the Temple for God and was using it for its rightful purpose. Tradition said that the Messiah would make a public appearance at the Temple.

Jesus told a parable about a man who planted a vineyard, then, as many land-owners did, he let it out to tenants, intending to send and claim his share of the produce when the grapes were harvested. When he did so, however, his messenger was beaten and driven away empty-handed. Even more brutal treatment was given to the second and third messengers. The owner then decided to send his beloved son (cf. the words at Jesus' baptism), for surely the tenants would respect and obey him; but when they saw him coming they said, 'This is the heir to the property. If he were dead we would have first claim to the vineyard', so they threw him out and killed him. The owner would return and destroy those wicked vine-growers (some versions call them 'husbandmen'), and hand over the care of his vineyard to others.

Jesus had no need to explain such a parable to his Jewish hearers. From Old Testament times the Jewish nation had been referred to as 'God's vineyard'. The Jews, and their leaders particularly, would recognize themselves as the tenants in the parable, working for God, the owner (e.g. Is. 5¹⁻⁷). The messengers, ignored and badly treated, represented the prophets who, throughout Israel's history, had been persecuted for speaking God's will. The Jews would realize that the owner's beloved son was meant to represent Jesus and that he was going to die. The parable also warned the Jews to expect suffering (which came in A.D. 70) and said that God was about to hand over their work to 'others', meaning perhaps the Christian Church which would include many non-Jews. Jesus' listeners did not like what the parable implied and said, 'God forbid!'

In drawing these parallels we make the story an allegory rather than a parable. Jesus emphasized the claim to his identity by quoting a verse from Psalm 118, 'The stone which the builders rejected has become the chief corner-stone' (Ps. 118²²). The psalmist was expressing his belief that no matter what enemy or adversity faced the nation, it was sure to come through as victor if God were on its side. Verse 18 echoes the statements made in Isaiah 8¹⁴ and Daniel 2³⁴ – those who come into collision with God's stone will be broken rather than break it. The verse may have been added by early Christian writers who felt that although the Jews had rejected Jesus and thought that they had destroyed him, he had become the most important person in history.

A question about tribute money (20¹⁹⁻²⁶)

Knowing that the parable about the vine-growers had been told against them, the priests and lawyers were anxious to get rid of Jesus as quickly as possible and they tried to think up controversial questions to which any answer would enrage one section of the community. They sent men, whom Luke calls 'spies', to pretend that they were interested in Jesus' teaching, and these watched every move that Jesus made.

In a flattering way they said, 'Teacher, we know that your teaching is sound and good. You favour no one, but speak honestly telling us what God expects of us. Now, do you think we should agree to pay tax to the Roman Emperor?'

Everyone who lived in a part of the Roman Empire had to pay for the privilege. Conquerors always issued their own coinage bearing the head and title of the conqueror and tax was payable in this coinage. The second Commandment forbade the Israelites to represent anything in sky, earth or seas in a picture or carving. (This is also forbidden in Islam.) The Jews bitterly resented having to use the Roman coins which showed Caesar's head. As well as offending the religious law the coins were a reminder of their lack of freedom.

Jesus asked to be shown a silver coin, meaning the Roman penny or denarius. He asked whose image was on the coin and was told 'Caesar's'. Then Jesus told his questioners, 'Give back to Caesar what belongs to Caesar, and give to God what belongs to God.' The Jews had a duty towards the Emperor and obeying this did not prevent them from also carrying out their duties towards God.

Jesus was well aware that this was another question set to trap him. If he said that his countrymen should pay tax to Rome he would lose the sympathies of the militant Jews. If he said they should not pay tax he would be arrested by the Romans as a rebel. Once again he had side-stepped trouble and also had made clear that he was not a political leader. He had also made it clear that one can serve God and the state, giving loyalty to both, for they each make their own demands. It was Rome's right to demand tax in any area where Caesar's head appeared on the coinage. Rome provided law and order, good roads and aqueducts – for which her subjects must pay.

Mark (12¹³⁻¹⁷) and Matthew (22¹⁵⁻²²) described the questioners as Pharisees and Herodians, an unusual alliance, for whereas the religious and intensely Jewish Pharisees resented the Romans, the political supporters of the Herod family were anxious to appease the Romans in order to hold on to their wealth and status.

General note about the Sadducees

The Sadducees and Pharisees were opposites in almost everything. The Sadducees, who became known about two hundred years before the time of Jesus, were the wealthy and conservative priestly group. Their name may have come from that of King David's priest in Jerusalem, Zadok. They accepted the Laws of Moses as found in the first five books of our Old Testament. These were the only scriptures they recognized, so they refused to bother about the hundreds of additional rules which had grown up to explain how one should behave in everyday life so as to obey Moses' laws. This was known as 'the tradition'. The Sadducees also refused to accept doctrinal developments that had grown up within Judaism in the last two centuries before Jesus. The Pharisees were in favour of these developments, the principal one being a belief in a personal after-life. The Sadducees did not believe in resurrection or angels. The Sadducees were in favour of living as peaceably as possible with the occupying Romans, perhaps for the safety of the nation, perhaps to avoid having their property and powerful positions taken away by Rome. They did not support the wish for a Jewish Messiah probably because he was expected to make a stand against the Romans. Naturally they were regarded by the Pharisees as collaborators with the pagan overlords.

More questions; What happens at resurrection? (20^{27-40})

Luke's gospel mentions the Sadducees at this point only. Some of them came to put before Jesus a question which challenged the belief in resurrection. Deuteronomy 25^5 stated that if a man died childless his name should be kept alive by his widow who should marry her husband's brother. The first son of this marriage must be known as the son of her first husband. The Sadducees pointed out that if a man had six brothers and each in turn died, his wife could marry in turn all seven brothers. If there was then a resurrection whose wife would she be in that future life? The Sadducees obviously felt that this teaching of Moses made it ridiculous to believe in a resurrection.

Jesus told them that one cannot compare life after resurrection with the life we know in this world, for those whom God considers worthy of life with Him do not die and do not marry as they did on earth. They are all as angels and sons of God. Then Jesus reminded the Sadducees that Moses himself had reported the words of God at the Burning Bush as, 'I am the God of Abraham, Isaac and Jacob' (Exod. 3^6). This suggested that those three were still in a living relationship with God. If the Sadducees believed Moses, they must also believe in resurrection, for 'God is not God of the dead but of the living'.

The lawyers, many of whom were supporters of the Pharisees, admired Jesus' ability to answer and said, 'Well spoken, Master!' There seemed no point in asking any more questions in an attempt to trap him.

Son of David (20⁴¹⁻⁴⁴)

Jesus had been questioned by the priests, lawyers and Sadducees, and the lawyers had congratulated him on the way he answered. He turned now to these lawyers and continued the type of argument familiar at that time.

All the psalms were believed to have been written by David. It was also believed that the Messiah would be a son of David, with the literal meaning here of 'descendant', not simply 'having the character of', but many Jews had grown to imagine the Messiah as a national and military leader like David had been. This was not Jesus' view of Messiahship. Here, and in the next sections, Luke indicates the differences between Jesus and the old Jewish parties, differences which inevitably lead to the coming crisis.

Jesus quoted to the lawyers the beginning of Psalm 110, one of the psalms the Jews regarded as referring to the Messiah: 'The Lord (God) said to my lord (Adonai), "Sit at my right hand until I make your enemies your footstool".' If David spoke of someone as 'my lord', he must have been thinking of someone greater and more exalted than himself, someone great enough to share God's throne, presumably the Messiah. Jewish children learned to obey the Commandment 'Honour your father and mother', but no father would refer to his own son as 'lord'. Jesus asked the lawyers, 'How can you say that the Messiah is son of David?'

Several times the New Testament refers to Jesus' own descent from David (e.g. Matt. 1²⁰, Luke 1²⁷, 2⁴, Rom. 1³), so it seems likely that Jesus was not throwing doubt on his family relationship with David, but was insisting that Messiahship meant a great deal more than being simply a descendant of David. Modern scholars believe that Psalm 110 was written after David's time, and that it was written for the enthronement of an Israelite king before the Exile. Such kings were regarded as appointed by God, sharing God's responsibilities for the people, adopted as sons by God and helped by God to defeat the enemies of Israel.

Jesus criticizes the lawyers (20⁴⁵⁻⁴⁷)

The lawyers have been mentioned already on pp. 43, 101. Here Luke includes more of Jesus' remarks about them, probably taken from Mark's gospel (cf. Mark 12³⁸⁻⁴⁰).

Jesus must have been expressing the thoughts of many people when he said that the lawyers enjoyed parading in long robes, receiving the respectful greetings of people in the streets and sitting in the seats of honour in the synagogues and at banquets.

They were supposed to give legal advice without charging a fee, and earn their living at some other job, but they taught that being generous to a rabbi or lawyer could help to get someone a place in Heaven, and thus they were offered fees for their advice. They took advantage of helpless, uneducated people, particularly widows who had no one to protect them. Payment of a lawyer's fee could mean the widow would have to mortgage her possessions. Such behaviour was against the law, but it was the lawyers themselves who decided the interpretation of the law! They were using a position of trust to exploit weaker people. They made a pretence of being pious by reciting lengthy prayers.

The widow's mite (21¹⁻⁴)

Widows were mentioned in the last section and perhaps this reminded Luke of an incident which had happened in the women's court of the Temple where thirteen trumpet-shaped collecting-boxes were fixed around the walls to receive money for various purposes. Into these, the Temple Treasury, wealthy people put large amounts of money, often making a great show of what they gave. Jesus noticed a poor widow dropping in two mites (probably each was a tiny coin known as a 'lepton', or a 'thin one'). The coins were almost worthless, but Jesus said, 'I tell you this, the widow has given more than any of the other people. They have so much that they didn't miss what they gave, but she has given all that she had left to live on.'

A gift should not be valued for the amount given, but for what it has cost to give it. The most valuable gifts are those given lovingly, willingly and sacrificially.

The destruction of Temple and city; What the future holds (21⁵⁻⁷)

The people were admiring the Temple at Jerusalem and from the

description left to us by the Jewish historian, Josephus, we can understand their admiration. (*Wars* 5.5 and *Antiquities* 15.11.3). In an effort to please the Jews, Herod the Great enlarged and decorated the building. At first the surrounding valleys made extension work seem impossible but Herod had great pillars put up to hold the new part of the base. People were amazed at the sheer size of the stone blocks used in the building. The work was begun in 20 B.C. and went on, after Herod's death, until A.D. 62. From a distance the Temple looked like a mountain of white and gold, a dazzling vision, particularly at sunrise. Each supporting pillar, forty feet high, was made from one single column of marble and over the door was Herod's gift, a great vine of solid gold, each cluster of grapes being as tall as a man. The rich votive offerings (offerings which people had vowed to give), added to the splendour, admired even by foreigners. Little wonder that Jesus caused consternation when he told the people, 'All these things you are admiring will be destroyed in a little while. Not one stone will be left standing on another.' The people asked him when this would happen. Would there be any warning signs?

It should have been obvious to them that the Romans would not go on tolerating Jewish revolts which could not hope to succeed against Roman might. If rebellions continued, as it seemed now they would, the Romans would march in and destroy the city and its beautiful Temple. This actually happened in A.D. 70, eight years after the Temple was completed.

Troubles and persecutions (21⁸⁻¹⁹)

Jesus warned the people against taking too much notice of so-called 'signs', for many would come claiming to be the Messiah and announcing that 'the Day' had arrived. Such men should be ignored. News of war and rebellions would not necessarily mean that the end of the world was near, said Jesus. There would be earthquakes, famines and plagues, and in the sky terrors and great portents (omens, signs). First, however, the followers of Jesus would face trials and persecution because of their faith. This would be their opportunity to testify. Jesus himself would inspire them with words. They must be prepared to be betrayed by their closest relatives and friends and some of them would suffer death. They would be hated for their loyalty to Jesus, but if they could stand firm they would gain true life and 'not a hair of their heads would be lost' (a saying obviously referring to spiritual and not physical safety).

The words of this section are not typical of Jesus and many scholars wonder whether he actually said them. Mark chapter 13 and Matthew 24^{1-51} contain similar words. These sections are apocalyptic in style. 'Apocalypse' is the Greek word for 'revelation' and the most famous literature of this kind is found in the books of Daniel and Revelation. Such writings claim to reveal future events and were often expressed as visions or in symbolic language. They were intended to encourage people at times of particular stress to keep their faith in God and go on doing good, for although troubles lay ahead a splendid person would soon come to rule on God's behalf and begin a new and better age. Imagery of the kind used here was much used by the prophets of Old Testament times who wanted people to realize that all was in God's plan. It was thought that nature was upset at any great upset of mankind. Apocalyptic writings were profuse and popular in the century before and the century after Jesus' birth, and it was natural that they should be found in the gospels, linking Jesus with God's plans for the future.

Old Testament prophets had spoken of such signs heralding the Day of the Lord. After a time of chaos and terror, God would come in glory to judge the people. It was natural that Jewish Christians should link such ideas to the expected return of Jesus. In the years that followed his death the people witnessed famine (Acts 11^{28}), earthquake (Acts 16^{26}), the destruction of Jerusalem, an eruption of Vesuvius in A.D. 79, and the terrible persecution of Christians under the Emperor Nero. It was natural that they should expect the return of Jesus and the end of the world to follow immediately, and many scholars believe that Luke included this apocalyptic section to correct that expectation. Either Luke has made many alterations to Mark chapter 13 or perhaps used another source, but the changes give a new character to the section. Mark's section was heavily influenced by Jewish apocalyptic writings and suggested that after the events described there would follow rapidly the return of Jesus in the clouds, then Judgement and the world's end. Mark's mysterious phrase, 'the abomination of desolation', perhaps described an attempt by the Emperor Caligula in A.D. 40 to put a statue of himself in the Temple. Mark may have compared it to 168–167 B.C. when Antiochus Epiphanes had set up a statue of the Greek god Zeus in the Temple, an event probably referred to by a similar phrase found in Daniel 9^{27}. Mark wrote before the fall of Jerusalem, but this tragedy had happened when Luke was writing and he saw it as the 'desolation'. He also witnessed the trials and persecutions of many Christians and spoke of them in the Acts of the Apostles. Luke (21^{9-13}) gives the explanation and purpose for the delay of Jesus' return – the end would not come immediately; Jesus had completed what he came to do but now there must be time and opportunity for the Church to take his message to all nations. Luke intends this to be known by everyone, and instead of Jesus' words being heard by only four disciples on the Mount of Olives, as Mark suggested (Mark 13³), Luke brings them into teaching given by Jesus in the Temple.

Jerusalem is destroyed (21²⁰⁻²⁴)

Jesus said that when armies surrounded Jerusalem the people would know that soon the city would be destroyed. Then the people living in Judaea should flee to the hills and stay right away from the city which had reached its time of judgement and punishment. It would be a terrible time for mothers with tiny babies. Many people would be killed with swords, others would be taken away as captives to other countries, and the city would be trampled by foreigners until their day had run its course (another reminder that there is still much time ahead before the end of the world).

Verses 20–24 are perhaps the answer Jesus gave to the question, in verse 7, asking if there would be any warning signs before the city's destruction. The historian, Josephus, described the horrible details of the time. In A.D. 70, after a long siege, the city fell to the armies of Vespasian and Titus. During the siege the Jews had no food and it is said that some ate their own children. Josephus wrote that over a million Jews died and 97,000 were carried away captive. The city was completely flattened and the Temple was pulled down and burnt (*Wars* 7.1. 1–3). Luke must have known such details, but instead of describing them as Josephus did, he kept closely to words like those of ancient prophets who had foreseen a previous destruction of Jerusalem. Like them he saw the defeat, invasion, destruction and captivity as God's way of punishing His disobedient people.

The return of Jesus (21²⁵⁻²⁸)

Even before the destruction of Jerusalem Jesus had brought about the beginning of God's Kingdom on earth in a more quiet and restrained way than many Jews had expected. Even now the world had not ended.

Here Luke says that only when the regular pattern of sun, moon and stars is in chaos and when the oceans terrorize people and engulf the earth, will the end be near. The Son of Man will come, not 'in the clouds' as in Mark 13²⁶, but 'on a cloud', meaning the shekinah, the glory of God's Presence. Then Jesus' followers can hold up their heads knowing that their salvation is near.

The language is again the picture-language of apocalyptic writings. The book of Daniel had spoken of the Son of Man in this way, but whereas some scholars believe it refers to the Messiah, others think it means human beings, the loyal Jews who had withstood persecution and were coming to God in glory to receive power and a kingdom. The early Christians, however, understood it to mean the Second Coming of Jesus. No doubt the fulfilment of his warning about Jerusalem, coupled with the colourful language of the popular apocalyptic of the Jews, added to their hope of his return in glory. The whole of this recent section, Luke 21⁵⁻²⁸, is a very difficult one and approached by individuals in their own ways.

A parable about a fig-tree (21²⁹⁻³⁸)

Jesus pointed out that when buds are seen on a fig-tree (or any tree) one realizes that summer will come soon. In the same way when they witnessed the events spoken of (see above section) they should realize that God's Kingdom was near. He said that some of his listeners would still be alive to see it all. His words would endure when 'Heaven and earth' had passed away. (The Jews used to say that their laws and beliefs were as everlasting as Heaven and earth. Perhaps Jesus meant that even Judaism would not have such everlasting value as his teaching.)

Jesus warned the people to be ready at any time for God's coming. They should not waste their lives in idleness, drunkenness or self-indulgence. They should ask God constantly to help them through the troubled times that lay ahead so that they would survive and prove able to stand in the presence of the Son of Man.

Many of the early Christians thought Jesus meant that he would return very soon. They assumed that he would take a leading part in the judgement of mankind and the organizing of a Kingdom for God. We know that, in the time of the first missionaries, some of the Christians St Paul wrote to were no longer bothered about their everyday jobs or anything as permanent as getting married, because they expected the world to end at any minute. Even Paul himself seemed to have this sense of urgent haste when he first became Christian, but he and Luke were to play an important part in teaching

Christians that there was no need to feel disillusioned and disappointed, for Jesus had finished what he had set out to do and time was now needed for his followers to take the gospel to the world. Some of this early missionary work in other countries is described in the Acts of the Apostles, which shows the gospel progressing from Jerusalem to the gentile world and to Rome, the centre of Roman power, authority and culture. Many of Jesus' hearers probably did live through the destruction of the city and Temple and also witnessed the exciting things that happened when the apostles began to spread the gospel (Acts ch. 2). No doubt many of them realized that God's Kingdom had come in a powerful way.

Every day now Jesus taught the crowds in the Temple precincts and the people arrived very early each morning to listen to what he said. At night he lodged at Olivet. This may mean that he camped in the open air as many pilgrims did, but John's gospel (11 and 12^{1-11}) shows that Jesus often stayed with friends at Bethany, a village on the slopes of the Mount of Olives.

(At this point some manuscripts of the Greek New Testament include a story about a woman accused of adultery, but most include it in John's gospel at 7^{53} to 8^{11} where it is usually considered to belong.)

General note concerning Luke's account of the Passion (Chapters 22 to 24)

The story of the last few days of Jesus' life is known as 'the Passion story'. The Jews used to meet to 'break bread together'. As they ate they looked forward to being in God's Kingdom which, they said, would begin with a feast prepared for them by God. As Jesus and the disciples ate their last meal he asked them to remember him in a special way whenever they broke bread together. Christians have commemorated that last meal ever since in the ceremony known as Holy Communion (or the Eucharist), and the early Christians must have repeated the words of the ceremony often enough to give it a definite pattern before anyone attempted a written account of the event. Both Matthew and Luke have based their accounts on Mark's story, but Luke has introduced his own material (L) freely, giving to it a different emphasis from that of Mark and Matthew. The result has much in common with the account in John's gospel.

Despite the emotion naturally found in Luke's story there is a stronger sense of triumph than of tragedy. In spite of his position as the condemned prisoner, Jesus remains calm and dignified, completely in control of the situation, praying not for himself but others, confident in Peter's eventual strength and leadership even though he knows that Peter will deny knowing him. Luke chooses to leave out the story of the disciples' desertion of Jesus and also Jesus' cry from the cross, 'My God, My God, why have you forsaken me?' He describes a conversation at the supper-table during which Satan is held responsible for Judas' betrayal of Jesus. One is conscious of this last great struggle between the goodness of God and the evil of Satan. Luke makes clear the hatred felt by the Jewish leaders, but tells of the efforts made by Pontius Pilate, the representative of Roman authority, to set Jesus free. For all his Gentile readers Luke shows that Jesus was no political rebel challenging the Romans' power, but the Prince of Peace challenging all individuals to become better people. In every way Jesus is presented as the perfect example in life and in death, and one who will be followed by many, such as Stephen whose martyrdom is described in Luke's second volume (Acts 7^{54-60}).

Passover and plots; Judas betrays Jesus (22^{1-6})

All Jews who could possibly manage it were expected to come to Jerusalem for the Passover festival, the most important of the year. Exodus 12 gave instructions about how it should be kept. About 1250 B.C. Moses had asked the Pharoah of Egypt to grant the freedom of the Israelites who were then slaves in his land. The Pharoah had continually changed his mind. Eventually Moses told every Israelite family to prepare for the long journey to freedom. They must kill a lamb, smear their doorways with some of the blood, then cook and eat the meat. That night, so the story says, the Angel of Death killed the first born child in every Egyptian home, but PASSED OVER the Israelite houses which were marked with blood.

At that same time of the year, on the night of the full moon (15th Nisan, our late March or early April), the Jews still keep 'Passover' to thank God for their escape. On Passover night they lay a table with a lamb bone, bitter herbs, unleavened bread and other reminders of the event. An ancient barley-festival, when for a week they also ate unleavened bread, began on the same date and soon the two festivals became thought of as one.

Each lamb sufficed for about ten people. Josephus, the Jewish historian of the first century A.D., described one Passover at Jerusalem when 256,500 lambs were sacrificed. This was stated to give his readers an idea of the importance of and attendance at this festival. The Jews also remembered at this time that God had chosen them as His special people and had brought them safely into Canaan to freedom. Remembering this they believed that God would free them from the present army of occupation, the Romans. National feelings ran high during this festival and special detachments of Roman soldiers were brought in to keep the peace, for a charismatic leader might easily incite a Jewish rebellion. When Jesus was a boy, two thousand Jews were crucified as punishment for a rebellion.

By now many Jewish leaders wanted to get rid of Jesus. Some of them resented the challenge he made to their age-old ways of religion. Some of them hated Jesus because he had openly criticized their hypocrisy. Others, perhaps, were genuinely concerned for their people and feared another mass-crucifixion if Jesus turned out to be another false Messiah. They wanted to get hold of Jesus before he could cause any more trouble, but the people around him might turn violently on anyone trying to arrest him. The problem was solved when Judas Iscariot, 'one of the Twelve' says Luke, offered to let the priests and Temple police know when Jesus was away from the protecting crowds. They were prepared to pay him for the information, and Matthew (26[15]) says they offered a reward of thirty pieces of silver.

People have wondered how a man who had lived and worked with Jesus could betray him. The reward was not really enough to tempt even a greedy man, though this is the motive suggested by Matthew (26[15]) and John (12[6]). Various explanations have been suggested. 'Iscariot' may have meant that Judas came from Kerioth, a town to the west of the Dead Sea. The other disciples seem to have been Galileans, so Judas, if from Kerioth, was something of an outsider to the group. Some readers suggest that 'Iscariot' meant that Judas belonged to the 'sicarii', the dagger-men, a nationalist group of Zealots prepared to murder Romans. Perhaps Judas hoped that the threat of arrest and death would rouse Jesus to fight, or that God Himself would be forced to send spectacular help to defend His Messiah. Other readers suggest that Judas, seeing his leader was in danger, decided to betray him in order to save his own skin. Like John (13[27]), Luke explains the betrayal by saying that Satan was influencing Judas. This emphasizes the idea that the battle between God and Satan, between good and evil, was being fought. Matthew (27[3-5]) says that Judas was filled with remorse when Jesus was condemned to death and that he threw back the money to the priests and elders, then went and hanged himself. Luke, however, in Acts 1[15-19], says that Judas used the money to buy some land and suffered a fatal accident there.

Preparations for the Passover (22⁷⁻¹³)

Again one realizes how carefully Jesus had planned ahead, for the story says that he told Peter and John to go into the city to prepare the disciples' Passover supper. This meant they would buy a lamb, sacrifice it at the Temple and roast it. They would need also to buy bitter herbs, unleavened bread and wine.

Jesus told them that on entering the city they would see a man carrying a water-jar, an unusual sight since water was usually carried by women. They should follow the man into a house and ask the householder to show them to the upstairs guest room, ready furnished and, so it seems, previously booked by Jesus. Ideally, the Passover supper should be eaten within the city and people loaned rooms, at no cost, to visitors. There the two should prepare supper.

Some readers have wondered if the house belonged to John Mark's family, for the earliest Christians often met in the upper guest-room of Mark's home (Acts 12¹²). There is no real evidence for this supposition, however.

The Last Supper; Jesus speaks of the betrayal (22¹⁴⁻²³)

The feasts of Unleavened Bread and Passover had becomed combined and were thought of as one celebration. Verse 7 says that the lambs were slaughtered also on this day. In fact the lambs were slaughtered on the day before Passover. It has been suggested that if the lambs were being killed on the day of the Last Supper then Jesus and his friends were eating the Passover Supper a day early. This was permitted when the Passover date fell on the sabbath. Other readers feel that Jesus' words at this supper suggest that it was not the Passover meal (see NEB footnote).

The Palestinian day ended at sunset and the evening was regarded as the beginning of the new day. Whereas we would say the Last Supper was eaten on Thursday evening, the Jews would think of it as the beginning of Friday. We cannot be sure whether Luke was counting the days in Jewish fashion or whether, since he was writing for non-Jews, he was counting the day from midnight to midnight as we do. (John's gospel puts the Crucifixion a day earlier than the Synoptics. Perhaps he was using a different calendar from that in use by the other gospel-writers, but most scholars think John's earlier timing was deliberate so that he could portray Jesus dying as the Passover lambs were being killed at the Temple.)

House with upper room

At supper, Jesus told the disciples, 'I have longed (or 'I longed') with all my heart to eat this Passover with you before I suffer, for I tell you I will not eat it again until it finds its fulfilment in the Kingdom of God.' Obviously Jesus had a special reason for wanting to be with them for this particular meal, and perhaps he had been afraid that arrest would make it impossible. He had kept secret the arrangements about the room, perhaps to avoid disturbance by soldiers. Soon we see how Jesus gave a new and special meaning to the Passover meal.

Often when Jewish people ate together they would speak about the feast they would one day eat together in God's Kingdom, a Kingdom which would be inaugurated when their Messiah arrived. Some believed he would make his first appearance at the Temple in Jerusalem. Good Jews made every effort to come to Jerusalem for the festival of the Passover, hoping each year would bring the Messiah. During the Passover meal the head of the family would pray before each of the four times he passed around the cup of wine. In the upper room Jesus, as head of his family of disciples, did this. As he passed the cup he said, 'Take this and share it between yourselves. I tell you that from now I shall not drink wine until the Kingdom of God comes.' Sometimes people abstained from wine to consecrate themselves for a special task, and Jesus knew that before God's Kingdom could be truly established his task involved great suffering. On the cross he did not accept the drugged wine offered to him, as if determined to experience fully the suffering of crucifixion right to the end (Mark 15[23]).

Then Jesus took some bread, gave thanks to God and, breaking it in pieces, passed it around to the disciples, but gave to it a deeper significance by saying, 'This is my body.'

Some manuscripts add extra words here, reading, 'This is my body which is given for you. Do this in remembrance of me.' In the same way he took the cup after supper and said, 'This cup, poured out for you, is the new covenant sealed by my blood.' These extra words may have been left out to make Luke's version more like the others. Even so the shorter version puts the wine before the bread, whereas Mark and Matthew put the bread before the wine. The longer version, with the extra words, may well be Luke's original and is similar to the earliest known words used in the Church (I Cor. 11[23-25]).

When the Jews asked God to forgive their sins they often offered Him sacrifices, or presents, to atone for those sins, because they had failed to keep their side of the agreement, or covenant, with God. Jesus' death was the once-and-for-all atonement, securing God's love and forgiveness for all time. He was arranging for mankind a new and better relationship with God, and sealing the promise with his blood, just as the ancient Jews sealed any agreement by pouring out the blood of a sacrificed animal (cf. Ex. 24$^{5-8}$). Blood represented life.

The first Passover in Egypt set the Israelites free from slavery. This one offered them freedom from being slaves to sin.

All Christian Churches, apart from the Salvation Army and the Society of Friends (sometimes called 'the Quakers'), take bread and wine together and remember the Last Supper in a service known as the Lord's Supper (or Holy Communion, or the Eucharist). The bread and wine are referred to as sacraments. A sacrament is explained as a visible symbol which brings about that which it symbolizes. It has also been defined as a visible sign which represents an invisible grace and becomes the channel of that grace. The Roman Catholic Church considers there to be seven sacraments – Baptism, Confirmation, the Eucharist, Penance, Extreme Unction, Holy Orders and Matrimony. Most Protestant Churches count as sacraments only the two which were commanded by Jesus himself – those of Baptism and the Lord's Supper.

Jesus then said, 'Listen. My betrayer is here. His hand is on the table with mine. The Son of Man must go the way planned for him, but woe to that man who has betrayed him!' Jesus saw his death as part of his work and quite inevitable, but this did not excuse Judas who helped to make it possible. On hearing this the disciples began to wonder which man in the group could do such a terrible thing. To betray someone after sharing the sacred fellowship of eating together was considered particularly treacherous.

Who would be most important? (22$^{24-30}$)

Even though Jesus had reminded them that soon he would die, the disciples seemed unable to understand, for soon they were busy quarrelling about which of them would be the important officials in the Kingdom over which Jesus was going to rule. Obviously they had not yet changed their view of his role as Messiah.

Eastern kings claimed that they were benefactors to their people because their subjects benefited from their reign, but in truth the subjects were usually used for the benefit of the king. Jesus did not want his friends to misuse their responsibilities in this way. They must not lord it over others. In Jesus' kind of kingdom the greatest person was the one who could most easily forget himself to serve other people. Jesus himself had spent his life serving other people. God had given him the powers of a king and he would bequeath that power to these men who had stayed with him in difficult times when others had deserted him (cf. John 6$^{66-70}$). The disciples would share in the fellowship of the Kingdom with him and would be in authority over the tribes of Israel, meaning that his teaching would be seen as superior to Judaism, but authority would come to them only when they had learnt to serve others.

Jesus foresees Peter's denials (22$^{31-34}$)

Still in the Upper Room Jesus said to Simon Peter, 'Simon, Simon, be careful. Satan has demanded permission to sift all of you like wheat, but I have prayed for you personally that your faith may not fail. When you have come to yourself, you must give strength to your brothers.' Originally Satan had been thought of as someone who tested people's loyalty to God.

Simon Peter was over-confident, not thinking for a minute that he could ever let Jesus down. He answered, 'Lord, I'm prepared to face prison and even death with you!' Jesus told him, 'I tell you, Peter, before cock-crow you will deny three times that you ever knew me.' Cock-crow may have referred to the crow of a cockerel at dawn. It was also the name given to the third of the four night-guard duties, so Jesus was saying to Peter, 'You will deny me before the night is over.'

Events were to prove Jesus right (see verses 54–61), for although Peter had the courage to follow the arrested Jesus right into the High Priest's courtyard, his nerve failed when he was accused of being one of the prisoner's companions, and he denied knowing Jesus. One suggestion is that Peter intended to try to rescue Jesus and to acknowledge knowing him then would give the game away.

Jesus realized that, when he was gone, the disciples would face fear, disillusionment and danger. They would need leadership and encouragement. Peter must be encouraged to get over his temporary failure. Having failed, he would be more able to understand and help others when they were finding things difficult. Jesus addressed him first as Simon, then as Peter, 'the Rock' who must stand firm.

(Mark's gospel describes the conversation between Jesus and Peter as taking place later, on the walk to the olive-orchard).

Future opposition (22$^{35-38}$)

Jesus was still speaking to the disciples in the upper room. 'When I sent you out barefoot, without money or luggage, did you ever go short of anything?' They answered, 'No.'

Then Jesus warned them that from now on things would be different. On their preaching tours people had welcomed them and given them food and shelter, but now they would be branded as friends of a criminal and no one would help them; they would have to rely on what they could provide for themselves. To emphasize the fact that they would meet opposition and danger, Jesus said, 'If you haven't a sword you'd better sell your coat and buy one.' They took him literally and someone said that they had two swords. (Perhaps they were referring to their fishermen's knives.) Jesus replied, 'That's enough of that!' Even at this stage Jesus would not countenance armed resistance. His words were symbolic and he did not mean his followers to use swords. (In 1302 the Pope, basing his statement on this text, declared that God had entrusted to the Church the two swords of civil and spiritual authority.)

Jesus told them that the scriptures saying that he was an outlaw who would die were about to come true. Never before had he said so clearly that he was following the way of the Suffering Servant described in Isaiah 53[12].

Jesus prays at Olivet; His arrest (22[39-53])

Each evening Jesus and the disciples left the busy city and found peace at Olivet, a hillside of olive orchards. They may have used a private orchard owned by a friend. Luke did not use the local name 'Gethsemane', perhaps because this would mean nothing to his non-Jewish readers.

From the evidence in the gospels (particularly John's gospel which mentions a number of visits to Jerusalem for annual festivals), we think that Jesus was now about thirty-three years old, a young man, but obviously accepting that soon he would be arrested and put to death. Even now he could easily have left Jerusalem and escaped, and perhaps his mind was torn between this and completing what he believed to be his mission for God, for he said to the disciples, 'Pray that you won't give in to temptation.' The death penalty could be administered only by the Roman authority, so death would be by crucifixion, a slow and agonizing death which Jesus may well have witnessed as a child.

By now it must have been very late and the disciples, tired after their long day in the city, were ready to camp down for a night's sleep. Jesus

Gethsemane A Franciscan monk meditating in the garden as it is today

went a stone's throw away from them and knelt down to pray. Mark said that Jesus fell on the ground, as if he wanted to express Jesus' feeling of weary helplessness, but Luke's choice of words is more reverent. His story has emotion but no feeling of desperation or desolation on Jesus' part. Even now Jesus seemed to be wondering whether or not this was the way God wanted him to take, and he prayed, 'Father, if it is your will, take this cup (of suffering) from me; yet not my will but yours be done!' Inwardly Jesus believed that only by dying could he show that God's concern for the world is deeper than we can possibly imagine, yet, as at his baptism, he needed to have this confirmed by God. This it would seem, was one of the 'opportune times' when the Devil returned to tempt him (cf. Luke 4[13]).

Luke says that Jesus' agony of mind was such that his sweat was as drops of blood falling to the ground. Doctors say that this can happen when people undergo great pain or mental strain. Some manuscripts omit this verse, perhaps because it might suggest that Jesus was weak or frightened. Luke alone says that an angel came to give him strength. It is Luke's way of saying that, far from forsaking Jesus, God was with him in his time of need. No doubt these words comforted many early Christians who were suffering when Luke was writing.

When at last Jesus returned to the disciples they were asleep. Luke excuses this by saying they were exhausted by grief. One wonders how this could be when they had seemed unable to appreciate the position (22[24]). Luke does not say that while Jesus prayed they fell asleep again and again instead of guarding him.

Jesus roused them suggesting that, instead of sleeping, they should be praying to be spared the mental struggle that he was experiencing, but even as he spoke a crowd of men headed by Judas came into the orchard. Luke alone mentions that as well as Temple guards there were chief priests and leading citizens. He is showing the seriousness of this matter. Judas stepped forward to greet Jesus as any eastern disciple would greet a teacher he loved, with a kiss, but, unlike Mark and Matthew, Luke seems to suggest that Jesus turned away from the kiss as he said, 'Judas, would you betray the Son of Man with a kiss?' By the time that Luke was writing, a kiss had become the accepted way of greeting a fellow-Christian, so perhaps Luke wished to avoid its association with betrayal.

When the disciples realized just what was happening they asked Jesus if this were a good time to make use of their swords, and, without waiting for an answer, one of them lashed out and severed the right ear of a servant who was employed by the High Priest. This incident may well have given the group a reputation as outlaws (see 22[37] and Is. 53[9]).

John's gospel (18^{10}) says that it was Peter who lashed out and that the servant was a man named Malchus. Jesus had no wish to resist arrest and replied, 'Let them do what they will', and he touched the servant's ear and healed it. Only Luke mentions the healing (cf. Matt. 26$^{51\text{-}52}$, Mark 14^{47}.

Jesus turned to the group who had come to arrest him and said, 'Do you take me to be a bandit that you needed swords and cudgels to arrest me? I've been in the Temple every day, but you didn't bother me then! However, this is your time – the time when darkness (evil) reigns.' Here again Luke's words remind one of John's gospel which often spoke of good and evil as 'light' and 'darkness'. As the struggle continued between God and Satan it must have seemed to the disciples that God was being defeated.

The Jewish trial; Before Caiaphas (22$^{54\text{-}65}$)

The soldiers took Jesus to the house of Caiaphas, the High Priest (see plan of Jerusalem, p. 145). Peter followed at some distance behind. The soldiers made a fire in the courtyard to keep themselves warm while Jesus was being questioned, and Peter mingled with them, anxious to find out what was going to happen. A servant girl, seeing Peter's face in the firelight, said that she had seen him around with the man who had been arrested, but Peter denied it, saying, 'Woman, I do not know him.' A little while later someone else said, 'You are one of them', and again Peter said, 'No, I'm not.' About an hour later someone, perhaps hearing Peter's accent, said quite definitely, 'Of course this fellow was with him. He's a Galilean', but Peter answered, 'Man, I don't know what you are talking about!'

As Peter said this a cock crowed. This may simply mean that it was dawn, or it may refer to the bugle which marked the end of the night's guard-duties. Perhaps Jesus was in the courtyard, perhaps in the building near a door or window, for he turned and looked at Peter who immediately remembered Jesus' words, 'Before the cock crows you will deny me three times.' Peter went out and wept bitterly.

The men who were guarding Jesus beat and ridiculed him. They had heard him referred to as a prophet, so they played a kind of Blind Man's Buff game with him, blindfolding him, poking him and saying, 'Now, prophet, tell us who touched you.' They insulted him in other ways.

Mark (14$^{53\text{-}65}$) and Matthew (26$^{57\text{-}67}$) give further details about Caiaphas' efforts to collect evidence against Jesus. In these two gospels the mocking takes place after the interview with the Sanhedrin.

The Jewish trial continues; Before the Sanhedrin (22⁶⁶⁻⁷¹)

During the night Jesus had been taken to an unofficial enquiry conducted by the High Priest. The eastern day began early, while it was still cool, and at dawn a hurried meeting of the Sanhedrin was called, though it must have been difficult to get the necessary quorum of twenty-three members together at this hour.

The Sanhedrin was the Supreme Court of the Jews, appointed to assist the High Priest. Since all aspects of Jewish everyday life were dictated by the religious laws it had been quite powerful, but the Romans had now limited its powers, probably to the extent that it could no longer carry out capital punishment (see John 18³¹; and Josephus, *Antiquities* 20.9.1.) The Sanhedrin consisted of seventy-one leading Jews – chief-priests, lawyers and elders. The High Priest presided and the court met in the Hall of Hewn Stone in the Temple area. Each member was expected to give an individual assessment and vote. The court was not allowed to meet between sunset and sunrise. All charges must be supported by two witnesses whose evidence must agree when they were questioned separately. If it seemed likely that the prisoner would be declared guilty the court must meet for a second day. If the death sentence were passed, twenty-four hours must elapse before sentence was carried out.

Such rules make it clear that, at best, the Sanhedrin was just and merciful, but the rules were obviously waived in the case of Jesus. The Jewish leaders wanted the case and the punishment over quickly since it was approaching the sabbath. They were keen to get together the kind of evidence that would move the Romans to act.

Jesus was challenged directly, 'Tell us, are you the Messiah?' If he claimed to be the Messiah, the Romans would realize that he could be a political danger and they would deal with him promptly as they had with other so-called Messiahs!

Jesus knew how they were thinking. His own idea of Messiahship was something quite different. For himself he had preferred the title 'Son of Man' and he had modelled his life on the poems describing the Suffering Servant of God (Is. 42¹⁻⁴, 49¹⁻⁶, 50⁴⁻⁹, 52¹³–53¹²), but it was hardly likely that the Sanhedrin would stop to discuss the matter with him, so he answered, 'If I tell you, you will not believe me; and if I ask questions you won't answer.' Then he reminded the Court of the words of Daniel (7¹³) saying that the Son of Man would rule and judge sitting on the right of Almighty God. The judging that really mattered would be done by Jesus, not by the court of the Sanhedrin. To anyone who wanted to understand, these words made it clear that the Kingdom which concerned Jesus was not an earthly, political kingdom such as Palestine or Rome.

Then they asked, 'Are you the Son of God then?' Such a claim would be considered blasphemy for which the Jewish penalty was death for insulting God. This could easily be linked with the idea of a militant Messiah in order to impress the Romans. Jesus answered, 'It is you who say that I am!', but this was enough for the Sanhedrin. The prisoner had not denied the suggestion, so he must be admitting it. They said, 'Surely we don't need to call witnesses. We ourselves have heard it from his own mouth!' This was a further waiving of the rules, for Jewish law said that a man could not be condemned by his own words. Obviously it had proved impossible to get two witnesses, but this was not going to stop them. Mark 14$^{55-59}$ and Matthew 26$^{59-61}$ speak of witnesses obviously not considered reliable.

The Roman trial; Before Pilate (23$^{1-25}$)

When Herod the Great died in 4 B.C. his kingdom was divided between his sons (see note on 3$^{1-20}$), but one of the sons, Archelaus, proved so unbearable that the Jews in his area asked Rome to do something about him. Archelaus was replaced by a Roman procurator, a kind of governor. The fifth of these procurators was Pontius Pilate who was in charge of Judaea, Samaria and Idumaea from A.D. 26 to 36. Pilate, in turn, was responsible to the Roman governor of Syria in which province Palestine was included.

It was to Pilate that the Sanhedrin brought Jesus. They realized that Pilate would not concern himself about a case of blasphemy against the Jewish God. They would need to make him understand the political connotation of the title 'Messiah' so that he would see Jesus as one who might lead a rebellion against the Roman army of occupation. The Sanhedrin thus made three accusations against Jesus, saying that he was: (a) putting ideas of rebellion into the minds of the people, (b) encouraging them to refuse to pay Roman taxes and (c) claiming that he was Messiah, a king. Anyone claiming to be a king was obviously a threat to the authority of the Roman emperor.

Governors often heard cases very early in the morning. Pilate questioned Jesus directly, 'Are you the king of the Jews?' Jesus replied, 'The words are yours.' It seemed, then, that Jesus was not claiming to be a king. Pilate told the priests and people, 'I find nothing to condemn in this man,' but they insisted, 'He is stirring up the people into rebellion through all Judaea. He began in Galilee and has brought his teaching as far as this area.' Mention of Galilee suggested to Pilate a possible way of evading the handling of this case. He asked, 'Galilee? Is this man a Galilean?' Galilee was well known for its rebels and the ruler of Galilee, Herod Antipas, was in Jerusalem for Passover. Perhaps Herod could make something of this case, so Pilate decided to send Jesus to him. Since the incident had arisen in Jerusalem, there was no need for Pilate to do this. Luke is the only writer who has mentioned the incident, perhaps because he wanted to show that the Roman authorities had nothing against Jesus.

Having heard of Jesus' miracles, Herod had been hoping to see some for himself, so he was pleased that Pilate had sent the prisoner to him. Only Luke mentions that Herod and Pilate had been at loggerheads. Pilate's gesture of friendliness brought friendship between them. Herod, however, did not seem to consider Jesus seriously at all and was the only person to whom Jesus made no answer, despite the constant accusations being made against him by priests and lawyers. Herod and his soldiers treated Jesus with contempt and ridiculed him. (Mark's gospel said it was Pilate's soldiers who did this.) They dressed him up as a mock-king and returned him to Pilate. The details may have come from the wife of Herod's steward, for she had supported Jesus' work (see 8³).

Pilate found himself again being forced to make a decision as to what to do with Jesus. Luke shows that he made three separate attempts to free Jesus (23¹⁴⁻¹⁶, ²⁰,²²). To the Sanhedrin and people Pilate said, 'You brought to me this man accused of encouraging you to rebel. As you see, I have questioned him before you and I find no case against him. Neither does Herod, for he has sent him back. He has done nothing to deserve the death penalty, so I will give him a flogging and let him go.' Pilate was keen to uphold the justice for which Rome was famous, but he was prepared to compromise to please the Jews.

The crowd, however, was not satisfied with only a flogging and shouted, 'Take this man away! Let Barabbas go free!' Verse 17 explains that there was a custom at Passover whereby the Romans allowed one prisoner to go free. Some manuscripts of Luke's gospel omit the verse which, perhaps, was put in by a later copyist to explain the situation. Barabbas had been imprisoned, accused of being a ringleader in an attempt to strike a blow for Jewish independence. He was also a murderer. Tradition says that Barabbas' name was also 'Jesus', but perhaps Christians were not anxious to use the name for two prisoners who were so different. 'Barabbas' means 'son of a father', perhaps an insulting nickname suggesting that no one knew the father of Barabbas. The crowd's wish to free him was itself enough to show that Jesus of Nazareth was not a political agitator, and again Pilate insisted that Jesus was innocent, but the crowd shouted him down calling, 'Crucify him! Crucify him!'

For a third time Pilate tried, saying, 'Why? What wrong has he done? I do not find him guilty of any capital offence; I will let him off with a flogging.' But they insisted, demanding the crucifixion of Jesus, and Pilate gave in to them. He released Jesus Barabbas and handed over Jesus of Nazareth to be killed. In this way Luke makes clear his opinion that it was the Jews, not the Roman authorities, who wanted Jesus put to death.

A Jewish scholar, Philo, who lived at Alexandria, described Pilate as inflexible, merciless and obstinate, yet in the case of Jesus he gave in to the Jews and allowed an innocent man to be crucified. The historian, Josephus, mentions certain events which may have made Pilate afraid to anger the Jews more than necessary. The Commandments forbade the making or worship of images (Ex. 20^{4-6}), so the Jews objected when Roman standards bearing the image of the emperor were carried into Jerusalem, because the emperor was worshipped as a god. They went to Pilate's headquarters at Caesarea to ask him to remove the images. After six days of waiting they were ordered to go away, otherwise they would be killed by Pilate's soldiers. The Jews knelt and bared their necks for death and Pilate, moved by their loyalty to their laws, removed the images. Some time later he decided to build an aqueduct to bring a new water-supply into Jerusalem and took money from the Temple treasury to pay for it. Thousands of Jews came to protest and were butchered by soldiers who had disguised themselves as Jews.

Reports of such indiscretions could bring about Pilate's dismissal and, on this occasion, he may have decided that one man's death was a cheap price to pay for peace.

In A.D. 36 Pilate's soldiers carried out a brutal and unnecessary massacre in Samaria and the emperor recalled him to Rome (Josephus, *Antiquities* 18. 3 & 4).

Jesus is taken to be crucified (23^{26-31})

The Roman Praetorium, or Judgement Hall, had previously been a palace of Herod the Great. From there Jesus was taken to be crucified. Mark's gospel says it was nine o'clock in the morning.

Roman crosses were usually T-shaped. The upright remained fixed in the ground to serve for many occasions. The crossbar, or patibulum,

Roman soldiers. One carries a standard

was carried to the site by the prisoner who was marched along inside a square of four soldiers. They took the longest route through the streets so that local people would see and take warning. A placard, on which the prisoner's crime was written, was carried ahead and in Jesus' case it read, 'This is the king of the Jews'. Later this would be fixed above his head on the cross.

Luke does not say that Jesus had been scourged, or flogged (Mark

15¹⁵, Matt. 27²⁶, John 19¹). This punishment sometimes killed a man or drove him insane, tearing the flesh of his back down to his waist. If Jesus had been flogged, this would explain why the Romans found it necessary to relieve him of the weight of the crossbar, for they commanded a bystander, Simon of Cyrene, to carry it. Cyrene is now known as Tripoli and is in North Africa. There was a large Jewish community at Cyrene and probably Simon was a Jew, attending the Passover celebration. Mark (chapter 15²¹) tells us that Simon had two sons called Alexander and Rufus, and one wonders if Rufus were the same person as the Rufus mentioned in St Paul's letter to the Christians at Rome (Romans 16¹³).

The group was followed by a crowd which included women who were weeping and already wailing for the dead in the typical eastern way (cf. Luke 8⁵²). Jesus turned to them and said, 'Daughters of Jerusalem, do not weep for me, but for yourselves and your children, for the time is coming when people will say "Happy are the women who have no children, who never bore or nursed a baby." They will wish the mountains and hills to fall on them and smother them.' In the east childlessness was considered a disgrace, but, when Jerusalem was being destroyed some years later, many would be thankful that they had no children to suffer the horrors of it. In 721 B.C. the Assyrian invasion of Israel was believed to be God's way of punishing the sinful Israelites, for prophets like Hosea had warned that it would happen. Here Jesus quotes some words of Hosea (Hosea 10⁸) which suggests that Jesus, too, thought of the destruction ahead as punishment brought on by sin. Jesus went on, 'If this happens to wood which is green, what will happen when it is dry?' Dry wood burns much more easily than newly-cut wood containing sap. Probably Jesus was thinking that if the Romans would crucify an innocent man there was no telling what they might do to people who rebelled against them. He may have meant the words to refer to the Jews, for if the Jews would condemn Jesus who had not provoked them what horrors would they commit when faced with conditions of siege?

Jesus is crucified (23³²⁻⁴³)

At last the procession arrived at the place called the Skull outside the city walls. Its Latin name was Calvary and its Jewish name was Golgotha, but Luke, writing for non-Jews, avoided the local name. Two criminals were being crucified, one of them on each side of Jesus. Mark and Matthew referred to them as 'bandits'. Jesus' mission was to sinners, and even in his death he was with them.

The soldiers would lie the cross bar on the ground and the prisoner's hands would be nailed or tied to its ends; then, using short ladders, they would haul man and bar up and drop the bar into a slot on the upright. On this upright there would be a small platform called a 'saddle' on which the victim could ease his weight, otherwise the nails could tear through his hands enabling him to fall free. Without the support of the saddle the body could hang freely and the pressure on the diaphragm would mean a mercifully quick death from suffocation. sometimes a prisoner would endure in agony for several days, through periods of insanity or unconsciousness, dying eventually from hunger and thirst in the blazing heat of the day and the cold of the night.

The escort set up Jesus' cross between those of the criminals. While he was on the cross Jesus said, 'Father, forgive them for they don't know what they are doing.' This saying is found only in Luke's gospel, and even here some manuscripts omit it. Most scholars regard it as a genuine writing of Luke who emphasized Jesus' concern for wrong-doers and outcasts. It would seem most obvious to assume that Jesus was asking forgiveness for the Roman soldiers who were nailing him to the cross. After all, they were simply obeying orders and could not be expected to realize the enormity of their action. Luke, in this gospel, however, stresses the love and forgiveness of God for all, and in his other volume the words of Peter and Stephen (Acts 3^{17-19}, 7^{60}) make it clear that this forgiveness is also for the Jews who, in ignorance, brought about the death of their Messiah. On the cross Jesus also offered forgiveness to the criminals by his side. The words of Jesus here (23^{34}) have always been given the widest possible application: Jesus offered forgiveness for those near him, but also for all humanity throughout all time.

While the prisoners hung in humiliation and agony the soldiers on duty were allowed to share whatever belongings were left. A Jew of that time usually wore a tunic, a girdle, sandals, a turban and an outer robe. The tunic, made from one unseamed piece of cloth, was perhaps the item for which the soldiers diced.

It is Luke who describes in most detail the reactions of the various bystanders. No doubt many had come out of a ghoulish curiosity and looked on as the Jewish leaders jeered, 'If you are the king of the Jews why don't you save yourself?' Luke says that the soldiers offered to Jesus some of the sour Palestinian wine that formed part of their rations. The gospels of Matthew and Mark say that Jesus was offered a drugged wine, presumably to ease his pain, but he refused it as if determined to fulfil to the end the role of God's Suffering Servant.

One of the bandits spoke with contempt, taunting Jesus, 'Aren't you the Messiah? Then save yourself and us!' The second bandit rebuked his companion, saying, 'Have you no fear even of God? We deserve this for what we have done, but this fellow has done no crime.' It is impossible now to guess exactly what he meant by saying, 'Remember me, Jesus, when you come as King!', but Jesus answered, 'I tell you this, today you shall be with me in Paradise.' There were several uses of the word 'paradise'. Originally it referred to a beautiful enclosed garden in which a Persian king would walk with a guest whom he wished to honour. The Greek version of Genesis referred to the garden of Eden as Paradise and many Jews tried to please God so that, after death, they might live with Him in Paradise. Luke alone reports Jesus' conversation with these robbers.

Even on the cross Jesus was being tempted to prove himself by spectacular miracles, as he had been at the time of the temptations in the wilderness (4^{1-13}). Despite the tragedy and humiliation Luke manages to show that Jesus was still the King, dignified, serene and fully in control of events, and at the same time fulfilling in many details the description of the Suffering Servant (Is. 53), and echoing the words of Psalms $22^{7,18}$ and 69^{21}, showing that all that was happening was in God's ancient plan for saving mankind.

The death of Jesus (23^{44-49})

All three synoptic gospels say that a darkness began at midday and lasted for three hours, and that the curtain of the Temple split in two from top to bottom. An eclipse would not cause such a long time of darkness and was not possible at Passover when there was a full moon. The curtain was a tapestry which screened the Holy of Holies, the dwelling-place of the invisible God, from the eyes of people worshipping nearby. The High Priest himself was the only person allowed to enter the Holy of Holies, and only once a year on the Day of Atonement. Some scholars have suggested that the violent desert wind called the 'khamsin' tore the curtain and swept in dust-clouds that caused darkness, but most regard the words as symbolic, emphasizing the seriousness of this crucifixion. It was believed that nature shared mankind's distress (cf. Amos 8^9, Joel $2^{10,30-32}$, 3^{15}, Hebrews 10^{19}) and such mysterious and frightening events were expected before the end of the world, when God was about to begin His time of Judgement. The torn curtain symbolized, perhaps, that God's Presence was now open to all mankind, an idea especially important to Luke, who may also have felt that the Temple was no longer necessary anyway, being too limited now that all nations were coming to God. (At this point in Matthew's gospel there are references to an earthquake, openings of tombs and dead people rising to life – probably Matthew's way of expressing Jesus' victory over death.)

When Jesus had been on the cross for six hours he cried aloud, 'Father, into your hands I give my spirit', and he died. The scourging, carried out previously, perhaps hastened his death. Perhaps he allowed himself to hang free from the saddle, so that life would not be prolonged.

The centurion on duty must have been deeply impressed by all he saw, for Luke says that he praised God and made the comment, 'There is no doubt about it; this man was innocent' (a fact already acclaimed by Pilate and the dying bandit). This is the translation given in the New English Bible, which suggests that the same section at Mark 15[39] and Matthew 27[54] could read 'Truly this man was a son of God' or (footnote) 'the Son of God'. We cannot tell whether the centurion was expressing his faith in Jesus as the Son of God. The words may have been the centurion's way of admiring the qualities he had seen in Jesus, qualities which would be much appreciated by someone like a Roman centurion.

Each of the gospel-writers has managed to tell this story in his own individual way, yet each account is restrained and dignified, unembellished with highly-coloured descriptions. Mark's story impresses us with the loneliness of Jesus at this time, his feeling of being forsaken even by God. Luke's story shows, instead, the sympathy of many who shared Jesus' sorrow, supporting him at this time – Pilate, the weeping women, the dying bandit, the centurion, the onlookers who had come to stare at a spectacle and went home sorrowful and upset. Instead of the cry that God has forsaken him (Mark 15[34], Matt. 27[46]), Jesus' words show his conviction that he has obeyed God's will to the end.

Jesus' personal friends stood some distance away to watch, for the Romans did not allow anyone too near to the crosses. Among these friends were some Galilean women who had been amongst his followers.

This story of courage and patience, obedience to God's will and willingness to forgive others, would encourage the many Christians who were being hounded and persecuted while Luke was writing. His story of the death of the Christian, Stephen, shows that Christians took Jesus as their example (Acts 7).

The burial of Jesus (23$^{50-56}$)

Also present at the Crucifixion was a wealthy merchant named Joseph who came from Arimathea, probably modern Rentis, a town about twenty miles from Jerusalem. Like the parents of John the Baptist (1^6) and old Simeon (2^{25}) Joseph of Arimathea was a good and honest person who longed for the Kingdom of God.

It was Roman custom to leave criminals' bodies to rot on the crosses or to be devoured by vultures and pariah dogs. However, an ancient Jewish law required the bodies of executed criminals to be buried before nightfall (Deut. 21$^{22-23}$), so in Palestine the Romans were prepared to throw the bodies into a common grave. Luke often took pains to show that the Jewish laws were kept by Jesus and his supporters and here he tells how Joseph of Arimathea, a member of the Jewish Sanhedrin, but one who had voted against the others at Jesus' trial, offered the use of a rock-tomb for the burial of Jesus (Matthew (27^{59}) says it was his own tomb). Perhaps Joseph was anxious to see that the law of Deuteronomy was obeyed, perhaps he wished to make it clear that he disapproved of Jesus' execution. Like the donkey which carried Jesus into Jerusalem, the tomb had not been used before, so was fitting for such a sacred purpose now. Joseph had the courage of his convictions for he went to the procurator, Pontius Pilate, to ask permission to bury Jesus' body. He also provided a bale of linen for the shroud in which Jesus' body could be wrapped.

The Passover sabbath was due to begin at six o'clock and, since no work of any kind was permitted on the sabbath, the burial had to be rushed, allowing no time for the usual anointing of the body with spices and perfumed ointments. The women took special note of the place so that they could return for the anointing as soon as the sabbath was over.

Legends exist that claim that Joseph the merchant traded in England and that, eventually, invited by the king of the area, he settled in Glastonbury where his staff took root and blossoms on Christmas Day. Having been given the wine-cup used at the Last Supper as a token of the disciples' gratitude he placed it in a little wattle church at Glastonbury. The cup disappeared and it became the dream of King Arthur and his knights that they should prove worthy of finding the cup which they called the Holy Grail. Tradition says that England's first Christian church was built at Glastonbury in A.D. 61.

The Resurrection (24$^{1-12}$)

Genesis 2$^{2-3}$ told how God, having created the universe in six days, rested on the seventh day and hallowed that day. Because of this the Jews were expected to obey the commandment which forbade work on the seventh day of the week. At the first light of dawn on the first day of the week after the Crucifixion (our Sunday) the women set off with their spices to anoint the body of Jesus. Rock-tombs were often cave-like structures, the openings of which were blocked with great stones like millstones, made to roll in a groove cut in front of the opening. This protected the tomb from animals and grave-robbers and it needed at least four men to move such a stone. When the women arrived, however, the stone had been rolled away already and there was no sign of the body inside the tomb. The women were at a loss to understand. Suddenly there appeared 'two men in shining clothes', a description which reminds us of the two men seen with Jesus in the story of the Transfiguration (9^{30}). (Mark's gospel speaks of a 'young man in white', Matthew speaks of 'an angel' and John's gospel has 'two angels'.)

The terrified women, afraid to look, lowered their gaze, but the men said, 'Why are you looking amongst the dead for someone who is alive? Remember how, in Galilee, he told you that the Son of Man would be given to the power of evil men, would be crucified and would rise on the third day.' (Mark 16^7 and Matt. 28^{10} say that Jesus intended to meet the disciples at Galilee.) The women remembered and went to report to the rest of Jesus' followers what had just happened. According to Luke these women were Mary Magdalene, Joanna the wife of Chuza who was Herod's steward, and Mary the mother of James (perhaps James, son of Alphaeus, since no mention is made of a brother John).

It is understandable that the gospel-writers vary in the details of this strange story which must have caused uncertainty and bewilderment. Mark names 'Salome' instead of Joanna and says that Jesus would meet his disciples at Galilee, but that the women were afraid to report what had happened at the tomb. Luke describes this and other resurrection appearances of Jesus all happening at Jerusalem, but says that the women told the disciples who dismissed the report as a lot of nonsense.

Some manuscripts of Luke's gospel include a verse 12, saying that Peter, wanting to see for himself, ran and looked into the tomb and when he saw that, apart from the cloth-wrappings the tomb was empty, he went home amazed. The verse is usually left out because most scholars believe it to be an addition by a later copyist who knew John 20³⁻¹⁰.

The Christians could not have got the idea of Jesus rising to life from Judaism, because Judaism had no belief of this kind. Stories of Jesus' appearances after the Crucifixion seem to have been widespread at a very early stage. In Acts 1³ Luke says that Jesus appeared on various occasions over a period of forty days, but in this final chapter of his gospel he mentions the Resurrection, appearances and Ascension as if they all happened on that same Sunday. Obviously the gospels have not accounted for all the appearances of Jesus, for St Paul (I Cor. 15⁵⁻⁸) says that Jesus appeared to James and to himself and, on one occasion, to a crowd of over five hundred people.

Jesus' followers had not expected him to come to them again. The women had expected to embalm his dead body, and the disciples did not believe the women's report that Jesus was alive. Yet something tremendous must have happened to change their ideas, especially since later they were ready to suffer torture and death rather than renounce their claim that Jesus was alive.

Jesus appears on the road to Emmaus (24¹³⁻³⁵)

Luke gives here a more detailed version of the event probably referred to at Mark 16¹²⁻¹³, a story about two people travelling from Jerusalem to Emmaus on that same Sunday evening. Various modern sites have been suggested for Emmaus, which Luke says was seven miles from the city. Present-day Koloniyeh used to be called Emmaus, but it is only four miles north-west from Jerusalem.

Cleopas may have been the 'Clopas, husband of Mary', mentioned in John 19²⁵. He and his companion were discussing the recent events that had happened in Jerusalem when Jesus himself joined them. Strangers often travelled together for company and safety. They did not recognize Jesus. Hoods may have covered their faces partially, but their failure to recognize him is probably best explained by the fact that they were not expecting to see him since he had died and had been buried.

The stranger asked what they were discussing and they remarked that he must be the only person to have been in Jerusalem who did not know what had happened there in the last few days! A powerful prophet, Jesus of Nazareth, who had said and done great things, had been handed over by the Jewish authorities to be crucified. It was a shame, because many Jews had hoped that he was the God-sent

Messiah who would free their people. Some women were now claiming that his tomb was empty and that angels had told them that Jesus was alive.

Their unknown companion told them it was obvious that they had not understood and believed the prophets whose words should have prepared them for all these things. He reminded them how the prophets had said that the Messiah must suffer before achieving glory. Then he went right through the Jewish scriptures explaining how the crucified Jesus had fulfilled them.

By now the three travellers had reached Emmaus and the house for which two of them were making. In the polite eastern way the stranger made as if he would continue on his journey, but since it would soon be evening, they persuaded him to stay rather than travel alone. He agreed to share their meal; then, as they sat together at the table, he took the bread and said the usual supper-time prayer, then broke up the bread and offered it to them. This task was usually performed by the host. As they watched his hands they suddenly realized that their companion was Jesus, but before they could do anything about it he was gone. Perhaps they saw nail-marks in his hands, perhaps they had seen him bless and share food on other occasions, such as the feeding of the great crowd (9^{16}). Perhaps the incident reminded them of reports they had heard about the Last Supper (22^{19}). Now they understood why they had felt so inspired when they listened to him on the journey! The fact that they had not recognized him on the Emmaus road must remain a mystery, as, also, the vanishing of Jesus.

Despite the long walk and the late hour they immediately hurried back to Jerusalem to tell Jesus' friends what had happened. There they heard that they were not the only ones who had seen Jesus, for Simon Peter had seen him too.

Jesus appears to his disciples (24^{36-43})

As they were talking, suddenly Jesus was there with them. They were terrified, thinking that he was a ghost, but he said, 'Why are you so bothered and unbelieving? Look at my hands and feet – it is I! Touch me and see! A ghost hasn't got flesh and bones as I have.'

They still couldn't believe it; it seemed too good to be possible. Then Jesus asked, 'Have you anything here to eat?' They gave him some cooked fish and he ate it, while they watched him, amazed.

Some of the Resurrection stories stress that, though Jesus now belonged to a different kind of existence from that of his previous life on earth, he still had the characteristics of an ordinary human person. Perhaps these were necessary to make himself known to his disciples. The important thing that the writers wish to say is that Jesus was capable of a living relationship with his disciples. Records that describe someone being alive after death are bound to be difficult to express and difficult to understand. The earliest followers of Jesus were Jews and Jewish people expressed even abstract ideas by means of something solid and tangible. To them if Jesus were really alive he must have a body. At the end of the first century there were people called Docetists within the Church. They claimed that God was not in the flesh-and-blood Jesus at his birth or on the Cross. The gospel-writers stressed that Jesus was at all times God in human flesh. Here Luke is concerned to emphasize that the risen Jesus was not a ghost or figment of the disciples' imagination.

This story is not told by Mark, but there is a reference to it in the last verses of his gospel which were added by another writer (16^{14}). Matthew does not mention it. John's gospel tells of three occasions when the risen Jesus came to his disciples (John $20^{19,20,26}$, 21^{1}).

The gospel for all the world (24^{44-49})

Jesus told his friends, 'This is what I meant when I told you that everything written about me in the Scriptures would come true.' Obviously he intended them to link their ideas about the Messiah with the descriptions of God's Suffering Servant. The Crucifixion was God's way of showing His love, and it offered forgiveness to all who would repent. God's offer was universal, to all people, but only when we are sincerely sorry for our wrongdoing can we make a response to that offer of forgiveness.

The disciples, who had witnessed all that had happened, had to wait in Jerusalem until they received the special gift of power promised by God, then, beginning in Jerusalem, they must proclaim the gospel of forgiveness to all nations. The giving of this gift of the Holy Spirit is explained in Luke's second volume (Acts chapter 2). The power enabled them to spread the message of Jesus from Jerusalem to Rome, the heart of the Empire.

Luke's gospel ends the story of the earthly life of Jesus in Jerusalem and Mark seems to do the same. Matthew and John end their versions of the story in Galilee.

The Ascension (24$^{50-53}$)

Jesus took his friends out to Bethany, the village on the Mount of Olives. He raised his hands in blessing as the priests would do, and as he did so he left them. Some MSS say he was 'taken up to heaven'. The people of those times believed that the earth was flat and that God's home was somewhere up in the sky, therefore it stood to reason that Jesus would go to be with God up there. Acts 1^9 says that a cloud removed him from their sight. To the Jews this cloud, or 'shekinah', was the sign of God's presence (see p. 80).

There had to be a time of parting and again there was the difficulty of how to express the experience. Whatever happened it enabled a small group of men in an obscure part of the world to go out and preach. Today the love of God as it was shown in Jesus has reached almost every country in the world and now, two thousand years since it all happened, the story still has the power to change people's lives.

Luke began his story with the old priest Zechariah, father of John the Baptist, praising God in the Temple. The gospel ends in the same place with the disciples praising God in the Temple, with no idea of breaking with Judaism. Luke's gospel is one of praise and joy and on this suitable note he ends this first volume of his writings. His second volume, the Acts of the Apostles, begins where his gospel ends and tells how the friends of Jesus took his message to the world.

Parables and Miracles Found in Luke's Gospel

Parables

7^{31-35}	Children at play
7^{36-50}	Two debtors
8^{4-15}	The sower
10^{25-37}	The good Samaritan
11^{5-13}	A friend at midnight
11^{21-22}	The strong man
12^{13-21}	The rich fool
12^{35-48}	Faithful and unfaithful servants
13^{6-9}	The fig-tree
13^{18-19}	The mustard seed
13^{20-21}	Yeast in the dough
14^{7-24}	Places at a feast. The dinner-party
14^{25-33}	The tower builder. A king going to war
15^{1-7}	The lost sheep
15^{8-10}	The lost coin
15^{11-32}	The lost son
16^{1-13}	The dishonest bailiff (or steward)
16^{19-31}	The rich man and Lazarus
17^{7-10}	The servant's reward
18^{1-8}	The judge and widow
18^{9-14}	The Pharisee and publican
19^{11-27}	The pounds
20^{9-16}	The vine-growers (wicked husbandmen)

Miracles

4^{31-37}	The man possessed by a devil
4^{38-39}	Simon's mother-in-law
5^{1-11}	The catch of fish
5^{12-15}	The leper
5^{17-26}	The paralysed man
6^{6-11}	The man with the withered arm
7^{1-10}	The centurion's servant
7^{11-17}	The son of a widow at Nain
8^{22-25}	The storm on the lake
8^{26-39}	The Gergesene madman
8^{40-42} 8^{49-56}	} Jairus' daughter
8^{43-48}	The woman with haemorrhages
9^{10-17}	The feeding of 5000
9^{37-43}	The epileptic boy
13^{10-17}	A crippled woman
14^{1-6}	The man with dropsy
17^{11-19}	Ten lepers
18^{35-43}	A blind man near Jericho
22^{47-51}	The High priest's servant's ear

Abbreviations

Acts	Acts of the Apostles	Ps.	Psalms
Chron.	Books of the Chronicles	Rev.	Revelation of John
Col.	Letter of Paul to the Colossians	Rom.	Letter of Paul to the Romans
Cor.	Letters of Paul to the Corinthians	Sam.	Books of Samuel
Dan.	Book of Daniel	Thess.	Letters of Paul to the Thessalonians
Deut.	Deuteronomy	Tim.	Letters of Paul to Timothy
Ex.	Exodus	Zech.	Zechariah
Ezek.	Book of the Prophet Ezekiel	Esdras	Books of Esdras (Apocrypha)
Gen.	Genesis		
Is.	Book of the Prophet Isaiah	Hosea	Hosea
Jer.	Book of the Prophet Jeremiah	Job	Book of Job
		Jonah	Jonah
Jud.	Book of Judges	John	Gospel according to John
Lev.	Leviticus	Kings	Book of Kings
Matt.	Gospel according to Matthew	Luke	Gospel according to Luke
		Malachi	Malachi
Num.	Numbers	Mark	Gospel according to Mark

Acknowledgements

The authors would like to thank the publisher's reader for his help and advice, also Christine Lee, Doris Fordham and Vera Smith for their patience in typing the manuscript.

Permission to reproduce copyright photographs has been granted by:

BBC Hulton Picture Library (pp. 26, 92, 128, 173); Camera Press (pp. 22, 70, 143, 166); Israel Government Tourist Office (p. 102); Popperfoto (pp. 39, 152, 161).

Index